# Communicating Family and Consumer Sciences

## A Guidebook for Professionals

by

**Elizabeth J. Hitch, Ph.D.**
Professor, Home Economics Education
Central Michigan University

and

**June Pierce Youatt, Ph.D.**
Associate Professor, Department of Family and Child Ecology
Michigan State University

Publisher
**The Goodheart-Willcox Company, Inc.**
Tinley Park, Illinois

Library of Congress Catalog Card Number 94-38397
International Standard Book Number 1-56637-166-X

2 3 4 5 6 7 8 9 10    95    99 98 97 96

**Library of Congress Cataloging in Publication Data**

Hitch, Elizabeth J.
  Communicating family and consumer sciences: a guidebook for professionals / by Elizabeth J. Hitch and June Pierce Youatt.

      p.  cm.
  Includes bibliographical references (p.     ) and index.
  ISBN 1-56637-166-X
  1. Consumer education—Study and teaching.
  2. Home economics—Study and teaching.
  I. Youatt, June Pierce.  II. Title.
  TX335.H49  1995
  640′,73′07--dc20                          94-38397
                                              CIP

## ABOUT THE AUTHORS...

Elizabeth J. Hitch and June Pierce Youatt have brought together their experience in teaching, administration, youth development, and community service in *Communicating Family and Consumer Sciences*. Both authors have advanced degrees in education and home economics and have been responsible for home economics teacher preparation at their respective universities.

**Elizabeth J. Hitch, Ph.D.**, is a professor presently serving as Director of Teacher Education at Central Michigan University. She is responsible for coordinating CMU's teacher preparation program by working with 27 academic departments on curriculum, policy, and procedures related to teacher education. As a member of the faculty, Dr. Hitch teaches graduate and undergraduate courses in methods of teaching in formal and nonformal educational settings, curriculum development, and evaluation techniques. Her involvement in a state-wide project to assist life management teachers in meeting state standards has included development of several public relations videotapes, brochures, and posters for use by teachers, a variety of instructional materials, and a curriculum guide designed to help teachers meet the needs of exceptional students in family and consumer sciences classrooms.

**June Pierce Youatt, Ph.D.**, is an associate professor at Michigan State University in the Department of Family and Child Ecology where she teaches graduate and undergraduate courses in family and consumer sciences. She is also a specialist with Michigan State University Extension. She has directed a multi-year, state-wide project to assist teachers in implementing life management education program standards. The project has included extensive efforts in the areas of professional development, curriculum development, and program evaluation. In addition, she has received several professional development and instructional development grants. Dr. Youatt was the recipient of a 1986 New Achiever Award from the American Home Economics Association, a 1990 State of Michigan Excellence in Teaching Award, and was named the Michigan Home Economist of the Year in 1991 and College Teacher of the Year in 1993.

# ACKNOWLEDGEMENTS

Many people contributed to this book and should be recognized. The following professionals reviewed the text and provided valuable input:

Dr. Sue Couch
Associate Professor
Home Economics Education
Texas Tech University
Lubbock, Texas

Dr. Wilma Pitts Griffin
Dean
Department of Home Economics
Baylor University
Waco, Texas

LaVonne I. Kurtz
Assistant to the Dean
College of Home Economics
South Dakota State University
Brookings, South Dakota

Dr. Sharon Redick
Chairperson
Department of Home Economics
  Education
The Ohio State University
Columbus, Ohio

Dr. Betty Sawyers
Associate Professor
Home Economics Education
Purdue University
West Lafayette, Indiana

Dr. Frances M. Smith
Professor
Department of Family and
  Consumer Sciences Education
Iowa State University
Ames, Iowa

Dr. Janice Wissman
Associate Dean
College of Education
Kansas State University
Manhattan, Kansas

This book could also not have been completed without the excellent production assistance provided by Barbara Parrish.

Finally, thanks are due to our husbands and families. Their encouragement, patience (and occasional impatience!) helped to keep us on task.

# INTRODUCTION

Family and consumer sciences content — content about the practical problems facing individuals and families — is taught or communicated in a variety of settings. In school classrooms, human service agencies, community outreach programs, and in business settings, professionals are providing formal and nonformal instruction in family and consumer sciences. While the instructional contexts may be different, professionals in these settings share a common need to understand diverse learners, develop relevant instructional plans, engage in instructional interaction, and evaluate outcomes.

*Communicating Family and Consumer Sciences* is a practical, skills-based guidebook that will assist students and professionals in designing, delivering, and evaluating family and consumer sciences instruction. Students reading this book will consider different models of instruction and various contexts for teaching. Professionals will have the opportunity to reflect on their practice and to refresh instructional and presentation skills.

Teachers, agents, leaders, and facilitators (or those preparing to be) will find a wealth of straight-forward information based on a sound body of research in teaching and learning. The processes described and illustrated in *Communicating Family and Consumer Sciences* are aimed at assisting professionals in a wide range of instructional roles, whether planning a teleconference, working with a classroom of adolescents, interviewing clients, or making a presentation at a professional meeting. The frequent examples and ideas for practical application should assist students and professionals in using this information to be better communicators of family and consumer sciences content.

# CONTENTS

$$\bigcirc\!\!\!\!1$$

# BECOMING AN EDUCATOR

Are you enrolled in the Department of Family and Consumer Sciences, a College of Human Ecology, or in a School or Department of Human Services? Graduates from these programs often work in classrooms, hospitals, public and private agencies, and businesses. Some work with youth, some with consumers, some with clients or patients, and others work with entire families. A key professional role for many of these graduates is to convey information from the family and consumer sciences. Fifty years ago, graduates of these programs would have identified themselves as home economists. Today, however, while some do identify themselves as *home economists,* others call themselves *human ecologists, family life educators, consumer specialists, community service professionals*, or *nutritionists*. Because we share a common heritage in home economics, it is important to understand how this history has shaped family and consumer sciences today. Understanding our past is important in shaping a professional philosophy for the future.

## LOOKING BACK

In Marjorie East's book, *Home Economics: Past, Present, and Future* (1980), home economics is described as both an area of study or a discipline and as a group of related occupations or a profession. According to East, the founders of the field of home economics, in the early part of the twentieth century, were influenced by a number of professional, disciplinary, and philosophical models. One predominant model emphasized the application of science for improving the near environment of the individual and family. They reasoned that if science could be applied to everyday life so that the environments where individuals grew, lived, and worked were improved, then the quality of life of the individual and families would be improved. At a practical level, founders were concerned with such daily life issues as nutrition and sanitation. Early writers and thinkers in the field stressed the interrelatedness of the individual and family to their environments. According to East, home economics was described as dealing with laws, conditions, and principles that were concerned with the immediate physical environment of humans, humans as social beings, and, specifically, the relationship between these two factors. (AHEA, cited in East, 1980). Brown (1981) says that this early, often-quoted definition of home economics describes the field as inclusive and ecological in nature.

Typically, early home economists were educated broadly across subject matter areas. These subject matter areas often included child development, nutrition, food preparation, aesthetics, clothing, housing, family economics, home management, and home nursing. If home economists were to understand and assist families with the practical problems of the day, they needed to be able to integrate information in ways that could address the problems. Dealing with problems, such as managing family finances, caring for children, providing for the daily "survival" needs of family members, and maintaining the health of family members, required (and still requires) knowledge and skills from a variety of disciplines.

As the field progressed, however, the trend toward specialization grew. A home economist might specialize in housing, nutrition, or child development. Many professionals from the 1950s to today have questioned whether a move toward specialization would sacrifice the integrative nature of the field, and if so, how specialists could be prepared best to view issues holistically.

Over time, in most institutions of higher education, subject specialization became more popular than the "general" or "integrated" degree in home economics. Rather than receiving a general degree in home economics, students began to major in one of the specific areas that make up the family and consumer sciences, such as nutrition, consumer economics, or textiles. Some of these specialized majors began to take on the names and characteristics of particular roles for which students might be prepared, such as merchandising management, interior design, or financial advising. In many institutions, the general home economics major may have had lower enrollments than the more specialized areas.

During the 1960s and early 1970s, home economics professionals spent a good deal of introspective time considering where the field was in relation to its original mission and where it should go in the next century. As a result of these reflections and debate, some colleges and departments moved toward "human ecology" and other name changes as a way of emphasizing the ecological and integrative nature of the field. As professionals embraced this perspective, new disciplines and subject matter areas beyond the traditional ones were recognized as important in dealing with the persistent, practical problems of families. In some colleges and universities, human ecology became a perspective within home economics. To others, human ecology was an entirely new discipline and emerging profession. Other institutions merely noted the human ecology movement as part of the evolution of the field.

In the early 1990s, the discussion within the profession renewed around issues of the breadth and scope of the profession and how the profession could assure its viability and vitality through the twenty-first century. Informal and formal deliberations on these issues resulted in the recommendation that the profession and the professional organization move from the name "home economics" to "family and consumer sciences." The name change represented an affirmation of an integrative approach to the study of the relationships among individuals, families, and communities and the environments in which they function.

## PREPARING THE PROFESSIONAL

Traditionally, the preparation of the home economics professional included not only background in a number of related subject matter areas, but the knowledge and skills required to deliver and apply content to the practical problems of individuals and families. This professional preparation included a strong emphasis in process skills related to communicating, problem solving, and program planning. The integration, synthesis, and application of knowledge is emphasized.

Other programs emphasized preparation primarily through in-depth study in one particular content area, with the primary emphasis being competence in a specific discipline or subject matter. These programs may or may not have spent time on the integration of their particular subject matter with other areas, or on how the content might relate to larger family problems or issues. Those prepared as content specialists may have viewed their roles as being responsive to a set of problems or issues as they were defined by the discipline. Students prepared with this model may identify strongly with the subject matter area and its particular practice, but not the broader field. These students may have described themselves as dietitians, interior designers, or fashion designers *rather than* as home economists with a *specialization* in dietetics or design. Whether or not these individuals saw themselves as home economists depended on their professional socialization and whether or not they adopted as their own the perspective, mission, and purpose of the home economics profession.

The professional preparation of those in family and consumer sciences can be organized so that both the content and process skills necessary to successfully facilitate the dynamic approach to family issues are developed. Kieran, Vaines, and Badir (1984) described the profession (home economics) from a systems view. They identified three interactive components of the profession that must be transmitted to students in preparation to practice family and consumer sciences. These are:

- The goal or mission.
- A body of knowledge.
- Practice (includes the methods of transmitting the body of knowledge).

Viewing the profession as a system provides an important perspective. It suggests that not only is the profession and discipline based on relationships and interactions, but that preparation involves integration. This dynamic model may also assist students in better understanding their own academic preparation and why academic programs consist of a variety of types of classes and educational experiences. To prepare an individual to function as a professional requires grounding in each of the components of the profession.

## THE GOAL OR MISSION OF THE PROFESSION

The goal or mission is the component that serves as a rationale for why the profession exists. It provides a guide or purpose for its members. All professions have some type of mission or purpose that guides members. Professionals in family and consumer sciences are guided by a commitment to enhancing the well-being of individuals, families, and communities by enabling individuals and families to reach their own goals and by helping to influence and shape societal change that will enhance the human condition. This mission is not bound by context. For example, the professional with a specialization in gerontology, family resource management, or design could equally aspire to this goal or purpose. Each would, however, assist families in different ways and perhaps work in very different agencies or institutions.

## THE BODY OF KNOWLEDGE OF THE PROFESSION

In addition to a goal or mission, the profession encompasses a *body of knowledge*. This second component depends upon the first for definition. Unlike mathematics or chemistry, there are no tight and clearly defined boundaries that surround family and consumer sciences content. Family and consumer sciences content is drawn from several disciplines, from chemistry to psychology to economics to art. Since the mission of this profession focuses on concern about the activities of the family and its relationship to its near environments, family and consumer sciences draws content from disciplines as it may relate to these interactions. Kieran, Vaines, and Badir (1984, p. 36) state: "The areas of study that make up family in the near environment include clothing, foods, textiles, nutrition, housing, and applied design." These examples of applied subject matter areas and their prerequisite conceptual bases in such disciplines as psychology, chemistry, economics, and sociology are intimately interrelated subsystems that make up the body of knowledge that are the family and consumer sciences.

## THE PRACTICE OF FAMILY AND CONSUMER SCIENCES

The third component of the profession is *practice*. This includes the methods of transmitting the body of knowledge to clients. Practice is not limited to the "how-to's" of teaching, advising, counseling, or consulting, but includes the reasoning and decision-making that are involved in the ethical transmission of knowledge. Kieran, Vaines, and Badir (1984) suggest that practice involves the human characteristics of the professional, as well as the role competencies and delivery skills required to communicate content.

## COMMUNICATING CONTENT

Since the focus of this text is specifically communication, it's a good idea to further analyze the third component — practice. As indicated, **practice** involves the application or transmission of a purpose and knowledge in a way that serves clients.

While not all professionals in family and consumer sciences are involved in the direct instruction of learners, it is interesting to note how many roles of family and consumer sciences professionals involve some aspect or element of instruction. Think about the professional role for which you are preparing or in which you are already working. Then look at the checklist in Figure 1-1. Notice how many of the tasks are performed by professionals in your career field. If you checked at least one of the tasks, you have or will have responsibility for communicating family and consumer sciences content! In fact, for most professionals in family and consumer sciences, instruction is at least one component of their professional roles.

Instructing is not necessarily standing in front of a classroom with a ream of lecture notes, although that may be the first image that comes to mind. Instruction or teaching occurs through a variety of strategies — consulting, advising, reporting, counseling, and training. It may involve personal interaction with learners or interaction through print or other media. Instruction that involves

**FIGURE 1-1. Communication Tasks Performed in Family and Consumer Sciences**

- Making presentations to clients about products and services.
- Teaching learners a particular process or skill.
- Training and evaluating other employees.
- Writing newsletters or other written media for the purpose of disseminating information.
- Making presentations at professional conferences or meetings.
- Providing instructions, directions, or information to clients.
- Explaining to clients how a product or process works.
- Assisting learners in making decisions or choices by providing reliable information and resources.
- Providing radio, television, or print interviews.
- Developing informational or educational materials.
- Explaining resources, services, or procedures to clients or other employees.

person-to-person interaction is the focus. Professionals in business, government, health care, education, human services, and media are involved to some extent in instruction. The different types of communicators, conditions, and types of communication most often used by each are shown in Figure 1-2.

**FIGURE 1-2. Careers for Communicating Family and Consumer Sciences**

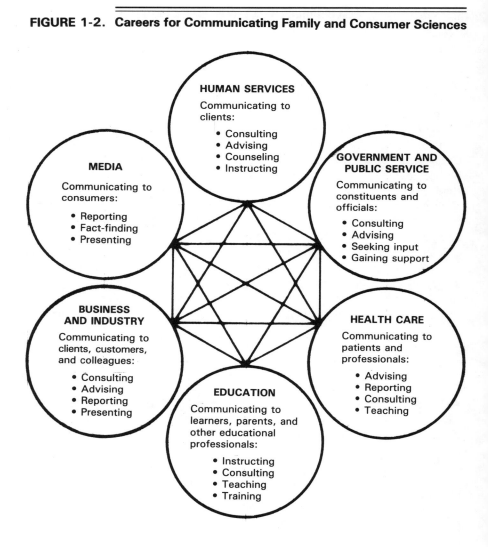

# FORMAL, INFORMAL, AND NONFORMAL COMMUNICATION

Education can be viewed on a continuum, from formal to nonformal to informal. You may be most familiar with **formal education**, such as is found in public and private schools. In formal instruction, the teacher establishes goals for instruction, determines the content and teaching strategies, manages instruction, and evaluates outcomes. Formal education is usually hierarchical. You progress from one level to the next. Formal education usually results in some type of diploma, certification, or degree. Formal education is teacher-directed and structured. Teaching in early childhood education programs, or life skills courses in middle schools, high schools, and in higher education are formal education activities.

**Nonformal education** is also planned and guided by the professional, but is usually less structured than formal education (Grandstaff, 1973; Ward & Detonni, 1974). In most nonformal education, the professional acts as the facilitator. Learners help establish the goals or objectives for learning, and may have more input as to how and what they learn. Learners may come and go in nonformal education experiences, while formal educational experiences generally require proceeding through a particular sequence or hierarchy of instruction. Community education classes, on-the-job training programs, 4-H clubs, nutrition counseling, financial planning seminars, and expectant parent classes are a few examples of nonformal education opportunities (Rainey, 1976).

**Informal education** describes activities that provide often unintentional or unplanned learning (Grandstaff, 1973). It has no formal structure. It may include activities like reading to a child, serving as a role model or mentor for a learner, allowing a neighbor to look over your shoulder as you demonstrate some household maintenance activity, or discussing the fiber content of a garment with a customer. "Teaching" in this way happens daily, whether we realize it or not!

It is this range of possible types of instruction that makes communicating family and consumer sciences content unique. The instructor may need to adapt his or her instructional style to formal or nonformal settings. Teaching may occur in a classroom with rows of desks and a chalkboard, in an office or boardroom, beside a hospital bed, in a retail store, or at the kitchen table of a client.

# COMMUNICATION COHERENT WITH MISSION

Like all professions, family and consumer sciences has a philosophy and mission. Communicating family and consumer sciences content is done within the context of the mission or purpose of the profession. The instructor is not merely concerned with the transmission of knowledge for its own sake, but is concerned that this knowledge and information will be applied and used. The instructor with a mission to enable individuals and families to make enlightened decisions is less concerned with formulas and prescriptions than with processes and practices. This involves helping learners achieve various levels of understanding; not just the technical (how to), but knowledge that assists individuals in understanding why (interpretive) and the emancipative knowledge that allows individuals and families to be self-directed (Brown & Paolucci, 1979). In recent years, educators have spent a great deal of time exploring how learners can be taught critical thinking skills, problem-solving strategies, and higher order thinking skills within the context of family and consumer sciences content.

Since the need for family and consumer sciences content cuts across all ages and stages, the professional may work with youth or adults, advantaged or disadvantaged, well-educated or undereducated. This makes the nature of communicating family and consumer sciences content vary considerably from professional to professional.

Consider the collection of subject matter that make up family and consumer sciences as well. Unlike some content, family and consumer sciences may be very close to the lives of the learners. Since it is applied subject matter, it is relevant to the learners. This requires instructional methods that convey its relevance and applicability, not just, for example, conveying isolated information on human development theory, but helping learners understand how the theory addresses their needs for understanding. Some of the content may be sensitive in nature; content that is highly personal to the learner. Conveying this content requires sensitivity to the learner, as well as an attitude of respect and acceptance for the learner. After all, if the professional is really committed to enabling families to become self-directed, his or her instruction must involve helping strategies like support, listening, or being a resource.

There are some unique aspects to communicating family and consumer sciences content, whether in a classroom, agency, institutional, or business setting. The professional must come to the practice of the profession with a commitment to the mission, a grasp of relevant subject matter, and a myriad of professional communication skills. There is no one professional "slot" for an individual prepared in the family and consumer sciences. He or she will find opportunities to work with individuals and families in a variety of public and private agencies, institutions, or organizations. Through the communicating of family and consumer sciences content, however, each has the opportunity to make a significant difference in the lives of his or her clients and learners.

# SUMMARY

Family and consumer sciences has an important philosophical and practical heritage in home economics. The discipline and profession began committed to the well-being of individuals and families through the application of science to everyday, practical problems. Today, family and consumer sciences uses an integrative approach to the relationships among individuals, families, and communities and the environments in which they function. The profession has declared its leadership role in improving the well-being of individuals, families, and communities, impacting the development, delivery, and evaluation of consumer goods and services, and shaping societal change that will enhance the human condition.

Many professionals in the family and consumer sciences will have, as at least one aspect of their professional roles, the responsibility of communicating content information. Communication may occur as a part of formal, nonformal, or informal education. Communicating content offers some unique challenges because of the diverse "consumers" of the knowledge in family and consumer sciences, the variety of settings in which that knowledge is provided, and the broad range of information that make up the family and consumer sciences. This book is about developing the skills required to effectively communicate that content.

## REFERENCES AND RESOURCES

Brown, M. (1981). Our intellectual ecology: Recitation of definition: A case in point. *Journal of Home Economics, 73,* 14-18.

Brown, M.M. (1985). *Philosophical studies of home economics in the United States,* (Vols. I-II). East Lansing, MI: Michigan State University.

Brown, M., & Paolucci, B. (1979). *Home economics: A definition.* Washington, DC: American Home Economics Association (mimeographed).

Combs, P.H. (1973). *New paths to learning.* New York: International Council for Educational Development.

East, M. (1980). *Home economics: Past, present, and future.* Boston: Allyn and Bacon.

Grandstaff, M. (1973). Are formal schools the best place to educate? In C. Brembeck (Ed.), *New strategies for educational development: The cross-cultural search for nonformal alternatives.* Toronto: D.C. Heath.

Istre, S.M., & Self, P.A. (1990). Toward a more unified discipline of home economics. *Journal of Home Economics, 82* (4), 4-9.

Kieran, D., Vaines, E., & Badir, D. (1984). *The home economist as a helping professional.* Winnepeg, Canada: Frye.

Peterat, L. (1986). *The conversation and company of educated women.* Urbana-Champaign, IL: University of Illinois, Urbana-Champaign, Division of Home Economics Education.

Rader, B. (Ed.). (1987). *Significant writings in home economics: 1911-1979.* Peoria, IL: Bennett & McKnight.

Rainey, M.C. (1976). Nonformal education: Definitions and distinctions. *Interaction 'ECO', 6* (1).

Ward, T., & Detonni, J. (1974). Nonformal education: Problems and promises. In Kleis, et al., *Nonformal education: The definitional problem.* East Lansing, MI: Institute for International Studies in Education, Michigan State University, 8-29.

# THE
# LEARNER

The professional preparing to communicate family and consumer sciences content has the opportunity to work with a variety of learners. Each year, literally millions of individuals are enrolled in Cooperative Extension and 4-H outreach programs, school family and consumer sciences programs, parenting and parent preparation classes, financial management seminars, wellness programs, nutrition clinics, and the list goes on! Each learner is unique. He or she is part of a one-of-a-kind ecological system. You may begin describing the learner by age or stage of development or ability level, but many of the characteristics of learners have a great deal to do with the environments in which they grow and interact. That initial environment, the family, has a major influence on the development of attitudes and values, including attitudes about education. The resources and other inputs to the family determine such factors as nutritional status, available health care, and educational opportunities. The school and neighborhood environment further influence opportunities, ideas about other people, even opinions on world events! No two learners are the same, and yet content needs to be relevant for each learner.

One of the most exciting realizations about family and consumer sciences is that it can be made relevant to all learners. There is a universality about the field if it is viewed as dealing with the **perennial practical problems** facing families. Brown and Paolucci (1979) used this phrase to describe those problems that every family faces, in every generation, across all cultures. For example, most families have faced questions such as: How should we manage our resources? How should we provide and care for elderly family members? How should we meet our food and nutritional needs? How should we guide and nurture our children? These are examples of perennial practical problems.

These are the types of significant, relevant issues that are the focus of family and consumer sciences.

While these issues or questions are common to nearly every family across time, space, and culture, it should be obvious that the answers to these questions will not be common for all learners. They *should not* be the same for all learners. The uniqueness of each family will determine how family members respond to these issues. Each learner has to find personal, practical, and relevant meaning in information in order for the information to influence his or her behavior (Combs, Avila, & Purkey, 1971). The professional in the role of instructor or facilitator, then, must acknowledge and respect the differences among learners.

Beyond respecting the diversity of learners, the instructor must know enough about learners to plan appropriate and effective instruction. Detailed and reliable information about diverse learners is essential to making rational decisions about communicating content (Williams, 1986). Effective instructors not only thoroughly understand the subject matter, but they understand the audience with whom they are working.

Learners are typically categorized by age (or developmental stage). Children, youth, and adults are obvious classifications. Thinking about learners in terms of developmental stage is reasonable, since there are some relationships between age and the ability to learn certain concepts. Another way to categorize learners links stage in the life cycle and learning needs. These topics will be discussed in the next two chapters. This chapter will focus on other aspects of diversity including lifestyle, ability to learn, and cultural and ethnic diversity.

## LIFESTYLE

**Lifestyle** can be defined as a way of living that reflects the values and attitudes of the individual. The lifestyle of a learner may be affected by factors such as his or her role in the family or society, available resources, religion and philosophy of life, and cultural or regional values.

## RELATIONSHIP BETWEEN LIFESTYLE AND LEARNING

Although instructors in any subject should take into account lifestyle variations when planning effective instruction, the consideration of lifestyle is critical in family and consumer sciences where values and attitudes are so closely tied to the content presented. It is tempting to assume that all learners live like you do — or want to live like you do — and to plan instruction so that it reflects your values. For example, a commonly used family and consumer sciences lesson in secondary schools dealt with wedding planning. Students comparison shopped for gowns and tuxedos, catered meals, and floral arrangements. As a finale, the ceremony itself was often enacted, with students playing the roles of bride, groom, and minister. While accepted as a traditional part of a family living class, consider the assumptions such a lesson makes about the "right" way to have a wedding. How might it conflict with the religious values of students? In what ways does it reinforce values of consumption? Is it appropriate, or even ethical, to model one type of ceremony for all learners, without consideration of socioeconomic status or cultural values?

The professional starting a small business in a new community provides another example of the importance of considering the relationship between lifestyle and learning. He or she should be especially interested in the lifestyles of community members as the new product or service is developed and marketed. Lifestyle will impact not only who will buy, but also how, when, and what products or services will be purchased. The content to be communicated about these products or services will need to be shaped by the consideration of the lifestyles of potential consumers.

## How Learners Approach Learning

Lifestyles also affect the *way* learners approach learning. Areas where the relationship between lifestyle and how a learner learns that are immediately evident include the home environment of the learner, previous experiences and opportunities of the learner, and the physical health and nutrition of the learner.

The **home environments** of learners can vary dramatically. For instance, a student from a large family, living in a limited amount of space, might need to make adaptations to his or her environment in order to study and learn. If a bedroom is shared with several siblings, the opportunity for study in that room may be limited. A student might choose to cope by "plugging in" to a stereo set while studying, studying at the library or in study halls, or not studying at all since it is so difficult.

The relationship between lifestyle and how a learner learns is also evident when you consider **lifestyle opportunities** of learners. Students who have experienced little outside the lifestyle of their immediate families and communities may find it difficult to try a new experience. The learner who has never seen an artichoke and has no idea it could be served as a food is very different from the student who has eaten calamari (squid) while on the Costa del Sol in Spain. These students are likely to be different in the way they learn about new foods just because of their lifestyles.

Likewise, learners will be influenced by the opportunities for learning they have experienced in their homes and families. Learners who have access to computers, literature, travel, and cultural activities often come to the learning environment with very different attitudes and skills than those learners who have had few experiences. Programs for young learners, such as Head Start, were developed for this very reason.

**Health** is another area where you can see the relationship between lifestyle and the way a learner learns. Learners with healthy lifestyles usually come to the classroom awake, alert, and ready to learn. Learners with unhealthy lifestyles or poor nutrition are often tired, unwell, and unlikely to either want to or be best able to learn.

## How Educators Approach Learners

As a formal or nonformal educator, you may be able to identify common lifestyle considerations that affect the needs and interests of your entire group of learners. The extension professional serving urban families, for example, might find that many of these families are apartment dwellers. In planning programs related to family financial planning, then, the extension professional would select appropriate examples for these learners by using rent as one component in the family budget.

The family and consumer sciences professional in business who is responsible for customer services or purchasing can readily understand the importance of client needs and interests. For example, providing late-night opportunities to purchase groceries is becoming more critical as family daytime hours are filled with school, work, and other activities.

Even though the family and consumer sciences educator may be able to make some assumptions or generalizations about a group of learners, lifestyle variations of individual learners must be considered. The teachers who plan Christmas projects as part of classroom activities have failed to take into account the diverse religions that may be represented in their classrooms.

## FAMILY DIVERSITY

Information about family diversity could be an important aspect in understanding the lifestyles of learners. Certainly no assumptions should be made about the family backgrounds of learners. There has been so much and such rapid change in families over the past 40 years that the instructor can only be sure that in any instructional setting, diversity in family structure will most likely be represented.

Instructors are likely to encounter increasing numbers of single mothers because of increased numbers of divorces and increasing numbers of births to never-married mothers. In 1987, 24 percent of births were to women out of wedlock. An estimated one of eight women was pregnant at marriage.

Besides those women who have never married and who are caring for and raising children, an increasing number of families are headed by single parents, and most of these are women. The number of families headed by women with no husband present doubled from 1970 to 1990 and represented 17 percent of family households in 1990. In 1990, 28 percent of families with children in the U.S. were headed by only one parent — over one-fourth of all families with children. These families were headed by a never-married, divorced, or widowed parent (Bureau of the Census, 1990).

Although not all single parent families are financially in need, many are. In 1989, 12.8 percent of the population of the United States lived below the official government poverty line. Of single parent families, about 46 percent were below the poverty level. While the average educational level of single parent families has risen over the last 40 years, a shocking number of these families remain economically disadvantaged.

If one-quarter of the families in this country are single-parent families, then three-quarters are two-parent families. It may be important to note, however, that many of these families are reconstituted or remarried families. In fact, almost half of the marriages annually in this country are second marriages. This means that many children in this country are part of stepfamilies. It has been predicted that one-third of children now under 18 are already stepchildren or will experience being a stepchild before they reach the age of 18 (Glick, 1988).

Whether part of single-parent or two-parent families, the majority of the women in these families are working. The increased number of women in the paid work force (especially mothers of young children) may be one of the most significant trends in the last 40 years. About 60 percent of women are currently in the paid work force, and it is predicted that by the year 2000, half of the paid work force will be women. Nearly 80 percent of divorced women are already in the workplace.

Another obvious demographic trend is increased lifespan. The lifespan has increased over 20 years since the turn of the last century. For the first time in history, people are living in a society in which most people live to be old. Consider what this means to formal and nonformal educators in terms of lifelong learners.

As has been noted, understanding the family is important to understanding the learner. The family serves as the first or primary context for the learner. It suggests educational needs, influences attitudes and values toward learning, and determines, in large part, the resources of learners. As families become more diverse, it will become more important to recognize this diversity and to try to understand how it affects the learner and how it may affect his or her learning.

## THE ECONOMICALLY DISADVANTAGED

Instructors should strive for a bias-free instructional environment for those learners who may have experienced the many disadvantages that are often the consequence of poverty, particularly urban poverty. Quite often instructors in urban settings encounter learners who are at risk because of economic disadvantage. These learners may come to the learning situation ill-prepared to be successful, with few material or personal resources to support their efforts to learn.

The typical response to economically disadvantaged learners has been to create a learning environment where instructors exert strong control, and the task of learners is to adopt appropriate behavior and to comply with instructor expectations. Further, since it is expected that the prerequisite to any other type of learning is "basic skills," major emphasis is usually placed on developing these basic skills in learners, whether or not they have any particular relevance to the world of the learner. While, in some ways, these assumptions about the need for control and an established, basic curriculum may appear logical, they violate what is known about learners who have experienced poverty and its consequences. Youth and adults who have grown up without developing a sense of trust in any system, and who have experienced limited success by following the conventional rules of those systems are least likely to fit in an environment that is not sensitive to their particular needs or interests.

Some descriptions of instruction that work with learners in poverty have been developed. These descriptions have been formulated based on what goes on in urban schools that have been recognized as exemplary (Haberman, 1992).

First, appropriate instruction is relevant to the learners. It deals with the real problems and concerns with which the audience is dealing. Rather than using abstract examples or issues as a basis for instruction, the challenges facing the learners are used as a basis for teaching. Real-life experiences are important, too. Field trips, observation, demonstrations, and other hands-on activities provide new opportunities for learning and reflecting.

Next, learners are encouraged to deal with big ideas, not just isolated facts. Facts and discrete information that may soon be outdated are inadequate to address real-life issues. Learners should be encouraged to make generalizations and use concepts and principles rather than merely memorize data.

Learners need to have the opportunity to make some decisions about their instruction. This may involve deciding on topics of study or how a unit of study will be conducted. This not only allows learners to experience some control over their environment (which may in itself be a new experience), but prepares them to make other choices. Realizing the consequences of these choices may be a critical learning concept for students who have, because of economic disadvantage, known little autonomy or freedom of choice.

These learners also need action learning, where they can take part in what goes on in the learning environment. Haberman (1992) contends that all learning should provide students with the opportunity to develop understanding and acceptance of others and to develop personal ideals and principles by which to live. Positive models of fairness and justice must be part of the instructional environment and must be demonstrated by the instructor.

Learners, too, must be encouraged to meet high standards through the improvement and refinement of their own work. The goal is to teach excellence through perseverance, an important lesson for life. The strategies that work when dealing with learners from impoverished backgrounds are summarized in Figure 2-1.

**FIGURE 2-1. Strategies for Working with Learners in Poverty**

- Make instruction relevant to learners.
- Encourage learners to deal with big ideas—not just isolated facts.
- Address real-life issues.
- Encourage learners to help decide what instruction is relevant.
- Use active learning strategies and hands-on experience.
- Exhibit fair and just behavior.
- Encourage perseverance to meet high standards.

# RESEARCHING LEARNER LIFESTYLES

Effective instruction allows learners to interpret ideas presented in light of their own lifestyles. In order to know something about learner lifestyles, it may be necessary to do some research about the individuals you expect to teach. This research need not be formal, but does need to be done systematically. One simple way to begin finding out about learner lifestyles is to explore the community in which learners live. This is simple for professionals who find themselves in a business that is located in the neighborhood it serves. Walks around the community can reveal a great deal about the lifestyles of the people who live there. Are there a number of churches or synagogues? Of what denomination? What is the predominant form of housing? Apartments? Single-family homes? What are the approximate sizes of lots? Do most families seem to have cars? Is there a regular bus route in the area? Is there a local restaurant where many of the neighborhood people gather for lunch? What other agencies or organizations are open to the community or neighborhood? What do the housing and dress of the community members suggest about their socioeconomic status? These are only a few of the questions about lifestyle that could be asked (and answered!) by viewing the community as an alert observer.

Professionals who find themselves serving more diverse and less constant groups can also find out something about lifestyles of learners in order to plan the most effective instruction possible. A quick questionnaire used at the beginning of a presentation can be tabulated on-site. Then the data can be used to help direct the learning. For example, the extension specialist asked to give a presentation on discipline techniques to be used with small children could pass out some simple questions on paper or ask orally about age of children, number of children, examples of behaviors presently being experienced, etc. With this data in hand, the specialist is more likely to identify appropriate content for the learners present.

Clearly, the needs and interests of individuals and the ways in which they learn may be influenced by lifestyle. Consideration of lifestyle must be a part of planning for instruction.

# ABILITY TO LEARN

The ability of learners to understand and apply content is probably one of the most obvious considerations in planning instruction. Within the school setting, discussions about the ability of learners most often refer to cognitive abilities, but within the context of family and consumer sciences there is opportunity and need to be concerned about the affective and psychomotor abilities of learners as well. Parent educators, for example, are as concerned with the social skills (affective skills) used in parenting as the cognitive information about parenting. Food service or hospitality supervisors must be as concerned with what learners can do as with what learners know. An adolescent in high school life management, who may have difficulty memorizing information, may be quite successful in the interior design course at the area vocational center. In other words, there are different types of abilities that may be built upon within the context of family and consumer sciences.

## VARIATIONS IN LEARNER ABILITIES

Since the abilities of learners are so varied, the instructor needs to expect variability within a group of learners. Not all fifth grade students in a latch-key program will be able to run a computer program on decision making after one demonstration. Not all college freshmen will understand the digestive process after four lectures. The community education class on house buying may be comprised of students of different educational levels and abilities. Even though the instructor is dealing with an adult audience with a common educational interest, assumptions cannot be made about the reading level, prerequisite knowledge, or cognitive ability of these learners.

While the instructor may not be initially aware of the varying learning abilities of individual clients or students, each learner already has a picture of him or herself as a learner. Previous school experiences, the messages of significant others, and the successes learners have experienced contribute to their own concept of their ability to learn. Some learners, over time, become very aware of particular learning difficulties or disabilities that may lead to low motivation or poor enthusiasm for learning new information or tasks. Adults who earned low grades in high school or other formal education may avoid other formal learning opportunities altogether because of earlier, negative experiences. These individuals are unlikely to voluntarily place themselves in a situation where they risk failure.

When the learning situation is involuntary for learners, as it is in middle school or high school, unmotivated learners may use disruptive behavior as a way to cope with their learning difficulties. A teenage girl who has difficulty reading may create any type of disturbance in order to be asked to leave the classroom before her turn to read aloud. A middle school boy may quietly disassemble a piece of classroom equipment out of boredom because he cannot read an assignment. He turns to an activity at which he is successful, even though this may be disruptive to the rest of the class. Teachers in formal classrooms need to look carefully at the circumstances that surround or initiate disruptive behaviors in classrooms to determine whether or not they may be linked to the student's ability to accomplish assigned tasks in the classroom.

The same principles apply to gifted learners. Gifted learners, too, have formed self-concepts related to their ability to achieve. They may feel a need to always be successful and may put pressure on themselves to achieve at a consistently high level at all times. Gifted learners may increase the demands on the instructor since it is important for these learners to be challenged. This may require different and additional learning experiences provided by the teacher. Among gifted adolescents and children, disruptive behavior may develop as a result of boredom. Assignments that are too short or too easy are quickly completed, leaving the gifted student with the time and imagination to develop his or her own activities.

## RESPONDING TO LEARNER ABILITY

In recognizing the varying abilities of learners, there are two important implications. First, it may be necessary for instructors to systematically individualize learner outcomes for different ability levels of learners. In the formal school setting, this is typically done by creating an individual educational plan. Teachers, counselors, and parents may identify the learning outcomes that are most appropriate for a learner, and these become the basis for his or her educational plan.

In nonformal settings, instructors can follow the same principle in consultation with the learner. What does he or she need to know? Where are the learner's interests, motivations, and/or abilities? It is probably somewhat easier to individualize a learning plan in nonformal settings, but it is no less important than in the context of a formal school setting.

The other implication for instruction is that teaching strategies selected by the instructor should meet the various learning styles of individuals. While Chapter 5 of this text (Learning Styles) deals more specifically with learner preferences in taking in information, it is important to emphasize this in view of learner abilities. Individuals have different preferences for learning and styles that help them best learn. Some learners have vivid recall of information after hearing a lecture, while others need to read or write the information in order to remember. These are examples of learning styles, and suggest the need to vary the type of instruction provided for learners.

Although not all family and consumer sciences professionals are trained to work with limited-ability learners, there are some principles that any instructor can employ that will increase success with learners who have difficulty. Tips for working with learners with limited ability are summarized in Figure 2-2.

First, instruction should be as concrete as possible. Because limited-ability learners may have difficulty dealing with abstractions, instruction should build on what is real. Actual materials, real-life examples, and practice in a realistic setting are important. To increase the likelihood that the learning will be transferred and used in the learner's life, instruction should be as close to real-life as possible. Instead of viewing a diagram on how to diaper a baby, the

---

**FIGURE 2-2. Tips for Working with Limited-Ability Learners**

- Make instruction as concrete as possible.
- Break ideas into simple concepts.
- Provide multiple opportunities for practice.
- Provide frequent feedback.

limited-ability learners need to see diapering demonstrated and then practice on an infant or life-size doll.

Content should be broken down into small segments so that learning can occur a "piece at a time." Teach one skill or concept, then build to the next. Allow the learners to focus on, practice, and master one segment at a time. Success with each step will increase motivation to continue.

There should be many opportunities for practice. Limited-ability learners generally profit from repetition. Practicing a skill over and over creates opportunity for learning and allows the learner to develop confidence in his or her ability. Through practice, the skill becomes part of the learner's repertoire.

There should be plenty of opportunities for feedback as well. Learners need correction, reinforcement, and praise. This helps learners stay focused on the task, and increases motivation.

## CULTURAL AND ETHNIC DIVERSITY

There is no doubt that family and consumer sciences professionals preparing for tomorrow's agencies, organizations, and classrooms will work with a more culturally and racially diverse population than professionals have in this century. In 1990, the U.S. population consisted of 80.3 percent white, 12.1 percent black, 9 percent Hispanic, 2.9 percent Asian/Pacific Islander, and .8 percent Native American/Eskimo (U.S. Bureau of the Census, 1990). Due to trends in birth rates and immigration, however, the U.S. will have a *minority majority* by 2060, according to demographer Leon Bouvier (1991). The 1990 census indicated 6 percent of U.S. counties have populations where the number of combined minority groups exceeds the number of non-Hispanic whites. The 1990 census also found that neighborhoods are more and more likely to be segregated by income level than by race. The trend is toward increasing ethnic and racial diversity.

The increased diversity in the U.S. population causes everyone from educators to marketing analysts to rethink how to do business. Certainly old definitions of minority groups are becoming meaningless. For those communicating family and consumer sciences content, this should mean a strong commitment toward being effective with all learners.

English is not always the primary language of learners. Increasing numbers of communities are becoming multilingual. One school system in suburban Detroit, for example, has students who speak 25 different languages! This phenomenon is not limited to larger urban environments, however. Many small towns are comprised of learners who speak languages other than English, too. The task of making instruction meaningful to all students becomes increasingly difficult without an understanding of the culture and backgrounds of these learners. Forcing bilingual students to abandon their language preference too often encourages the abandonment of cultural pride as well.

Ideally, there would be professionals who would be prepared to work with learners in their native languages. Where that isn't possible, instructional materials should be used that reflect the culture of the learners. With youth, family involvement should be encouraged. Involving families makes them a part of the instruction and may create positive attitudes toward the learning environment and learning. Using volunteers who speak the languages of learners and who represent their culture may also help make learning experiences more relevant.

Racial and cultural ethnicity should be considered and taken seriously in preparing instruction for learners. The consideration, however, has less to do with how to make instruction different for different groups, and more to do with being nonbiased across diverse populations.

Some distinctive differences in communication patterns exist across cultures. The need to establish a relationship before conducting business, preferences related to personal space or distance when talking, or in eye contact may be related to cultural differences. Instructors working with Asian populations, for example, should discover by what name learners prefer to be addressed since the order of names is not conventional with typical U.S. patterns (first name, last name). Instructors working with Arabic students may discover differences in the physical closeness or distance they prefer when having personal conversations. Coming to understand the communication patterns of any culture, however, is really part of the larger principle of coming to respect and appreciate all learners. Creating an environment of respect allows each learner to work and grow, free of limiting stereotypes and expectations. Instructional strategies that recognize diversity are shown in Figure 2-3.

## SENSITIVITY TO GENDER

Over the past two decades, major strides in eliminating obvious sex bias from instructional programs and materials have been made. Most textbooks now, for example, are balanced in portraying men and women in various occupational roles. Efforts have been made to eliminate language that suggested scripting by sexes. For instance, the fireman, policeman, and stewardess have been replaced by the firefighter, police officer, and flight attendant. These changes in language and image are neither insignificant nor trivial. They each

---

**FIGURE 2-3. Some Strategies for Encouraging a Learning Environment Recognizing Diversity**

- Learn and use the methods of addressing and greeting people from the learners' cultures.
- Identify and use customs surrounding gift-giving at introduction and/or parting.
- Discover and respect preferred social distances during conversation.
- Recognize variations in eye contact.
- Acknowledge holidays and other significant religious events or cultural celebrations.
- Learn about dress as an indication of values, status, or customs.
- Use learning materials that portray all cultures in a positive way.

represent concrete attempts to portray broader options for both men and women. This is particularly important in educational settings. Examples of language that can be exclusionary or negative and how to "neutralize" such language are given in Figure 2-4.

The more subtle forms of sex-role stereotyping and sexism may still be present. Professionals dealing with learners have a responsibility to become aware of these and to take deliberate action to overcome the behaviors or to modify any materials that restrict male or female learners.

During group instruction, instructors should be responsive to the classroom climate. Research indicates that males are more likely to dominate discussions and that males often receive more constructive criticism than do females (Gage & Berliner, 1988). Instructors must be aware of the patterns that may develop in groups and consciously balance instructional time and attention.

Instructors must also examine the assumptions they have about learners that may influence their interaction with learners and their instruction. Who, for example, is assumed to have the primary responsibility for rearing children? Who is most responsible for earning the primary income? What assumptions are made about work hours or leisure-time? The beliefs held by instructors regarding these issues may influence when instruction is scheduled, assumptions about prerequisite knowledge, or areas of educational need or interest.

All materials and media should be examined for equity. Males and females should be portrayed as participating equally in physical and intellectual ac-

## FIGURE 2-4. Examples of Language Usage

| EXCLUSIONARY LANGUAGE | NEUTRAL LANGUAGE |
|---|---|
| The policewoman patrolled | The police officer patrolled |
| As man searched for answers | As people searched for answers |
| The female judge presided | The judge presided |
| The typical senator sends his constituents | The typical senator sends constituents |

| NEGATIVE FEMALE LANGUAGE | NEUTRAL LANGUAGE |
|---|---|
| Girl talk | Small talk |
| Girls in the secretarial pool | Secretarial staff |
| Old maid | Woman |
| Employees with wives and children | Employees and their families |

| NEGATIVE MALE LANGUAGE | NEUTRAL LANGUAGE |
|---|---|
| Ken helps with the children | Ken cares for the children |
| His son was a real cry-baby | His son was easily upset |
| The breadwinner | The wage earner |
| Tom respects his old man | Tom respects his dad |

tivities. Men and women should be shown in both domestic and occupational roles. Both males and females should also be portrayed with a wide range of human responses, including tenderness, aggression, fear, and appreciation. Materials and media that represent this balance are less likely to restrict the expectations and attitudes of learners.

As with other types of equity, the key to sex equity is treating each learner with respect. The sex, economic status, or cultural background of the learner is only a factor as it directly relates to understanding the educational needs of the learner. These factors are less likely to be significant than the characteristics of the individual learner. A quick check to determine the presence of gender bias that can be used by professionals is given in Figure 2-5.

**FIGURE 2-5. A Quick Check for Forms of Gender Bias**

**Directions:** Rate yourself on each of the statements below.

**Attitude**
— I think it is important to treat males and females equally.
— I do not joke about males' or females' abilities or roles.
— I do not ''put down'' people of either gender.

**Expectations**
— I expect similar behavior from males and females.

**Duties**
— I make assignments based upon ability rather than gender.

**Environment**
— I use visual materials that are nonsexist and nonracist.
— I use visual materials that show men and women in a variety of roles.
— I use visual materials that reflect the varied interests of men and women without showing stereotyped examples.

**Curriculum**
In planning curriculum, I ensure that:
— the needs and interests of all students (male and female) are considered.
— the contributions of both sexes are acknowledged.
— all students are able to explore the wide range of career options and roles available to them.

Considering the statements above, check the continuum below to assess your gender bias awareness.

| Always | Often | Sometimes | Rarely | Never |
|---|---|---|---|---|
| Basically gender fair | | Need some improvement | | Need much improvement |

Consider your overall rating. List some specific goals for yourself to help achieve gender equity in your areas of professional responsibility.

# CREATING A BIAS-FREE
# LEARNING ENVIRONMENT

Creating a bias-free environment means guarding against some stumbling blocks, as well as consciously adopting some bias-free behaviors and attitudes. The stumbling blocks to a bias-free environment may include language, class-related values, cultural values, nonverbal communication, and stereotypes.

Language can reflect attitudes and values, so positive communication must make every effort to avoid biases. Biases through language creep in via words, images, qualifiers, and tone of voice. Words that have racist meanings or suggestions should be avoided. Expressions that might reinforce stereotypical images of any group should not be used. Avoid generalizations that refer to ethnicity or comparisons that are based on ethnicity. Again, these encourage the development or reinforcement of stereotypes. Not all Hispanics, Asians, or Africans are alike anymore than all of the persons within any other population group. In fact, avoid referring to the ethnic, racial, or cultural background of a person unless it is relevant. What is the purpose in describing an individual as the African American judge, the Hispanic teacher, or the Asian musician? These descriptors are rarely relevant. Consider, too, messages that take lightly stereotyping and bias. There is nothing humorous about limiting others through perceptions or expectations.

Any publications or media that you use should adequately and honestly represent a diverse population. That is, textbooks, videotapes, and other materials should fairly represent gender, racial, and ethnic groups. It is important that tokenism also be avoided through these materials. Featuring only one African American learner or one Asian homemaker just for the sake of doing so is patronizing. Fairly representing persons from various groups is a movement toward bias-free communication. Various types of bias to avoid are listed and defined in Figure 2-6.

As instructors work with learners of various backgrounds, it is important to concentrate on the performance of the individual rather than on the characteristics of the individual. The expectations for achievement and the opportunities to achieve should be equally available to all learners. Duties and responsibilities assigned to learners should be made on the basis of ability rather than race, ethnicity, or gender. Learners, too, should be expected and required to treat each other as equals.

So much of biased communication and behavior has become part of a pattern that it may not at first seem noticeable — except, of course, to the person who is being disadvantaged by the messages and treatment. When in doubt about language, substitute your own name for the group you're describing. Consider how you would like the label you're applying to others. Explore whether or not the limitation or expectation you perceive has to do with ability or with factors related to race, ethnicity, culture, or gender. The key to creating a bias-free learning environment is to treat all people with equal respect and consideration.

**FIGURE 2-6.** Forms of Bias in Curricular Materials

| BIAS | DEFINITIONS | IMPLICATIONS |
|---|---|---|
| Omission | Underrepresentation of certain groups | • Group does not have a significant role to play or contribution to make |
| Stereotyping | Assigning traditional and rigid roles, behaviors, or attributes to a group | • Limits the abilities and potential of the stereotyped group<br>• Denies learners the knowledge of diversity, complexity, or variation of a group<br>• May lead learners to internalize stereotypical ways and fail to develop their full potential |
| Imbalance/ Selectivity | Representing only one interpretation of an issue, situation, or group of people | • Restricts knowledge and perspectives of learners<br>• Distorts reality<br>• Ignores complex and differing viewpoints |
| Unreality | Unrealistic portrayal of contemporary life experience | • Denies learners the information needed to deal with such issues |
| Fragmentation/ Isolation | Separating issues related to minorities or one sex from the main body of the text | • Implies issues are less important |
| Linguistic Bias | Discriminatory language | • Attributes roles unfairly |

Source: Sadker, M.P. & Sadker, D.M. (1982). *Sex equity handbook for schools,* New York: Longman.

## SUMMARY

Family and consumer sciences deal with the perennial, practical problems of families—those problems that face all families across time and culture. Although the problems addressed are not the same, instruction and content must be relevant to learners of varying lifestyles, cultures, and values. With the rapidly changing demographics within the United States, family and consumer sciences professionals are assured that they will have the opportunity to work with diverse learners.

The lifestyle, culture, and values of individual learners may influence their attitudes toward learning and their resources for learning. Understanding factors like economic disadvantage or poverty are critical to creating learning environments that meet the unique needs of learners. Learners' abilities are also important in instructional planning; an understanding of the ability to learn and preferences for learning have implications for both what is communicated and how it is communicated.

The critical guideline for designing and developing effective and appropriate instruction is respect and understanding of learners. All learning environments should be bias-free; that is, the learning environment should not restrict, through expectation or limitation of opportunity, the potential of any learner. One goal for family and consumer sciences professionals should be to encourage every learner to find personal and practical meaning in the content.

## REFERENCES AND RESOURCES

American Demographics Desk Reference, Series, No. 1. (1991). *American Diversity*, June.

Betances, S. (1991). Diversity. *Vocational Education Journal*, 66(8), 22-23.

Bouvier, L. (1991). American diversity. *American Demographics Desk Reference Series*, *1*, June.

Brown, M., & Paolucci, B. (1979). *Home Economics: A definition.* Washington, D.C.: American Home Economics Association (mimeographed).

Bullard, S. (1992). Sorting through the multicultural rhetoric. *Educational Leadership*, *49*, 4-7.

Combs, A., Avila, D., & Purkey, W. (1971). *Helping relationships: Basic concepts for the helping professions*. Boston: Allyn and Bacon.

deColon, M., & Velez, H. (1988). Puerto Rican culture: transition and change. In *Empowerment through difference*, AHEA Home Economics Teacher Education Yearbook. Chicago: Glencoe.

Gage, N.L., & Berliner, D. (1988). *Educational psychology*. Boston: Houghton Mifflin.

Glick, P. (1992). American families as they are and were. In A. Skolnick & J. Skolnick (Eds.). *Family in transition*. New York: Harper/Collins.

*Guidelines for the creative use of biased materials in a nonbiased way* (Contract No. 3007 70460). U.S. Office of Education.

Haberman, M. (1991). The pedagogy of poverty versus good teaching. *Phi Delta Kappan*, *73*, 290-294.

*How we're changing*. (1990). (Special Studies Series No. 170, p. 23). U.S. Department of Commerce, Bureau of the Census.

Newcombe, E.I. (1979). Survey on bias. In *The Teddyffrin/Eastown program, state on manual: Preparing for change*. Washington, D.C.: Women's Educational Equity Act Program, U.S. Department of Education.

Noddings, N. (1992). The gender issue. *Educational Leadership, 49*, 65-70.

Pickett, A., & Gillespie, M. (1988). Minority youth at risk. In *Empowerment through difference*, AHEA Home Economics Teacher Education Yearbook. Chicago: Glencoe.

Riley, M.W. (1992). The family in an aging society: A matrix of latent relationships. In A. Skolnick, & J. Skolnick (Eds.), *Family in transition*. New York: Harper/Collins.

Williams, S. (1986). Home economics learners. In *Vocational home economics curriculum: State of the field*. AHEA Home Economics Teacher Education Yearbook. Peoria, IL: Bennett & McKnight.

## 3

# CHILDREN AND YOUTH
# AS LEARNERS

Educators in family and consumer sciences have the opportunity to work with a variety of learners. Learners may vary according to age, lifestyle, and abilities. Each of these aspects of the learner is important to recognize and to understand. The ethnic and cultural diversity of individuals and families is important, too, and should be considered in instruction. Likewise, the "age and stage" of learners is an important variable in instruction and instructional planning. The age and stage differences in learners will affect what content is communicated and how it is communicated.

Consider, for example, financial management concepts that might be appropriate for 10- to 12-year-old children as compared with adults entering retirement. Not only would the type and complexity of the information vary, but the methods by which the content is taught would also vary. If you are to be successful in communicating content, understanding with whom you communicate may be as important as understanding what you communicate.

For learning to occur—the type of learning that changes the behavior or attitudes of learners—the *content* must have relevance to the individual. The learner must be able to find some meaning in what is being taught. This implies that the learner is capable of learning what is being taught. Thus, there is a need to understand the intellectual, social, emotional, and physical development of learners in order to appreciate what they may be ready to learn.

Many individuals enter the field of family and consumer sciences expecting to teach in middle schools, junior high schools, high schools, or colleges and universities. Others will work in nonformal settings, for example with 4-H youth of varying ages. Some professionals may find themselves working in child care programs, working with youth recreation programs, or counseling or advising youth. Others may work in retailing, in a business focused on youth, or in family community services. In all of these settings, it is important to understand the abilities, needs, and interests of youth.

## DEVELOPMENTAL CHARACTERISTICS
## OF YOUTH AS LEARNERS

Various theorists have helped describe the ways individuals progress and grow through the life cycle. Many have taken a single aspect of development and sought to explain its progress. Perhaps the most notable, Jean Piaget, developed a model to explain **cognitive (intellectual) development** (1963, 1974). His model suggests that cognitive development is more than just collecting and adding new information as a person grows; instead, changes occur related to the organization, adaptation, and the assimilation of knowledge. Piaget identified four stages of cognitive development that are related to chronological age (maturity) as well as experience or activity and social transmission. It is important to note that cognitive development has not been tied merely to chronological age. Educators dare not make assumptions about cognitive developmental stage based only on age, even though this may be one indicator.

Piaget suggested that the ability to learn particular facts or ideas is directly related to the "mental tools" a person brings to the learning situation. These tools are a function of the cognitive developmental stage. In the daily practice of instruction, this means that learners cannot learn what they are not yet prepared to learn. For example, many upper elementary age students may not be able to think in abstract terms. Instructors working with this age group should probably avoid dealing with case studies or problems that have numerous variables or issues that require extensive hypothetical thinking.

A more in-depth understanding of Piaget's work and other cognitive development theorists (Klahr, 1978, Flavell, 1977, Hetherington & Parke, 1979) may be important for the instructor concerned about matching content to cognitive readiness.

A theory of **emotional development** was formulated by Erik Erikson (1963). Building upon the work of Freud and others, Erikson identified eight life stages, each of which requires a significant emotional accomplishment. The successful negotiation of each stage is dependent upon the achievement of the preceding stages. For example, somewhere in the elementary and middle school years, children begin to develop a sense of industry, an understanding of the relationship between perseverance and outcomes, and the satisfaction inherent in this. If, however, children fail to develop this sense, inferiority develops. With this in mind, the 4-H agent may want to make sure that projects for children in this stage are those that lead to feelings of accomplishment and success.

Projects should allow learners to take responsibility and be short enough in duration for learners to maintain interest and come to closure.

Other theorists and researchers have looked more specifically at particular aspects of **social and personal development**. Kohlberg (1963, 1975) has proposed a sequence of stages of moral development that range from stage one, when individuals obey to avoid punishment, to stage six, when internal or personal ethics serve as the basis for moral decision making. More recently, Gilligan (1982) and Noddings (1984) have developed models that take a slightly different perspective. Both authors emphasize women's views of ethical and moral development.

Another theoretical approach to human development was conceptualized by Robert Havighurst (1981). He proposed that each person must accomplish "developmental tasks." These tasks involve social and emotional concerns related to growth and development that must be accomplished at various stages. During early childhood, for example, individuals develop the ability to interact with age-mates. One developmental task of adolescents is accepting one's physique and using the body effectively. In each developmental stage, the requisite task must be effectively accomplished in order to function most effectively in the next life stage. While these tasks are somewhat culture-bound, they do represent some of the changes in the lives of learners brought about by life experiences and individual growth and development.

The preceding discussion has focused on individual growth and development, but it is important for the educator to note that individual learners are part of family systems that also proceed through developmental stages. This, too, influences the interests and attitudes of the learners. For example, a 50-year-old, first-time father caught up in the "expanding years" of the family life cycle (when children are added to the family) may share many of the educational needs of his 20-year-old counterpart who is in the same stage of the *family life cycle*, even though they may be at two very different *individual* stages of development.

There are several reasons why it is critical to understand the developmental stages of learners. First, you can better anticipate the educational needs and concerns of the learners. The operating principle here is relevance. What is important to the learner today? What is currently of interest? What life events are impacting on the learner? These life events may suggest educational needs. The adult learner anticipating retirement, for example, may find more relevance in community education offerings that deal with financial management rather than career development. Another example here relates to the type of housing content that could be included in a senior high school level consumer education course. While home buying may not be an appropriate topic, shopping for apartments or other rental housing, selecting a residence hall, and examining lease agreements may be appropriate. These activities are probably closer to the life experiences of the students than purchasing their own homes. The home buying content, however, may be of great interest to adult audiences through community or extension education.

Second, understanding the developmental stages of learners will allow the instructor to better plan instructional strategies. This involves not only recognizing the cognitive level of students, but their level of social/emotional development as well. The youth leader working with early adolescents may find that learners at this developmental stage need concrete, hands-on activities to better understand abstract concepts. The leader may also realize that early adolescents have an abundance of physical energy and need to be active. But recognizing social/emotional development may be as important as considering the physical and cognitive development just described. Because early adolescents are struggling with peer acceptance, the leader will not create a learning environment where youth are likely to be embarrassed or asked to take major social risks. Instead, learning activities may be planned that enhance cooperation among youth and give them opportunities to succeed and achieve, especially in front of their peers.

Planning instruction requires understanding the learner for whom it is being planned. Consideration must be given to the developmental stage of the learners as well as their life roles and lifestyles.

The following sections address the intellectual (or cognitive), social/emotional, and physical growth characteristics of children and youth. The age divisions of "middle childhood" and "adolescence" are somewhat arbitrary, but are based on the most typical divisions used for programming and curriculum development. Programs are most often directed to elementary age children (those in middle childhood) or to middle or junior high school or high school age youth (those in adolescence).

## MIDDLE CHILDHOOD

Children from ages six to eleven are generally considered to be in "middle childhood." Middle childhood is a time of rapid change for youth. Their world expands as they discover school, peer groups, clubs, sports teams, and other extracurricular activities. Their intellectual, social/emotional, and physical growth allows them to develop a sense of competence — a feeling that they can exert some control over their environment. Their self-concept is becoming more defined as they try new things, get feedback from others, and measure their performance and abilities against those of their peers. The skill development that occurs during middle childhood contributes to their sense of competence, too. Skill development includes everything from reading to throwing a football to learning to resolve conflicts with friends (Schiamberg, 1988).

The development of children is typically discussed in terms of their intellectual, social/emotional, and physical development. Each of these dimensions influences their ability and interest in learning family and consumer sciences content.

### Intellectual Development

Intellectually, youth in middle childhood are entering into what Piaget described as the formal operations stage. Formal operations are actually mental activities that serve as a basis for thinking. These include being able to organize or categorize objects (classification), being able to return to the beginning point of a thought process (reversibility), and being able to order objects according to value along a continuum (seriation). These operations now make it possible for children in middle childhood to deal with concepts, understand causality, and conservation (the understanding that two equal quantities remain the same if nothing is subtracted or added).

For example, children in this stage of development can group the advantages and disadvantages of a particular course of action. Further, they can categorize families by their structure, rate products, and understand how to balance a budget. Each of these tasks requires that students have developed to the point of being able to undertake formal operations.

By the end of middle childhood and the beginning of adolescence, youth are well able to deal with symbols that represent experience — words, numbers, and objects. They also understand cause and effect, but logical thought processes are applied only to real (concrete) objects or experiences.

For example, youth in middle childhood are generally able to plan a project that involves collecting and distributing canned goods to families in need. They are much less likely to be able to hypothesize about the complexity of circumstances that may cause families to become needy. As youth move from the egocentrism of early childhood, they develop an orientation that allows them to begin to see other perspectives and to imagine and understand the points of view of others.

## Social/Emotional Development

Socially, children are developing a sense of right or wrong, a sense of "good behavior" vs. "bad behavior." Rather than modify behavior simply to please adults or avoid punishment, youth at this age are beginning to develop an internal sense of control, and eventually to develop a sense of self-control.

The peer group is an important part of the social development of youth in middle childhood. The peer group is a source of identification, as youth begin their first steps toward independence from parents. Peers also provide acceptance and a sense of belonging, as well as spurring healthy competition (Jorgensen, 1986).

## Physical Development

Physically, youth in middle childhood are improving gross motor skills, including running, jumping, and throwing. With the improvement of physical coordination and balance, many children become interested in vigorous bodily activities, especially team sports such as baseball, football, volleyball, and basketball. Overall, girls and boys are not far apart in this development, but girls tend to show slightly better coordination, flexibility, and balance while boys have greater overall strength (Cratty, 1979).

Fine motor skills, a focus area for development in early childhood, are fairly well developed in youth in middle childhood. By ages 8 to 9, most children are capable of playing video games, swinging a hammer, and doing other tasks that require hand-eye coordination.

## ADOLESCENCE

Adolescence is generally considered to begin with the onset of puberty. Puberty usually begins in U.S. girls between the ages of about 9 and 12 and a few years later in boys.

### Intellectual Development

As youth move from middle childhood into adolescence, their cognitive development is characterized by growing intellectual capabilities and the ability to perform higher-order problem solving. During adolescence, youth move from the concrete operations stage of middle childhood to the new stage of formal operational thought. This stage was described in the previous section about Piaget's developmental theory. Basically, adolescents are at a stage where they are able to grasp the hypothetical.

As youth progress through adolescence, they are typically able to not only think about the theoretical possibilities given a particular situation or set of circumstances, but also to think about relationships between abstract concepts and ideas. This represents a significantly higher level of conceptualizing than that of the early adolescent. Older adolescents cannot only consider themselves in terms of somewhat abstract psychological qualities, but can think about their own reasoning processes and consider why they believe as they do. As a result, older adolescents are likely to be more tolerant and more understanding of other points of view because they have the capacity to stand back and examine their own ways of thinking and those of others.

### Social/Emotional Development

Youth at this age are very concerned about the opinions of their friends. Middle school-aged youth are often described as having a "herd" instinct. Choosing their own friends, being with friends, and being accepted by friends are important to the growing adolescent. At the same time, youth this age are becoming more independent and pulling away somewhat from family. They have a growing need and desire for privacy and want to spend time alone and with friends. Hours spent on the telephone, listening to music, or in front of a mirror are behaviors consistent with the social and emotional development of adolescents.

Adolescents typically feel almost invincible, out of reach of most of the real dangers of the world. Since they may see themselves as nearly immortal, they may make poor choices about their physical safety. While they seem unconcerned about physical risk, they are extremely concerned about social risk and what their friends or other youth think about them.

As youth progress through adolescence, their need and drive for independence grows. There is ongoing change in the balance of affiliation with peers and parents. They are moving further away from childhood and closer to the social independence of adulthood. Adolescence typically brings concerns about career plans and further education, relationships with the opposite sex, and their own social roles. Adolescents struggle with what it means to be a man or woman, and how to integrate the intellectual, emotional, social, and physical changes that move them toward adulthood. Adolescents are refining their social skills and acquiring and testing a set of ethics or values to guide their own behavior.

In later adolescence, peer relationships are likely to include settling into a relationship with a person of the opposite sex. Time with family may continue to decrease as youth maintain peer relationships and increase the time spent in school-related activities and work-for-pay. One study found that students spent 25 percent of their time with families as high school freshmen, but only 15 percent of their time with families as high school seniors (Csikszentmihalyi & Larson, 1984). Many of the social attitudes and behaviors that were exhibited in early adolescence, however, remain constant throughout later adolescence. For example, teens' feelings about themselves and their lives tended to remain stable across adolescence, as did behaviors like dependability, responsibility, and sympathy (Csikszentmihalyi & Larson, 1984). Generally, teenagers at this stage continue to enjoy sports and activities, provided there is a reasonable match between the skills of the adolescent and the challenge of the activity.

## Physical Development

Dramatic physical changes are evident in the early adolescent. The development of physical skills continues. Middle school age boys and girls may display awkwardness or restlessness as a result of their dramatic, but uneven, physical growth. Still, youth at this age may spend long hours attempting to learn to skateboard or dance. Their pattern of growth also results in periods of great energy, often followed by periods of fatigue or times of "doing nothing." Rapid bone and muscle growth in early adolescence result in real "growing pains," and youth at this age need opportunities to move around, to walk, and to stretch. The arrival of secondary sex characteristics can result in adolescents being somewhat self-conscious about their bodies and concerned about physical attractiveness to others.

Older adolescents have generally reached physical and sexual maturity, although growth may continue in males until 17 to 20 years of age. Internal organs and physiological systems continue maturation through early adulthood. These physical and sexual changes have a significant impact on the attitudes and behaviors of adolescents. The combination of physical development and social learning plays an important role in the development of sexual interest and activity. The weight gain of early adolescence may still influence body image of males and females, with females especially developing or maintaining concerns about self-image as it relates to body weight. Differences in patterns of growth and development among youth may still be evident in later adolescents, but most, by this time, have adjusted to their "adult" bodies.

# LEARNING ACTIVITIES AND YOUTH

No matter what area of family and consumer sciences content is to be communicated to youth, it is important to consider the developmental stage of the individuals with whom you work. What are their intellectual capabilities? What are their academic skills? What are their problem-solving abilities? What physical skills are they developing or refining? What are their social needs? What are their emotional needs? Learning activities developed in light of the learners for whom they are planned are more likely to be effective.

## FIGURE 3-1. A Framework for Life-Span Family Life Education

| Age Levels | TOPIC AREAS AND KEY CONCEPTS* | |
|---|---|---|
| | Human Development and Sexuality | Interpersonal Relationships |
| Children | • Physical, emotional, social, and sexual development<br>• Similarities and differences in individual development<br>•Perceptions about older people (adolescents, adults, elderly)<br>• Understanding people with special needs<br>• Uniqueness of each person<br>• Responsibility for keeping healthy (nutrition, personal hygiene)<br>• Social and environmental conditions affecting growth and development<br>• Aspects of human reproduction (prenatal development, birth, puberty)<br>• Body privacy and protection against sexual abuse | • Building self-esteem<br>• Identifying and enhancing personal strengths<br>• Respecting self and others<br>• Dealing with emotions<br>• Communicating with others<br>• Sharing feelings constructively<br>• Learning from and teaching others<br>• Making, keeping, and ending friendships<br>• Sharing time, friends, and possessions<br>• Handling problems with others<br>• Acting with consideration for self and others |
| Adolescents | • Types of development: physical, cognitive, emotional, personality, moral, social, and sexual<br>• Patterns of development over the life span (conception to death)<br>• Interaction among types of development (e.g., social and sexual development)<br>• Accepting individual differences in development<br>• Stereotypes and realities about adulthood and aging<br>• Developmental disabilities<br>• Social and environmental conditions affecting growth and development<br>• Effects of chemical substances on physical health and development<br>• Responsibility for personal health (nutrition, hygiene, exercise)<br>• Body privacy and protection against sexual abuse<br>• Communicating about sexuality (personal values, beliefs) | • Building self-esteem and self-confidence<br>• Assessing and developing personal abilities and talents<br>• Respecting self and others<br>• Changing and developing one's thoughts, attitudes, and values<br>• Dealing with emotion<br>• Dealing with success and failure<br>• Communicating information, thoughts, and feelings<br>• Initiating, maintaining, and ending relationships<br>• Assessing compatibility in interpersonal relationships<br>• Understanding the effects of self-perceptions of relationships<br>• Understanding the needs and motivations involved in dating<br>• Accepting responsibility for one's actions<br>• Acting in one's own and others' best interests |

*(continued)*

The National Council on Family Relations built upon this principle of learning in developing their *Framework for Life-Span Family Life Education*. See Figure 3-1. The framework identifies topic areas and key concepts by the age at which the information is most appropriate or meaningful. The framework identifies content appropriate for children, adolescents, and adults.

**FIGURE 3-1.** *Continued.*

| Age Levels | TOPIC AREAS AND KEY CONCEPTS* | |
|---|---|---|
| | **Human Development and Sexuality** | **Interpersonal Relationships** |
| **Adolescents** | • Normality of sexual feelings and sexual responses<br>• Human reproduction and contraception<br>• Varying family and societal beliefs about sexuality<br>• Choices, consequences, and responsibilities of sexual behavior | • Understanding the basis for choosing a family lifestyle (values, heritage, religious beliefs)<br>• Factors influencing mate selection (social, cultural, personal)<br>• Understanding the dimensions of love and commitment<br>• Exploring the responsibilities of marriage |
| **Adults** | • Dimensions of development: physical, cognitive, affective, moral, personality, social, and sexual<br>• Patterns of development over the life span (conception to death)<br>• Interaction among dimensions of development (e.g., social and sexual development)<br>• Factors influencing individual differences in development<br>• Promoting development in self and others<br>• Myths and realities of adulthood and aging<br>• Dealing with disabilities<br>• Social and environmental conditions affecting growth and development<br>• Responsibility for personal and family health<br>• Communicating about sexuality (personal values, beliefs, shared decision-making)<br>• Normality of sexual feelings<br>• Human sexual response<br>• Contraception, infertility, and genetics<br>• Responsible sexual behavior (choices, consequences, shared decision-making)<br>• Prevention of sexual abuse<br>• Varying societal beliefs about sexuality | • Building self-esteem and self-confidence in self and others<br>• Establishing personal autonomy<br>• Achieving constructive personal change<br>• Communicating effectively<br>• Dealing with emotions<br>• Dealing with crises<br>• Types of intimate relationships<br>• Exercising initiative in relationships<br>• Developing, maintaining, and ending relationships<br>• Understanding the effects of self-perceptions of relationships<br>• Varying influences on roles and relationships (ethnic, racial, social)<br>• Recognizing factors associated with quality relationships<br>• Taking responsibility and making commitments in relationships<br>• Evaluating choices and alternatives in relationships<br>• Changes in the marital relationship over time<br>• Acting in accordance with personal beliefs with consideration for others' best interests<br>• Creating and maintaining a family of one's own |

*Communicating, decision-making and problem-solving have not been listed as separate concepts but should be incorporated into each topic area.

# LEARNING ACTIVITIES FOR MIDDLE CHILDHOOD

When planning learning activities for youth in middle childhood, consider their growing sense of competence and self-esteem. Activities should allow youth to test their skills, stretch their abilities, and to achieve success. These types of activities contribute to the development of self-esteem and sense of competence. These outcomes are more likely achieved through projects, cooperative team activities, or other types of active involvement rather than through work-sheets or traditional "seat work." Youth need feedback and correction, but this should always be incorporated in the learning activity.

Learning experiences for youth in middle childhood should be real and concrete. Since youth at this age are not yet adept at dealing with the abstract, it makes sense to have students "doing" and "seeing," rather than just "hearing." The use of equipment for experimentation, field trips, audiovisual aids, technology, and manipulatives are appropriate choices for youth in middle childhood.

Leaders, teachers, and facilitators can encourage the development of self-control by establishing clear limits within the group or classroom. Leaders may want to have youth help in determining the rules or guidelines. Youth at this age need opportunities to practice pro-social behavior. Group work, therefore, that encourages cooperation, negotiation, and helping, is important in the social development of youth. Still, youth need time to work alone and at their own pace. Therefore, instruction should contain elements of large group, small group, and individual work.

Sometime during middle childhood, youth begin to have an understanding of the points of view of others. They realize that not everyone sees things as they do, nor do they do things quite the way they do. The point at which youth can see beyond themselves is the point when professionals can begin to use community service and other service projects and programs. Applying family and consumer sciences skills to the service and assistance of others is an excellent form of concrete practice. It also teaches responsibility and other social skills that are so important to youth at this stage of development. Service projects can be used with youth through adolescence and may even provide important career exploration opportunities for older youth.

# LEARNING ACTIVITIES FOR ADOLESCENTS

When planning learning activities for older youth, consider the developmental characteristics of the adolescent learner. Because early adolescence is a time of significant physical change, it often is a time of self-consciousness and self-centeredness on the part of the adolescent. Youth at this age particularly enjoy personal inventories, self-report activities, and/or other reflective exercises that allow them to consider their own points of view without risking too much. These are strategies or activities that help learners focus on themselves and to relate the content directly to themselves.

Adolescents need and enjoy opportunities to interact with peers. Since peers are so important to the adolescent, large and small group activities, team projects, and committees are appropriate models for instruction. Adolescents, too, need regular opportunities to practice cooperation, team work, negotiation skills, and other group interaction skills.

Since the approval and acceptance of peers is so important to adolescents, it is also important that they not be embarrassed nor be put at risk with their peers. Instructional strategies that can cause a teen to look foolish, vulnerable, or incompetent in front of peers should be avoided. Adolescents may be willing to risk failure or disclosure with peers, but only after a strong level of trust has been established in the peer group. A classroom teacher, for example, should not expect teens to share with the class their most embarrassing moment on the first day of the Personal Living Class. Club leaders may find adolescents resistant to role playing, presentations, or answering questions until they are sure that they will be accepted by the group.

Adolescents often experience a strong need for independence. Instructional strategies, therefore, that allow them to make decisions and assume some responsibility for their own learning may be the most successful. The dietitian, for example, might meet more enthusiasm if he or she stresses with youth good decision making about dietary choices rather than a rigid set of guidelines. Youth leaders may elicit more cooperation and enthusiasm among youth who select their own projects or events versus having them selected for them. Computer programs with paths, reports with several possible topics, or goal-directed projects with many available strategies are all good options for adolescent learners.

Because youth, particularly in early adolescence, are growing quickly but unevenly, leaders, facilitators, and teachers should be prepared for a variety of individual differences in a group of adolescents even if they are all of the same age. There are dramatic differences, for example, among 12-year-old girls. This diversity demands various instructional techniques. A variety of learning experiences should be used within any area. For example, the professional working with a 13-year-old as an apprentice should demonstrate, explain, allow the learner to do guided observations of others performing the same function, provide for supervised practice, etc.

As adolescents grow and change, the educator should expect to work with the learner on more than just the tasks at hand. Young adolescents, in particular, may frequently turn to an adult other than a parent to talk about their concerns, anxieties, and dreams. The professional working with youth of this age should be accepting and willing to work with the "whole" learner.

## YOUTH AND THE FACILITATOR

Professionals working with youth in middle childhood and adolescence have many opportunities to influence the growth and development of youth.

Whether working in formal, nonformal, or informal settings, teachers, leaders, directors, or facilitators may serve as role models to youth.

Professionals may influence the performance of youths in a variety of ways. Although there is disagreement on just how and why it happens, there are several theories that suggest that the leader's or teacher's expectations of a youth influence what that youth will actually do.

Consider the ways in which youth are placed in groups, the amount of attention they are given, and the types and levels of praise, encouragement, criticism, or remediation that are offered. Leaders or teachers who have high expectations for some youth and not for others may transmit those expectations in a variety of ways. These expectations may be internalized, so that each person performs at the level expected. For example, a professional running an after-school recreation program is told not to be too concerned about a particular family—they just do not "participate." As a result, the professional may choose other children to lead certain activities, spend additional time working with other children, make a point of providing feedback to the parents of other children—but not the youth from the family that "just doesn't participate." What is the consequence to these youth?

Family and consumer sciences professionals need to be particularly sensitive to their own biases and attitudes so that all youth have equal opportunities to perform. Research on teacher behavior, for example, has found that classroom teachers interact more with boys than girls (Sadker & Sadker, 1982) and ask boys more questions (Jackson & Lahaderne, 1967).

The family and consumer sciences educator as teacher, leader, counselor, or facilitator also serves directly as a model of behavior to learners. Models affect behavior in a variety of ways. Gage and Berliner (1988) categorize the ways in which models influence behavior into three categories: models who teach new behavior, facilitate behavior, or inhibit and disinhibit behavior.

The family and consumer sciences professional may teach a new behavior intentionally or unintentionally through modeling. Because learning through imitation is so successful, the educator needs to become adept in "showing" skills, for example, demonstrating. Youth may model social and personal skills of the family and consumer sciences professional, too. Thus, the educator working with youth has a professional responsibility to model appropriate personal behaviors.

The family and consumer sciences professional as a model may also facilitate behavior or inhibit or disinhibit behavior. The area of "inhibiting" behavior is an interesting one. Consider, for example, a youth who has been socialized in a family where aggressive behavior is a typical response to disappointment or discouragement. The absence of an aggressive response by the educator may actually serve to inhibit the behavior in the youth. Of course, sanctions against that type of behavior in the group, club, or classroom may also inhibit the behavior. Conversely, when students see demonstrated behaviors like empathy, caring, or talking openly about their feelings, the model can disinhibit their behaviors; that is, the model may free them from inhibitions related to the behavior. When youth see that it is all right to talk about their feelings or emotions, they may learn to do so.

The teacher, leader or facilitator often sets the tone in the group or classroom. He or she becomes the model for enthusiasm and motivation. How learners respond to a tough challenge, hard work, discouraging tasks, or difficult material is often modeled after the group leader. Family and consumer sciences professionals communicate more than just family and consumer sciences content.

## FAMILY AND CONSUMER SCIENCES CONTENT AND THE YOUNG LEARNER

It is a major challenge to plan and provide instruction to learners at a level and in a way that is appropriate. The professional working with youth may find that adolescents bring a great deal of enthusiasm and motivation to learning. Consider again the development of youth and then family and consumer sciences content. At a time when the individual is striving for independence, concerned about self, working on new relationships, and anticipating adulthood, what could be more appropriate than family and consumer sciences content? Family and consumer sciences content can meet some very critical learning needs for the individual. Youth want to know and need to know about human development, health and wellness, interpersonal relationships, resource management, and other survival skills. The ease of transition from youth to adulthood depends upon how well the individual is prepared for adulthood. Family and consumer sciences knowledge can make the difference in whether or not the individual successfully negotiates the developmental tasks of adolescence in preparation for adult living.

## SUMMARY

Just as there is no "typical" U.S. family, there is probably no typical 10-year-old or 16-year-old. Each learner brings to the learning environment a unique set of needs, abilities, and interests. However, there are some commonalities for which the family and consumer sciences professional must anticipate and plan. As learners move through middle childhood and then adolescence, you can expect certain intellectual, social, emotional, and physical skills to develop. To be most effective in communicating family and consumer sciences content, the educator should consider what the learner is ready to learn and under what conditions he or she is most likely to learn.

## REFERENCES AND RESOURCES

Berla, N., Henderson, A., & Kerewsy, W. (1989). *The middle school years.* Washington, DC: National Committee for Citizens in Education.

Bredekamp, S. (Ed.). (1987). *Developmentally appropriate practice in early childhood programs serving children through age 8.* Washington, DC: National Association for the Education of Young Children.

Brooks, J.B. (1987). *The process of parenting.* Mountain View, CA: Mayfield.

Cratty, B. (1979). *Perceptual and motor development in infants and children* (2nd ed.). Englewood Cliffs, NJ: Prentice-Hall.

Csikszentmihalyi, M., & Larson, R. (1984). *Being adolescent.* New York: Basic Books.

Erikson, E. (1963). *Childhood and society* (2nd ed.). New York: Norton.

Flavell, J.H. (1977). *Cognitive development.* Englewood Cliffs, NJ: Prentice-Hall.

Gage, N.L., & Berliner, D. (1988). *Educational psychology* (4th ed.). Boston: Houghton Mifflin Company.

Gilligan, C. (1982). *Mapping the moral domain: A contribution of women's thinking to psychological theory and education.* Cambridge, MA: Harvard University Press.

*Guidelines for family life education programs over the life span.* Minneapolis: National Council on Family Relations.

Havighurst, R.J. (1981). Life-span development and educational psychology. In F.H. Farley & N.J. Gordon (Eds.). *Psychology and education: The state of the union.* Berkeley, CA: McCutchan.

Hetherington, E.M., & Park, R.D. (1979). *Clinical psychology: A contemporary viewpoint.* New York: McGraw-Hill.

Jackson, P., & Lahaderne, H. (1967). Inequalities in teacher-pupil contacts. *Psychology in the Schools, 4,* 204-208.

Jorgensen, S. (1986). *Marriage and the family: Development and change.* New York: Macmillan.

Klahr, D. (1978, March). *Information processing models of cognitive development: Potential relevance to science instruction.* Paper presented at the annual meeting of the American Educational Research Association.

Kohlberg, L. (1963). The development of children's orientations toward moral order: Sequence in the development of moral thought. *Vita Humana, 6,* 11-33.

Kohlberg, L. (1975). The cognitive-developmental approach to moral education. *Phi Delta Kappan, 56,* 670-677.

Mattessich, P., & Hill, R. (1982). *Family development and life cycle research and theory revisited.* Minneapolis: Minnesota Family Studies Center, University of Minnesota.

Mattessich, P., & Hill, R. (1987). Life cycle and family development. In M.B. Sussman & S.K. Steinmetz (eds.), *Handbook of marriage and the family* (pp. 437-469). New York: Plenum.

Noddings, N. (1984). *Caring: A feminine approach to ethics and moral education*. Berkeley: University of California Press.

Piaget, J. (1963). *Origins of intelligence in children*. New York: Norton.

Piaget, J. (1974). *Understanding causality*. (D. Miles, & M. Miles, Trans.). New York: Norton.

Sadker, M.P., & Sadker, D.M. (1982). *Sex equity handbook for schools*. New York: Longman.

Scanzoni, J. (1983). *Changing gender roles and redefinitions of family development*. Paper presented at the thematic session of the annual meeting of the American Sociological Association, August, 1983, Detroit, MI.

Schiamberg, L. (1988). *Child and adolescent development*. New York: Macmillan.

Spanier, G.B. & Glick, P.C. (1980). The life cycle of American families: An expanded analysis. *Journal of Family History, 5*, 97-111.

## 4

# ADULTS AS LEARNERS

The instructor of family and consumer sciences content may encounter the adult learner in a variety of settings — the college classroom, a community group, a workshop, a seminar, or across the desk. While adult learners vary greatly in their interests, abilities, and attitudes about learning family and consumer sciences content, adults as a group have distinct characteristics that differentiate them from the school-age learners you might think of as "students." Their age, previous education, and varied life experiences cause their approach to learning to be quite different from that of the young child or adolescent. Because adults tend to approach learning differently than young children and adolescents do, it is important to understand the implications for providing instruction for adults.

## ADULTS' MOTIVATIONS FOR LEARNING

Much of the instruction of children and adolescents is compulsory; students may enroll in a family life class or a nutrition class because it is part of their academic program. Other young students might be motivated by a prize or award and engage in some learning activities for these extrinsic rewards. However, adults are generally voluntary learners and come to an educational experience out of a "need to know" or a "desire to know."

## THE "NEED" TO KNOW

Adults' motivations to learn are more likely to be intrinsic as adults realize that a gap exists between what they know and what they need to know. This gap can be addressed or remediated via education. The education may be formal, such as a class, workshop, or seminar. Learners may seek nonformal experiences, such as a retail store demonstration or a computer-accessed database. Education may be informal, such as reading an extension service bulletin. Tough (1971) identified what he called **independent learning projects** where adults make significant efforts to learn some needed information or skill independent of formal instruction. These projects involved reading, asking questions of experts, experimentation, using audio and video cassettes for information, etc. For example, the business executive traveling to Japan may gather information about the company to be visited, the customs of the country, and simple Japanese words and phrases to use while traveling. Another adult learner may decide to add a deck to his or her home. He or she might obtain instruction booklets and talk with others who have undertaken such a project. Both of these are examples of independent learning projects.

The educational needs that prompt both formal and informal learning efforts emerge from the social and developmental context of the individual (McClusky, 1971). For example, the developmental tasks of a particular stage may prompt an educational need. Expectant parents may find themselves in need of education on pregnancy and the birthing process—topics that may have been of little interest or concern in their earlier life stages. Adults facing retirement may perceive a need to understand the systems that will provide benefits and support to them in their next life stage. Individuals faced with having to cope with an emerging health condition—diabetes, heart disease, arthritis—have a need to know about diet and other health care practices. These are examples of educational needs that develop as a result of the developmental and social context of the individual.

As adults grow and conditions around them change, it is likely that there will emerge needs for additional family and consumer sciences information. This new information may enable adults to cope with new situations, allow them to make particular contributions and function more effectively in particular roles, or to handle change more comfortably. Because of the relationships between the educational needs perceived by adult learners and their voluntary participation in educational experiences, adult learners are often described as **problem-centered learners**; that is, learners who want to learn in order to solve a particular problem.

## THE "DESIRE" TO KNOW

While the changes in the lives of adults generate educational needs, they also prompt educational wants. Not all of our efforts to learn are motivated by "needing" to know—some are inspired by just wanting to know. People often become interested in learning new skills or gaining new information not because of a problem, but due to some sort of stimuli in the environment. The homemaker may be intrigued by a series of sessions on strengthening family traditions, a parent enticed by a brochure on activities to do with young children, or a worker curious about what really goes on in a stress reduction workshop. These desires or preferences are less predictable than some of the needs you can anticipate based on developmental stage, but they are just as motivating to adults. The myriad of noncredit community education courses in many communities are a type of response to adult educational "wants." Many of the offerings teach leisure or enrichment activities. These cater to the learning desires and preferences of adults.

Whether adults come to a learning experience from an educational need or want, it is probably important to remember that they bring with them certain expectations about what the experience will be like and what they will get out of it. Some adults anticipate the satisfaction of attaining new information and skills, a sense of personal accomplishment, or the ability to do something new or better. Other adults may value the social rewards that might include the esteem of friends or acquaintances and the interaction with other learners. The anticipation of these social and psychological rewards from a learning experience serve to motivate adults. The better you understand what prompts adults to a learning experience, the better you will be able to satisfy the adult learner and tailor the educational experience to meet the intended learner outcomes. See Figure 4-1 for some additional examples of family and consumer sciences-related "needs" vs. "wants."

## IMPACT OF DEVELOPMENTAL CHARACTERISTICS ON ADULT LEARNING

At first, it may seem unusual to think about adults as having similar characteristics. Take, for example, a group of adults who are attending a training session on working as respite caregivers for families who have a family member with Alzheimer's disease. In this group are men and women from 27 to 68 years of age. Some in the audience have advanced degrees; some never finished high school. Some have had experience dealing with individuals with degenerative diseases, while some know nothing about caring for someone with a disability. They represent various ethnic groups, various races, and different

**FIGURE 4-1. Family and Consumer Sciences-Related Educational Needs vs. Educational Wants**

| Educational Needs | Educational Wants |
|---|---|
| Food stamp availability/use | Family structures in other countries |
| Organizing for a household move | Gourmet cooking |
| Retirement planning | Following the stock market |
| Designing a pre-nuptial agreement | Dressing for success |
| Child care options | Planning a family vacation |
| Talking with your child about death | Flower arranging |

personalities and temperaments. Beyond their interest in serving families in need, do they have anything in common?

Many theorists believe that adults do, in fact, progress through common stages of development. While each person is an individual with unique experiences, there may be some experiences common to individuals as they develop. As you have already seen, these ages and stages may prompt certain educational needs. These stages also have implications for adult learning preferences.

Levinson (1978) described 10 stages through which adults progress, each stage roughly corresponding to an age band, Figure 4-2. With each stage emerges a certain character development, a tendency toward an interpersonal style, and a cognitive style (way of thinking about things). Levinson describes the tasks in each developmental period. For example, at the "settling down" stage, ages 33 to 40, Levinson claims that adults invest themselves in work, family, friendships, community. They establish a niche in society and strive to "make it" or to achieve their personal dreams that they formulated in their early 20s.

Sheehey (1974) popularized the age-related developmental model (based on the work of Levinson and others) in her book *Passages*. Other theorists include Erikson (1950), who describes the stages of humans as being a "continuous sequence of events through which everyone passes," and Neugarten (1971), who focuses on psychological development in his model.

These developmental theories give rise to some interesting implications for adult education. What might you expect to be the needs, interests, and preferences of learners if, as Levinson suggests, at the age 30 transition, individuals are evaluating early choices and making new ones as needed?

Individuals are not only at some point in their own development, but are often part of families that are progressing through a life cycle. Duvall (1962) and others have proposed various models that look at the family life cycle. These cycles begin with the formation of a family, through the adding of children, the launching of children, and the death of one spouse. Duvall's conception of life cycle attached changes in relationships and patterns to the passage of time. Responsibilities, interests, and needs were attached to each stage. These stages, however, were initially based on marital status and the introduction of children into the family. It has been recognized that, in fact, not everyone marries, has children, and then experiences the "empty nest" as children leave home—and even for those who have these experiences, it may or may not happen in the linear model first described by Duvall. Many interested in families have formulated new ways of looking at the relationship of family changes or development to the passage of time. These sociologists or family theorists (Spanier & Glick, 1980; Scanzoni, 1983) have made accommodations in the traditional life cycle that more accurately reflect current social realities. Figure 4-3 shows a contemporary family life cycle model. Models such as this one can be used to explore the variety of family contexts for adult learners.

**FIGURE 4-2. Major Tasks of Each Developmental Period Proposed by Levinson**

| Development Period | Age | Tasks |
|---|---|---|
| Early Adult Transition | 17-22 | Terminate pre-adulthood, and move out of pre-adult world, taking preliminary steps into the adult world. Explore possibilities and make tentative commitments. |
| Entering the Adult World | 22-28 | Create a first major life structure, which may include marriage and a separate home, a mentoring relationship, and the Dream. Attempt to pursue the Dream. |
| Age 30 Transition | 28-33 | Become aware of the flaws of the first life structure and reassess it. Reconsider earlier choices and make new ones as needed. |
| Settling Down | 33-40 | Create a second adult life structure; invest yourself in work, family, friendships, community. Establish a niche in society and strive to "make it," to achieve the Dream. |
| Midlife Transition | 40-45 | A bridge from early to middle adulthood: Ask basic questions, such as "What have I done with my life?" or "What do I want for myself and others?" May or may not involve crisis. |
| Entering Middle Adulthood | 45-50 | Create a new life structure, often (but not always) with a new job, new marriage, or change in nature of work life. |
| Age 50 Transition | 50-55 | Similar in function to the Age 30 Transition; a more minor adjustment to the middle adult life structure. However, if no crisis occurred at Midlife Transition, one is likely to occur now. |
| Culmination of Middle Adulthood | 55-60 | Build a second midlife structure, analogous to Settling Down in middle adulthood. May be a particularly satisfying time if the adult has successfully adapted the life structures to changes in roles and self. |
| Late Adult Transition | 60-65 | Termination of middle adulthood, and bridge to late adulthood. Conclude the efforts of middle adulthood. Prepare for retirement and the physical declines of old age. A major turning point in the life cycle. |
| Late Adulthood | 65+ | Create a new life structure that will suit the new patterns in retirement and the increasing physical declines. Cope with illness. Deal with the psychological issue of loss of youth. |

Bee, 1987

# FIGURE 4-3. A Contemporary Family Developmental Life Cycle

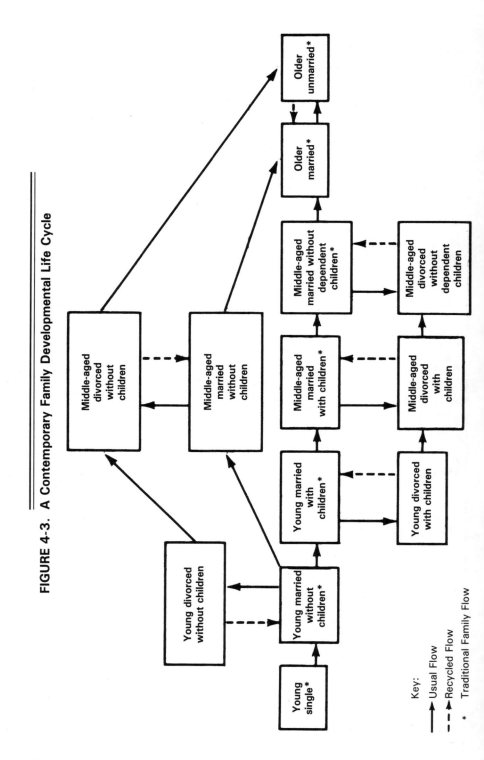

Key:

→ Usual Flow

--▶ Recycled Flow

* Traditional Family Flow

**FIGURE 4-4.** National Council on Family Relations (NCFR) Curriculum as Correlated to Developmental Stage

---

## FAMILY INTERACTION

### CHILDREN

- Families as sources of protection, guidance, affection, and support
- Families as possible sources of anger and violence
- Family similarities and differences
- Individuality and importance of all family members
- Responsibilities, rights, and interdependence of all family members
- Changes in families (births, separations, deaths)
- Family members as individuals
- Getting along in the family
- Expressing feelings in families
- Family rules
- Family problems
- Impact of change on families
- Family traditions and celebrations
- Personal family history

### ADOLESCENTS

- Families as sources of protection, guidance, affection, and support
- Families as possible sources of anger and violence
- Family differences (membership, economic level, role performance, values)
- Different needs and expectations of all family members
- Rights, responsibilities, and interdependence of family members
- Becoming an adult within the family
- Interaction between family members
- Communication in families
- Managing feelings in families
- Family rules
- Coping with internal change and stress in the family
- Personal and family decision-making
- Intergenerational relationships
- Interaction of friends and family
- Influence of family background and history
- Family traditions and celebrations
- Changes in family composition (births, divorce, death)

### ADULTS

- Families as sources of protection, guidance, affection, and support
- Families as possible sources of anger and violence
- Differences in families (membership, economic level, role performance, values)
- Changing needs and expectations of all family members
- Rights, responsibilities, and interdependence of family members
- Family transitions (marriage, birth, divorce, remarriage, death)
- Individual and family roles
- Individual development in the family
- Intimate relationships in the family
- Effects of family on self-concepts of its members
- Factors affecting marital and family relationships
- Giving and receiving affection
- Power and authority in the family
- Family rules—overt and covert
- Sources of stress and coping with stress
- Intergenerational dynamics throughout the life span
- Lifestyle choices
- Family history, traditions, and celebrations
- Varying influences on family interaction patterns (ethnic, racial, social)

It should be clear from this discussion that stage development has implications for determining instructional content. The National Council on Family Relations (1987) has developed a comprehensive family life curriculum that correlates to stage development. They have identified content that they believe is most appropriate at various stages. A partial outline for that curriculum is shown in Figure 4-4.

The implications of looking at adults in the context of a developmental stage seem clear: you would expect that individuals in a particular stage of the life cycle might experience some common educational needs or wants, and have some common preferences. For example, parents with teenage children often find a need to modify their parenting behaviors as children become more independent and capable. Parents of teens may share many similar parenting education needs, even though as individuals they may be very dissimilar. Individuals in the "midlife adjustment stage" might find common interest in exploring career changes, or marriage enrichment. Understanding the life stages or family life stages of adult learners can increase your understanding of their possible educational needs and wants.

## IMPACT OF MENTAL AND PHYSICAL CHANGES ON ADULT LEARNING

Preferences in how, when, where, and what adults learn are also influenced by the aging process and its effects on individuals. It is obvious that aging causes physical changes in adults, but it may be less obvious how these changes influence learning and learning preferences.

Most people believe the only way aging influences learning is by eroding intellectual powers. You have probably heard the sayings, "You can't teach an old dog new tricks," and "Never too old to learn." Are they based on fact? There is a large body of research to suggest that, in spite of some decline in certain types of cognitive abilities, adults can and do continue to learn effectively, with much smaller and later declines in mental abilities than earlier believed (Bee, 1987).

The ability to perform speeded tasks and short-term memory are areas of intellectual performance where there do seem to be decline. In general, performance on speeded tests begins to decline earlier in the adult years than does performance on unspeeded tests (Jarvik & Bank, 1983). For example, as they age, adults would be less likely to perform well on a task that requires verifying a checkbook balance if the task must be completed within 10 minutes.

There is also decline in short-term memory (Botwinick & Storandt, 1974). Older adults do not appear to be able to recall information or rearrange information on short-term memory tasks as effectively as younger learners. Researchers are unclear about why this is true and whether it has to do with how information is stored (encoding) or how it is retrieved. Retrieval does become slower with age (Cerella, 1985; Madden, 1985). This, obviously, has an impact on instruction. Giving a complex set of directions for the use of a new home appliance orally, then asking the older learner to repeat these directions is unlikely to be successful. Older adults would be less likely to recall these directions or to be able to selectively recall and repeat certain portions of the directions.

Physical changes, too, may influence the adult learner. As people age, there is a decline in physical strength and stamina due to changes in muscles and bones. Changes in the skin make people less tolerant of heat and cold. Aging affects sensory acuity, including vision, hearing, taste, and smell (Bee, 1987). As people age and the risk for chronic illness increases, adults are more likely to experience other physical disabilities. The rate and severity of many of these changes is related to personal health habits and heredity, yet you should anticipate these effects if you work with older adult learners. Again, there are very real implications for responding to learner needs. Consider a series of workshop sessions for retired persons. What type of physical environment would be most comfortable? What kinds of instructional aids might you use? It is probably obvious that details like the temperature of the room, the size of the print

**FIGURE 4-5. Examples of Mental and Physical Changes Affecting Adult Learning**

| POSSIBLE CHANGES ASSOCIATED WITH AGING | EXAMPLES OF PLANNING FOR INSTRUCTION |
|---|---|
| **Mental Changes:** | |
| Decrease in ability to perform speeded tasks | Do not "rush" adult learners; allow learners to proceed at own pace. |
| Decline in short term memory | Provide printed sheets of detailed instructions; allow plenty of time for each task. |
| Slower retrieval of information | Wait longer for students to answer questions in discussion; allow more time for tests. |
| **Physical Changes:** | |
| Decline in physical strength | Provide energy-saving devices when possible. |
| Decline in stamina | Do not require long periods of standing; plan short, discrete tasks. |
| Decreased tolerance to heat and cold | Maintain comfortable room temperature for learners; monitor regularly. |
| Decline in sensory acuity:<br>- Vision<br><br>- Hearing | - Provide materials in large type (at least 11 pt. type size for printed materials).<br>- Select room with good acoustics; use microphone if necessary. |

of instructional resources, the length of the session, and the degree of physical exertion required make a difference in planning instruction. Figure 4-5 gives examples of mental and physical changes in adults and their implications for learning and instruction.

## ANDRAGOGY VS. PEDAGOGY

Imagine the enthusiastic and animated behavior of the kindergarten teacher with a class of five-year-olds, or the calm, but firm manner of the junior high school mathematics teacher. Now transfer either of these persons to a room of adult learners. If you sense the "misfit" then you have some insight into how the approach in working with adults must be different than that used with children. While the term **pedagogy** is used to describe the instructional process with children, Knowles (1980) assigned the term **andragogy** to the process of facilitating learning with adults. The central thesis of andragogy is that adults differ from youth as learners in certain critical aspects, and thus a different approach is required to assist their learning.

He makes four assumptions about adults as learners. First, adults are self-directed. In other areas of their lives, adults take responsibility for their behavior and decisions. In their roles other than that of learner or student, they make daily decisions about family, finances, work, health, and safety. They have some measure of control over their lives. They are independent. If one assumes that adults have these abilities, attitudes, and characteristics, then instruction and the instructional environment must be different than that of an elementary or secondary school. Consider the ways young students in formal educational environments are required to be accountable for their time and activity, from incentive charts to hall passes to requests to use the restroom. Imagine these same rules with adults who are, in "real life," parents, bank presidents, and volunteer firefighters. Clearly, you would expect adults to take responsibility for much of their learning and for the instructor to serve as helper and facilitator rather than director or leader.

Second, Knowles indicates that adults have a rich background on which to draw. While most adults would acknowledge that children do not go to school as "empty slates," you must certainly discard that idea when working with adults. Most adults have previous educatioal, interpersonal, and usually vocational experiences, all of which are important to them and how they perceive themselves.

Adults have some previous experiences with formal education, and these experiences will influence their expectations about and attitudes toward later instructional experiences. Adults who have had successful formal school experiences and who feel positive about school and learning are likely to welcome and feel confident about new learning opportunities. Adults who have had negative experiences, however, may be reluctant to enter into learning activities, particularly if those are reminiscent of earlier, unpleasant experiences. Think about a group of high school noncompleters who are required by a human service agency to attend some instructional sessions. They enter the classroom and sit down in desks arranged in long rows. There is a teacher's desk. The instructor comes in and stands behind the desk, passing out papers and lecturing. These adults are suddenly back in an environment that may have very negative connotations. Having had previous negative experiences is likely to influence their attitudes toward and expectations of the present experience.

On the other hand, the life experiences of the adult learner can make a rich contribution to the learning experience. Imagine discussing the care of a child with a disability in a group where some adults have had first-hand experience. Their experience expands and enriches instruction and provides a frame of reference for their own learning. Many of the terms, concepts, or examples that would have to be carefully explained to children are part of the experience of adults who come with a rich background of skills and abilities.

This experience can, however, serve as a roadblock if instruction contradicts previous experience, traditions or beliefs. Take, for example, a workshop on food preservation. As the cooperative extension agent explains the importance of pressure-cooking low acid foods, he or she is interrupted by a homemaker who explains he or she NEVER uses the pressure canning method and no one in his or her family has yet had a food-borne illness! This suggests the importance of understanding and acknowledging the previous experience of learners.

A third assumption about adult learners is that they are problem-oriented. They want to know because they need to know NOW. The educational need or want that has presented itself requires relevant information that can be immediately applied. While tenth grade students may be convinced to endure geometry because they will need it "some day," adults want to know because they need it today. If this is true, you would expect adults to be interested in the practical side of most issues and to be interested in theory primarily as it supports what they need to know. It is a safe assumption that voluntary adult learners will not continue instruction if the instruction is not relevant and helpful to them.

A fourth assumption made by Knowles relates to the educational needs and wants being related to stage of development. Knowles indicates that the content and skills desired by adult learners are likely to be related to their developmental stage (as noted in a previous section of this chapter). Stage brings with it a teachable moment, when people are ready and willing to learn.

## TECHNIQUES FOR WORKING WITH ADULT LEARNERS

Given what is known about adult learners, how can you best facilitate their learning? How do you teach adults? Adult education involves careful planning of the learning environment, diagnosis of learning needs, cooperative planning and design of learner outcomes and activities, and evaluation of outcomes.

# PLANNING THE LEARNING ENVIRONMENT

The learning environment or climate includes physical and social/psychological dimensions. The following factors should be considered when planning for the physical environment. Instruction for adults should be planned in a facility that is physically comfortable for adults. Meetings or classes should be located so that they are geographically convenient for the learners. The room should have comfortable chairs (avoid elementary classrooms with small-scale chairs) and have adequate heat and light to be pleasant. It may be important to check the accessibility of restrooms, refreshments, and parking.

The environment should also provide psychological comfort. Will everyone feel comfortable and confident in that location? Think, for example, about individuals unfamiliar with a university who are expected to attend a workshop on campus. Their concerns may range from what to wear to how to locate the right building. While the local school, church, or police station might be appropriate for some meetings, each of these places could create discomfort for some groups of learners.

The instructor does, of course, create a climate for learning by his or her manner and behavior toward learners. Friendliness, respect, and a genuine interest in the learner are important to adults. Whether the instructor is working with one client or with a large group of learners, it is important to try to get to know the learners and something about their experiences. Taking time to share names, past experiences, and expectations may be important in setting the tone for instruction. In the end, whether or not the instructor really does facilitate learning will depend upon how willing the learner is to accept "help" from the instructor. This is largely dependent upon the relationship established between the instructor and learner.

The relationship between adult learners is important, too, and in group instruction, the instructor needs to establish procedures or guidelines that assure the respectful and equitable treatment of all learners. This may mean rules for group discussion, guidelines for the critique of others' work, limits on areas that can be discussed, or systems for making sure everyone has an opportunity to participate.

# ANALYZING THE NEEDS OF THE ADULT LEARNER

In addition to preparing the climate for learning, the instructor must prepare for the learning episode by assessing the needs, interests, and abilities of learners. What are the expectations of learners? For instance, in a room full of adults who have come to learn about beginning a home business, what do they expect to learn? Some may want ideas for home-based businesses. Others want to hear about the legal and tax implications of beginning a home business. Some are interested in how to balance family and work when everyone works at home. Still others want to hear about recordkeeping and bookkeeping. Yet everyone came to learn about starting a home business!

Not only did these adults come with a variety of expectations, but their abilities also vary. In the same group of would-be entrepreneurs is a young person with an undergraduate degree in business, a displaced homemaker, and a highly creative retired person with limited reading ability. While it is not necessarily advisable to pre-test learners as you might in a formal learning environment (with paper/pencil testing), it is advisable to determine the ability level of learners.

Expectations and abilities can be ascertained in a variety of ways. Perhaps learners would be willing to talk about themselves. Ask them what they hope to learn, why they came, how they heard about the course, their own goals upon completion of the course, etc. In large groups, instructors may ask these types of questions by having people respond in writing, by raising their hands, or forming small discussion groups. Individual interviews with learners or formal advisory groups can also provide information.

A caution here is not to make assumptions about either abilities or expectations. For example, suppose the instructor of the home business course had given students a short survey. The directions read: "Indicate in priority order topics you are most interested in discussing. Number 1 should be the topic in which you're most interested; number 2, your second highest interest, etc." After these directions, the following topics are listed: recordkeeping, balancing family and work, great ideas for the home business, marketing your home-based product or service. Although all the learners might respond to the survey, they were limited by what was listed. In fact, the majority of those who came to the home business workshop were interested in the legal and tax implications of starting a home business, but this was not an option.

To extend the example, suppose that the instructor, seeing that most participants have indicated "marketing your product" as a top priority, begins with a very elementary explanation of how to publicize. The instructor may have seriously underestimated the level of existing knowledge among learners, thereby missing the aspect of the information they most need. This illustrates the need to accurately determine the needs and abilities of learners. Whether a paper/pencil instrument, discussion group, interview, or advisory committee is used to determine need or to sample ability, it needs to allow maximum input and participation of the adult learners.

The self-directed nature of adult learners suggests that they be encouraged, where possible, to help determine the goals and content of the educational experience. This may, of course, not always be appropriate. If learners are working toward a particular license or certification, then the content of the program is most likely tied to these requirements, and dictated outside the instructor-learner relationship. Where possible, however, adults need to have opportunities to suggest what it is they want and need to learn. What are their desired outcomes as the result of this educational experience? These can become the intended learner outcomes for instruction.

# PROVIDING INSTRUCTION TO ADULT LEARNERS

The preceding discussion on the developmental characteristics of adult learners and their mental and physical changes should imply the types of instructional strategies that would be appropriate for adult learners. For instance, since adults tend to desire relevant and concrete skills and information, activities that allow for practice, direct observation, and participation are probably best suited to the adult. Discussion is a valuable strategy since it allows learners to contribute through their own experience and to be an active part of the learning process.

Strategies that put learners "at risk" need to be used with caution. For example, while role playing is an effective way to practice new skills, it may cause discomfort or anxiety for some adults. The same is true of oral reports, reading aloud, and extensive "homework" assignments. Instructors should carefully consider the previous experience and abilities of learners before assigning lengthy reading materials and/or difficult assignments.

Instructional aids should be considered carefully, too. The discussion in later chapters will suggest criteria for the selection of instructional resources, but some additional considerations may be appropriate for adult learners. For instance, what are the learners' previous experiences? Would they be comfortable or intimidated using a computer? Can they see a projected overhead transparency? Is the audio of the videotape clear enough to be easily understood? Can everyone sit close enough to the front of the room to see the chalkboard? Are maps, charts, or diagrams easy to read or would they appear confusing and cause anxiety for some learners? Would hand-held calculators assist, or are there learners who don't or can't use them?

It is clear that andragogy emphasizes the individualism of the adult as learner and the particular educational objectives most relevant to him or her. It is not easy to determine educational needs, cooperatively plan objectives, or consider individual instructional preferences when working with groups of learners, but it is critical to do so with adults. Figure 4-6 summarizes the techniques appropriate for working with adults.

# FOLLOW-UP OF OUTCOMES

It can be difficult to determine the impact of instruction when working with adults. How do you determine whether or not instruction has been successful? If adults have developed a product or acquired a new skill, it may be possible to conduct a product or performance evaluation. If the learning activity is completely voluntary, it may be wise to simply focus on the degree of satisfaction learners had with the experience. Paper/pencil testing of adults should be reserved for those learning experiences for which there is a need for documentation of learning. For example, if learners have to demonstrate particular competency in an area to receive a type of certification, to complete a requirement, or to receive academic credit, then paper/pencil testing may

**FIGURE 4-6. Summary: Providing Educational Experiences for Adult Learners**

Many of the following are considerations for all types and ages of learners, but should be carefully addressed when working with adults.

**Planning the Learning Environment**

- Physical Dimensions
    - Geographically convenient location
    - Easy to locate classroom or meeting room
    - Appropriate size furniture
    - Adequate heat and light
- Psychological, Sociological Dimensions
    - Appropriate location for topic being presented to audience
    - Friendly, open manner of the instructor
    - Instructor respect for learners
    - Opportunities for learners to get to know each other are provided
    - Guidelines and procedures allow all learners equal opportunity to participate in learning

**Preparing the Learning Episode**

- Assess learners' needs
- Assess learners' interests
- Assess learners' abilities/previous knowledge
- Encourage learner participation in establishing goals and content of the learning experience

**Providing Instruction**

- Encourage high learner participation
- Emphasize relevant and concrete skills
- Plan time for learner "practice"
- Avoid "high risk" instructional strategies/initially
- Use instructional resources that "fit" learners' past experiences/needs
- Use technology if learners are comfortable with it
- Plan audiovisuals that all can see and easily interpret

be an appropriate strategy. Otherwise, learners should be allowed to participate in the evaluation of the experience, sharing their response to the experience, and the degree to which it met their needs.

## SUMMARY

At first, there may seem to be very little purpose in contrasting the teaching of adults to the teaching of children. In fact, adults and youth learn in many of the same ways. People learn best if they have the prerequisite knowledge; if things are concrete; if content is broken into small pieces; if what they learned is used and reinforced; if they have an opportunity to practice; if it seems relevant. While adults and children learn in many of the same ways, the characteristics of adults suggest that learning should be facilitated in different ways. In working with adults it becomes important to understand who they are, what they can do, and what they have done. The instructor has a responsibility to respond to the learner as an adult, providing maximum opportunity for participation in planning, guiding, and evaluating instruction. As technology allows us to live longer, healthier, more leisurely lives it can be predicted that adults will have more opportunity to pursue both the "nice to know" and "need to know" types of family and consumer sciences content over the life cycle. The challenge for the instructor is to communicate in ways that make it helpful and fun for the adult learner.

## REFERENCES AND RESOURCES

Bee, H. (1987). *The journey of adulthood*. New York: Macmillan.

Botwinick, J., & Storandt, M. (1974). *Memory, related functions and age*. Springfield, IL: Charles C. Thomas.

Cerella, J. (1985). Information processing rates in the elderly. *Psychological Bulletin, 98*, 67-83.

Duvall, E.M. (1962). *Family development* (2nd ed.). New York: Lippincott.

Erikson, E.H. (1950). *Childhood and society*. New York: Norton. (Reissued 1963).

Erikson, E.H. (1959). *Identity and the life cycle*. New York: International Universities Press. (Reissued by Norton, 1980).

Jarvik, L.F., & Bank, L. (1983). Aging twins: Longitudinal psychometric data. In W.K. Schair (Ed.), *Longitudinal studies of adult psychological development*. New York: Guilford Press.

Knowles, M. (1980). *The modern practice of adult education: From pedagogy to andragogy*. New York: Association Press.

Levinson, D.J. (1978). *The seasons of a man's life*. New York: Knopf.

Levinson, D.J. (1980). Toward a conception of the adult life course. In J. Smelser & E.H. Erikson (Eds.), *Themes of work and love in adulthood*. Cambridge, MA: Harvard University Press.

Lifespan family life education. (1987). *Journal of Family Relations, 36*, 5-10.

Madden, D.J. (1985). Age-related slowing in the retrieval of information from long-term memory. *Journal of Gerontology, 40*, 208-210.

McClusky, H.V. (1971, February). *Background report on education*. Washington, DC: White House Conference on Aging.

Neugarten, B.L. (1977). Personality and aging. In J.E. Birre and K.W. Schaie (Eds.), *Handbook of the psychology of aging*. New York: Van Nostrand/ Reinhold.

Sheehey, G. (1974). *Passages*. New York: E.P. Dutton.

Tough, A. (1971). The adult's learning projects. *Research in Education Series No. 1*. Toronto: Ontario Institute for Studies in Education.

# 5

# LEARNING STYLES

Two students settle down to complete an assignment for their consumer education class. One student turns up the radio, scatters books and papers across the desk, picks up a pencil, and begins to write. The second student shuts the door to reduce the noise, takes out note cards and begins systematically leafing through one reference at a time. If you observed their classroom behavior, you would note that there, too, they approach learning and instructional tasks differently. However, both are high achieving learners; both do well and earn good grades. What is described here may be attributed to differences in learning style.

## WHAT IS LEARNING STYLE?

Over the past two decades, research has demonstrated that every learner learns differently. Each learner demonstrates characteristics of his or her preferred style. Although some of the characteristics of a learning style change as the learner grows from child to adult, other characteristics appear to remain constant over time. Learning style influences how the learner gathers information, sorts it, creates meaning from it, and makes decisions. It would appear that these characteristics can affect the academic achievement of the learner.

A National Association of Secondary School Principals task force worked throughout the mid-1980s to create a model of learning styles. They defined learning styles as:

> . . .the composite of characteristic cognitive, affective, and physiological factors that serve as relatively stable indicators of how a learner perceives, interacts with, and responds to the learning environment. It is demonstrated

in that pattern of behavior and performance by which an individual approaches educational experiences. Its basis lies in the structure of neural organization and personality which both mold and is molded by human development and the learning experiences of home, school, and society. (Keefe & Languis, 1983)

Early research in this area looked at "cognitive style" rather than learning style. This work was not concerned necessarily with the practical areas of learning or training, but with explaining cognitive processes such as perception or information processing (Kirby, 1979). Later, researchers began to look at the relationship between cognitive style and personality, and other variables like nonverbal intelligence. The stage was set to begin to explore the relationship between cognitive style and the learning process. What developed was an understanding that in addition to the cognitive factors, there were social and physical elements that influence the learning process (*Student Learning Styles and Brain Behavior*, 1982).

Researchers began to explore ways in which the learning styles or preferences could be determined and mapped. The result would be a profile of the learner. **Learning style** has become a way to describe what types of physical, social, environmental, and sociological elements or factors help an individual to learn effectively.

## WHY UNDERSTAND LEARNING STYLES?

Understanding the learning styles of individual learners and having some idea of the learning style preferences of groups allows the instructor to tailor instructional strategies, instructional resources, and the instructional environment to learners. "Exploratory studies indicate that selected instructional methods, resources, and programs appear to complement specific elements of an individual's learning style. When these methods, resources, and programs are matched with the learning style characteristics, academic achievement increases and general attitudes improve. When they are mismatched, achievement decreases and attitudes deteriorate." (Dunn, 1979, p.1)

The following example illustrates this point. Suppose a professional is addressing employees at a staff meeting on a topic requested by the employees. Yet, as the presenter speaks, some employees are having difficulty following along. They attempt to take notes, but have difficulty listening, selecting the key points, then writing them down. They raise their hands and ask to have points restated. Someone suggests that the presenter slow down. Another asks if he or she would explain something again; could he or she illustrate the point using a chalkboard? Thirty minutes into the oral presentation, some employees are beginning to squirm and move about. The presenter wonders where he or she has gone wrong. After all, the presenter believed he or she was talking about a topic of high interest to the employees.

The reactions of these employees are not necessarily indicators of disinterest, disrespect, or boredom. They may be indicators, however, of various learning styles. Once you understand how individuals learn most comfortably, and under what conditions, you can begin to develop and adjust your instructional plans accordingly. In the scene described above, for example, the instructor might have needed to provide visual cues or opportunities to touch and manipulate models.

In another situation, certain environmental factors such as noise or temperature may negatively influence the learning process. The physical environment for learning can be modified based on this information.

Information about individual and group learning styles might also tell something about the types of learning strategies that are successful with students: those that require movement, abstract thinking, group interaction, inductive or deductive reasoning, listening, viewing, active experimentation, simulations that involve emotions and feelings, or creative endeavors. While another chapter in this text describes how to use these various strategies appropriately, the key is to use them appropriately with the *right* learners — those most inclined to benefit from the strategy.

The same is true about the selection and use of instructional resources. While there are a myriad of available resources and aids, and sound guidelines for their selection (see Chapter 12), particular resources are likely to be more effective with some learners than with others. Researchers speculate that this is related to learning style. Insight into learning style can help in creating an instructional environment, developing instructional plans, and selecting instructional resources that help to communicate as effectively as possible, family and consumer sciences content to the individual learner.

Of course, using learning style information to create a comprehensive environment is only one approach to its use. Other researchers and practitioners advocate making individual diagnosis of learning styles via a formal instrument, and then tailoring instruction to the needs of the individual. Although there has been some controversy about the use of formal instrumentation and the validity of various types of instruments, individual assessment is one way of arriving at individual learning style information. Besides assessments specifically for the purpose of identifying elements of learning style, there are also tests that look at skills that correlate to learning style.

## FACTORS THAT MAKE UP LEARNING STYLE

Learners can be described in terms of their styles — how and under what conditions they prefer to learn. What are the elements or factors that make up style?

Early researchers and theorists who studied cognitive style focused on how individuals perceived information, or how they accessed information. Witkin (1967) looked at how much individuals separated themselves from the environment in order to perceive what is really happening. He described learners as either **field dependent** (when the environment is critical to the learner's understanding or learning) or **field independent** (when environment is less important to a learner). Witkin, as well as other researchers, often viewed learners as "either/or."

Cohen (1967) looked at people as "lumpers" or "splitters." This distinction describes those who look at the big picture (**lumpers**) or those who focus on details (**splitters**). He claimed that the lumpers were more inclined to find out how to do something by watching someone else do it, while the splitter preferred obtaining information through a series of marked steps, and perhaps preferring to learn on his or her own.

While cognitive style usually focuses on just one dimension, learning style entails many elements, and these may not be simply either/or. Learning style research has attempted to obtain specific indicators of how a person learns so that instruction can be tailored to that learner. French (1975), for example, developed a matrix to be used by instructors in categorizing learner behaviors into styles of learning. Instructors were to look at sensory intake, including dependence on reading and writing, level of speaking, listening, use of visual stimuli and visual representations, movement, and use of taste and smell in learning. They also analyzed concept formation; for instance, whether students perceived in orderly relationships, relied on impulse, used processes of reasoning to reach conclusions, etc. After the analysis, the instructor was referred to a set of suggested learning prescriptions that corresponded to the learning style.

Joseph Hill referred to his area of research as **educational cognitive style**. He attempted to diagnose the complex, personal, cognitive style of a learner on 27 variables or elements in areas including how information is perceived, how individuals filter perceptions and how information is processed. Again, these elements were identified by having learners report their preferences related to reading vs. listening, reliance on senses, preferred groupings for learning, etc.

The work of Dunn and Dunn (1978) includes not just a method for diagnosing learning styles, but suggests options for teaching individuals with different learning styles. Dunns' inventory looks at 24 elements of learning style. These include *elements in the environment*, such as sound, light, temperature, and design; and *emotional elements*, such as motivation, persistence, responsibility, and structure. They also looked at *sociological elements*, such as whether the student prefers learning alone, is peer-oriented, prefers learning with adults, or prefers learning though a variety of ways. The *physical elements* include such things as auditory or visual preference, time of day the learner functions best, and need for mobility during a learning episode. While much of the Dunns' work has been with children, there are implications for adult learners as well.

In the 1970s, David Kolb advanced learning style theory by suggesting that most people approach learning situations (or almost any new situation) in one of two ways: either by *feeling* or by *thinking*. From this, he developed a model that categorized learners into four groups: **imaginative learners** (who integrate experiences and approach problems reflectively), **analytic learners** (who develop theories based on what is known and are engrossed with ideas), **common sense**

**learners** (who integrate theory and practice and like to tinker and experiment with things), and **dynamic learners** (who learn through trial and error and arrive at accurate conclusions, even in the absence of strong logic).

Kolb's work became the basis for the **4MAT System** developed by McCarthy. The 4MAT System is based on the premise that there are four basic methods of teaching: concrete experience, reflective observations, abstract concepts, and active experiment. When using the 4MAT System, an instructor is encouraged to use all four methods *systematically*, in the course of instruction, in order to reach the four different types of learners described by Kolb.

Gregore, another involved in learning style research in the 1970s, also discussed learning style as an indicator of systems of thought. He believed that learning style indicated how a learner approaches reality and identified approaches to learning as concert sequential, abstract sequential, abstract random, and concrete random.

The early researchers and theorists began modern learning styles theory by focusing on how individuals learned differently, for example, how individuals have different cognitive patterns or styles for storing information. By the 1970s, emphasis had shifted, somewhat, to how individuals learn differently. Current discussion centers strongly on *thinking*. Figure 5-1 summarizes the work of some of the major researchers.

Researchers in the area of learning style (the above highlights only a few) have developed inventories to determine learning style. Dunn, Dunn, and Price (1975, 1979, 1981, 1985, 1989) have developed very sophisticated instruments to measure learning style. Proponents of formal learning style assessment suggest that instructors cannot correctly identify all characteristics of learning style (Dunn, 1990) and that some behaviors may be misunderstood or may

**FIGURE 5-1. Examples of Considerations in Learning Style**

| Cohen (1967) | French (1975) | Hill (unpublished) |
|---|---|---|
| Lumper<br>Splitter | Sensory intake (reading vs. writing)<br>Level of speaking<br>Level of listening<br>Response to visual stimuli<br>Need of movement<br>Use of taste and smell | Reading vs. listening<br>Reliance on senses<br>Preferred groupings, etc. |

| Dunn and Dunn (1978) | Kolb (1976) |
|---|---|
| Environment (sound, light, temperature, design)<br>Emotion (motivation, persistence, responsibility, structure preferences):<br>• Learning alone vs. with other workers<br>• Learning with adults<br>• Learning in a variety of ways | People-oriented vs. task-oriented<br>Talking vs. listening<br>Animated vs. reserved<br>Experimenting vs. digesting, etc. |

be misinterpreted. There is research to support the reliability and validity of various instruments (Curry, 1987; DeBello, 1990), but all of these studies have been done with K-12 grade learners within the formal classroom. These inventories are generally self-report instruments that require 10 minutes to several hours to complete. Many can be teacher-scored. Some of the commercially prepared materials link specific instructional advice to their learning styles. Obviously, it is not always feasible or appropriate to test for learning styles. While it might be worth it for the secondary teacher who will be with a particular class of students for one semester, it probably is not appropriate in working with the individual learner, workshop or seminar audiences, or with groups that may have several purposes, only one of which is educational.

## OBTAINING LEARNING STYLE INFORMATION

The learning preferences of learners can be identified. This identification can come formally through the use of an inventory or other self-report instrument, through the assessment by a professional, or through more informal observation of learners.

Instruction will be better tailored to any group if there is some understanding of learning styles and preferences, even if it is not possible to obtain this information through the use of elaborate inventories. The instructor may obtain some of the general information through the use of a few prepared questions. These may relate to the use of instructional strategies or resources. For example:
- "Would you like me to write on the transparency as I talk about these points?"
- "Shall we take two short breaks or one long break today?"
- "How many of you would like a copy of my notes at the end of my talk?"
- "Would you like to complete the task individually or in small groups?"
Although these may seem like fairly innocuous questions, they help to identify learning style preferences such as reading vs. listening, need for movement, and level of social interaction. Instructors can make an assessment of learners using some of these types of questions without relying upon prepared inventories.

In some circumstances, the instructor may choose to gather information about learning through direct observation of learners. Purposeful observation provides valuable data, even when more formal measures are used.

The observation of learners should include their reactions and responses to many of the types of stimuli already described. First, observe the level of attention of learners. How do they look? Do they seem restless, bored, confused, alert, or sleepy? Does productivity and cooperation seem to decline during particular times of the day or in certain temperatures? Do learners seem to prefer some seating arrangements over others? There are obvious cues for each of these conditions, and they may suggest something about learning style.

For example, the Dunn inventory looks carefully at the time of day learners function best. Perhaps your client has difficulty focusing on detailed information during a morning appointment, but is able to be more attentive and listen more closely to directions after lunch. This is a facet of learning style.

Besides the attentiveness of the learners, pay careful attention to the questions they ask. Some trends may become evident. Many questions about procedure, directions, or process may mean that the learners need more structure. Learners who need oral repetition of information may be having difficulty learning by listening; they may need written materials. Frequent requests for help may suggest that the learner is teacher-motivated and prefers to have the guidance and help of the instructor.

Listening to learners about their degree of satisfaction with aspects of instruction is important, too. How helpful do they perceive intermediate deadlines to be? peer mentors? incentive programs? snacks or breaks? background music? While this may seem like a laundry list of unrelated factors, preferences for them do provide clues about how people want to learn and under what conditions they learn best.

In addition to observing and listening to learners, you can also monitor their responses and reactions to the types of instructional activities and strategies you develop. How do they react to small group work? Do they really listen to and learn from films, or do they just enjoy the break? What happens when learners are unsupervised? Which activities do learners join in enthusiastically and in which are learners reluctant to engage? Under what conditions do learners seem most productive? most relaxed? most interested? These observations can be made informally or kept in the form of anecdotal records. Figure 5-2 summarizes the quick ways of assessing learning style elements.

It would be naive to suggest that there is always a linear relationship between what you observe and learning style. For example, learners who beg to hold class out-of-doors may not prefer learning in that environment, but merely prefer that environment to the classroom! Similarly, not wanting to read assignments, sleeping through a presentation, or irresponsible behavior cannot and should not always be interpreted as the result of learning style. Again, it is not possible to observe all characteristics of learning style. These behaviors can be clues, however, and should be considered.

**FIGURE 5-2. Quick Ways to Assess Learning Style Elements**

- Simple written inventory
- Oral questioning
- Observation
- Analysis of student questions
- Learner reports of satisfaction/dissatisfaction
- Monitoring responses to activities/learning strategies

# USING LEARNING STYLE INFORMATION
# WHEN PLANNING INSTRUCTION

Because all learners or clients do not learn in the same way or prefer to learn in the same way, it would seem logical not to teach them in the same way. However, is that possible, especially in large groups where learning styles of the group members may vary considerably?

It is probably important for communicators of family and consumer sciences content to begin by thinking about their own styles and preferences. If your strengths are brainstorming, looking at things from a variety of perspectives, and being interested in many different areas, it may be difficult to realize that the rest of the world does not share the same learning style. Instructors need to identify their own styles first, and acknowledge that others may not share those styles. This emphasis on "know thyself" and "know the other person with whom you are working" is advocated by persons like Gregore, who believe an important use of learning styles is recognizing individual styles and building on personal strengths.

Instructors also need to acknowledge that there is no "best" learning style. Research has failed to support any real relationship between learning style and intelligence quotient (IQ) (Kirby, 1979). Students who learn in a particular way are not necessarily more intelligent than other learners, although some research has linked particular learning preferences to achievement in certain content areas.

Some researchers have suggested that, ideally, learners would be matched to instructors or presenters with the same learning/teaching style. Researchers, like Dunn and Dunn and Carbo, who espouse the diagnostic/prescriptive approach, believe that instruction and materials need to be matched to individual learning style. That is, if it were determined that the instructor was an **assimilator** (preferred to collect and analyze data and devise models) and made assignments that required the use of **inductive reasoning** (moving from details to generalizations), then that instructor would be matched to students with similar preferences. One difficulty with this proposal is that many instructional settings do not provide the option of various instructors, even if it were possible to determine everyone's teaching and learning style. Even if it were possible, it denies learners an opportunity to adapt their styles and preferences to other modes.

Because several learning styles are likely to be present in any audience, instructors need to balance instructional plans by selecting strategies and resources that cater to a variety of learning styles. This means moving beyond only those with which the instructor is comfortable to include the range of activities that meets the learning style needs of others. In concrete terms, this means planning *every* instructional episode (presuming there are learners with varying styles) to include a variety of instructional strategies. This is the aspect of learning styles that emphasizes application to all aspects of program planning and instruction. This way of applying learning styles allows for adapting instruction to major or broad learning differences and is the approach taken by McCarthy, Butler, and others.

For example, suppose a family and consumer sciences instructor is speaking with the parents of newborns about infant care. The instructor may begin by describing the procedures and explaining why these are important. Next, he or she demonstrates how these are done. A discussion follows on how and why these procedures are used and how they may be modified by the new parents. Learners then practice individually or in small groups. The instructor moves around to help individuals as they request or appear to desire assistance. Finally, the instructor provides written materials that summarize the content of the presentation. As noted in later discussions of learning theory, this type of varied presentation is likely to be effective because it builds on the principles of how people learn, and the ways in which people learn best.

Another strategy for meeting the individual learning styles of learners is to, where possible, individualize instruction. This may mean allowing learners to select from among various activities in which they can participate, selecting their own projects, assignment topics, or assignment formats, etc. While it is not always possible to completely individualize instruction (instructing each individual at his or her own pace with individual learner outcomes and instructional plans), there are many opportunities to allow personal choice in the instructional process. When given a choice, learners are likely to select an option that matches their particular learning styles. (See the chapter on Instructional Planning for more details on this strategy.)

As instructors attempt to meet the individual learning style needs of audiences it is helpful to periodically check with the learners about the degree of satisfaction with instruction. This type of evaluation or feedback is not directed at how well learners like the instructor or how much they have learned, but at how satisfied they are with the instructional process. Questions about their level of comfort, activities they have enjoyed most and least, resources that have been most and least helpful, what they would like to do again (or never do again!) and what they've enjoyed most are helpful to ask when planning and modifying instruction. Again, not all of these can be guaranteed to be directly related to instructional style, but the opinions and preferences of learners provide important insights to the instructor trying to effectively communicate family and consumer sciences content.

## SUMMARY

Learning style influences how a learner perceives information, gathers information, sorts it, and makes decisions. Every learner has his or her own learning style. The learning style describes what physical, social, environmental, and sociological elements or factors help an individual to learn effectively. Various researchers have examined these considerations in learning style. Understanding the learning styles of individual learners or groups of learners allows the professional to tailor instructional strategies, instructional resources, and the instructional environment to learners. Studies have shown that by doing so, academic achievement increases and general attitudes improve.

Learning style information can be identified formally through the use of an inventory or other self-report instrument, through the assessment of a professional, or through more informal observation of learners. Various methods can then be used to match instructional methods to the learning styles of learners.

## REFERENCES AND RESOURCES

Brandt, R. (1990). On learning styles: A conversation with Pat Guild. *Educational Leadership, 48*(2), 10-12.

Butler, K.A. (1988). Learning styles. *Learning, 88*, 30-34.

Carbo, M., Dunn, R., & Dunn, K. (1986). *Teaching students to read through their individual learning styles.* Englewood Cliffs, NJ: Prentice-Hall.

Cohen, R.A. (1967). *Primary group structure, conceptual styles and school achievement.* Unpublished doctoral dissertation, University of Pittsburgh.

Curry, L. (1987). *Integrating concepts and cognitive learning styles. A review with attention to psychometric standards.* Ontario: Canadian College of Health Science Executives.

Curry, L. (1990). A critique of the research on learning styles. *Educational Leadership, 48*(2), 50-53.

DeBello, T. (1990). Comparison of eleven major learning styles models: Variables, appropriate populations, validity of instrument, and the research behind them. *Journal of Reading, Writing and Learning Disabilities International, 6*(3), 203-222.

Dunn, R. (1979). *Learning: A matter of style.* Alexandria, VA: Association for Supervision and Curriculum Development.

Dunn, R. (1990). Rita Dunn answers questions on learning styles. *Educational Leadership, 48*(2), 15-18.

Dunn, R., Dunn, K. & Price, G.E. (1975, 1979, 1981, 1985, 1989). *Learning style inventory.* Lawrence, KS: Price Systems.

Dunn, R., & Dunn, K. (1978). How to design programmed learning sequences. *Instructor, LXXXVIX*, 124-128.

French, R.L. (1975). Teaching strategies and learning processes. *Educational Considerations, 3*, 27-28.

Gregore, A.F. (1984). Style as symptom: A phenomenological perspective. *Theory into Practice, 23*(1), 51.

Hill, J.E. *Cognitive style as an educational science.* (Unpublished manuscript) Bloomfield Hills, MI: Oakland Community College.

Keefe, J. & Languis, M. (1983). *Operational definitions.* Paper presented to the NASSP learning styles task force. Reston, VA.

Kirby, P. (1979). *Cognitive style, learning style, and transfer skills acquisition.* Information series No. 195. Columbus, OH: National Center for Research in Vocational Education.

Kolb, D. (1977). *Learning style inventory: A self-description of preferred learning modes.* Boston: McBer.

Kolb, D. (1976). *Learning style inventory technical manual.* Boston: McBer.

*Learning Styles: Putting Research and Common Sense into Practice.* (1991). Arlington, VA: American Association of School Administrators.

McCarthy, B. (1990). Using the 4MAT system to bring learning styles to schools. *Educational Leadership, 48*(2), 31-36.

*Student Learning Styles and Brain Behavior.* (1982). Reston, VA: National Association of Secondary School Principals.

Witkin, H.A. (1967). A cognitive style approach to cross-cultural perspective. *International Journal of Psychology, 2*, 233-250.

# 6

# DECIDING WHAT TO COMMUNICATE

Every instructor of family and consumer sciences content comes face to face with the question, "What should I teach?" Professionals may ask, "What do my clients need to know?" Sometimes the question is less confounding. A session outline, a program curriculum, a selected textbook, a job description, or an agency's competencies or objectives may provide guidance. In other settings, there may be little direction other than topics such as, "A course in child development" or "A session on improving your home interior on a shoestring budget." At some level, all instructors have to decide what to teach — what content to communicate.

There is no simple solution to this quandary. The decision about what to teach is based on a variety of factors. Communicators will, of course, want to consider learner needs and expectations, as well as the expectations, philosophy, and requirements of the sponsoring institution or agency. However, other, more personal factors also come into play, including instructor competence, preference, and philosophy. What you know about your content area, about your learners, and about your world is screened through your personal philosophy and your philosophy of education. These screens help in deciding what to teach or communicate.

## YOUR PHILOSOPHY OF EDUCATION

As either a formal or nonformal communicator of family and consumer sciences content, you have an idea of your purpose or mission. Through professional preparation, most professionals come to agree on some basic tenets of purpose or mission. However, even if all agree on *what* communicators of family and consumer sciences content are trying to do, it is safe to say that there are some major differences in *how* professionals believe that should be done. These differences in "how" actually represent some differences in philosophy.

## TYPES OF PHILOSOPHIES

Most professionals in family and consumer sciences can agree that what they are trying to do is to improve the quality of families' lives, but different philosophies guide instructional decision making. These philosophies include a focus on development of the individual, basic skills, technical skills/competencies, or critical thinking.

Some family and consumer sciences educators approach their goal of improving the quality of families' lives by trying to maximize the potential of each individual. These educators believe that the starting point is to facilitate in each person a strong sense of self, an understanding of personal strengths and weaknesses, and strong interpersonal skills. They believe that learners must come to appreciate and care for one another, to develop nurturing and caregiving skills, and to come to understand their own values and to respect the values of others.

Other professionals believe that every learner requires strong academic and basic skills. Basic skills are the foundation for all other learning and for success in everything else a learner will attempt to do. These basic skills might include reading, writing, and computational skills as applied to life situations. If a learner has strong basic skills, other types of achievement are possible.

Another view is that every learner requires certain technical or life skills. There are certain functions and roles over the life cycle that each of us might have to perform—the roles of parent, spouse, worker, community member. The key is to analyze these roles and determine what competencies a person needs to be able to perform in these roles. Upon determining these competencies, educators can break each competency into tasks that must be accomplished in order to perform the competency. With this approach, the educator can teach any skill, from how to prepare a meal to how to care for an elderly family member. The key is to analyze the job, function, or role, and to break the big job down into manageable, teachable parts.

The final view or philosophy insists that learners need to be able to think. Skills and knowledge aside, the family and consumer sciences learner needs to be able to make informed, rational choices that lead to enlightened action. This requires being able to understand and consider different kinds of knowledge, to consider consequences, to weigh alternatives in both a rational and ethical manner, and to make decisions or judgments in light of personal and public welfare. Educators who hold this view believe that the tool for changing the quality of life for all families and their societies is to be able to think critically—then act—on problems and issues.

The four examples described here loosely depict persons with humanistic, academic, technical, and social reconstructionist philosophies (McNeil, 1977). While these examples greatly simplify what each of these philosophies repre-

## FIGURE 6-1. Philosophical Screens

| To a person with a philosophy that emphasizes: | Instruction should: |
| --- | --- |
| Humanism | • maximize the potential of each individual. |
| Basic skills | • emphasize basic skills that are the foundation for other achievement. |
| Technical skills/ Competencies | • focus on building specific competencies that can be ''put together'' to achieve certain necessary tasks for a particular role. |
| Social reconstructionism/Critical thinking/Practical reasoning | • help learners develop decision-making skills/higher order thinking skills for positive social outcomes. |

sent, they serve to introduce how individuals with a common mission can believe the mission is best served in a variety of ways. These philosophies are summarized in Figure 6-1.

## RELATIONSHIP BETWEEN PHILOSOPHY AND WHAT TO COMMUNICATE

Perhaps, as you have read the brief descriptions of each of these philosophies, you have tried to match yourself to one or the other. While few people are purists, you may hold to one philosophy more than the others. The philosophy you hold serves to mold what you decide to teach or communicate.

Consider, for instance, the topic or concept of family planning. Four professionals with four very different philosophies set about to teach this topic to a group of young, adult learners. The professional with the humanistic philosophy is concerned about the learners' feelings toward contraception, their attitudes and values about the use of contraceptives, and the ways these attitudes and values will influence their choices of contraceptives. The educator with the technical philosophy is apt to spend less time on how learners feel. More time will likely be spent on descriptions of the various methods of contraception—the "how to's." The educator with a social reconstructionist point of view may emphasize the decision-making process and the factors that should be considered when making a decision. These factors might include everything from the values of the decision makers, to the potential long-term health impact, to the ethical considerations of one method over another.

Clearly, all the decisions you make about what to communicate are screened through this personal philosophy, but is there a "right" philosophy for those who communicate family and consumer sciences content? Perhaps it is easier to think about certain philosophies being more compatible with certain goals and/or instructional settings. Educators who work in vocational skills centers or career centers in food service, child care and guidance, clothing management services, or institutional management may often find themselves using materials that are built on a technical model. In these cases, the goal of the program is to teach students a marketable *skill*.

Educators providing leadership to clubs or youth programs may find these programs more "learner-centered," where the emphasis is really on the personal development of the individual. Learners and program leaders may be less concerned with the cognitive outcomes of learners than with the interactions with and among the learners. The educator with the humanistic philosophy may be at home here, unless there is a strong emphasis on a product created by the learners.

In certain clubs, organizations, or businesses, the success of the participants is judged on level of performance or quality of product. In these settings, the leader may have to adopt a philosophy that emphasizes product over process.

Some settings appear to dictate the type of model that will be used. In a graduate nutrition course, for example, the selection of content will depend less on the philosophy of the instructor than on the complex concepts that have to be transmitted.

Philosophy has been discussed first because the philosophy of the communicator colors the way in which everything else is viewed. There are other factors—factors less obtuse—that also influence what educators decide to teach. Some of these (the learner, the setting, etc.) are discussed in other chapters in this text.

This discussion of educational philosophy has greatly over-simplified this complex dimension of teacher decision making. It may have helped, however, to illustrate the relationship between professionals' views of their roles and what they decide to communicate.

## CONCEPTS AND GENERALIZATIONS

Once you have a sense of your philosophy, the learners you are serving, and the main topic you want to communicate, you are ready to decide on the information or subject matter your students or clients need to know. While there is a variety of models available, concepts and generalizations have the broadest application to formal and nonformal settings.

## CONCEPTS

A **concept** is an idea that can be expressed in a word, phrase, or sentence. It expresses in a simple, verbal expression all a person knows, thinks, and feels about a topic or subject. Consider the concept "healthy lifestyle." What comes to mind when someone indicates that he or she has, or desires to have, a healthy lifestyle? Perhaps you think about good dietary habits, regular exercise, or a reasonable number of hours of sleep each night. Maybe a person prizes a healthy lifestyle and thinks it is important to maintain. All of these thoughts and feelings relate to an individual's conceptualization of a healthy lifestyle.

Each individual has his or her own set of concepts. Your idea of a healthy lifestyle may be quite different from someone else's idea. Your conceptualization of the world is affected by your background and experiences. For example, if you grow up in a home where food choices take into consideration cholesterol and regular exercise, your concept of what a healthy lifestyle is will be affected by that.

## A Concept Outline or Framework

Since concepts represent units of thought, they are useful in organizing the world of objects and events into categories. Categories of concepts may then be subdivided, grouped, or arranged into hierarchies following an outline format. Depending upon the nature of the outline being generated, you might organize concepts along any of several dimensions, for example, from simple to complex, concrete to abstract, vague to clear, or from limited to extended applicability.

This ability to arrange thoughts and ideas in some kind of organized way is what makes concepts useful in planning instruction. If you can identify the important concepts, their relationship with one another, and their importance to the learners, you can make an outline or framework for instruction that will help you in your instructional planning.

A simple concept outline that might be used by an instructor is shown in Figure 6-2. In developing the outline, the instructor first listed all of the concepts that came to mind when thinking about the topic of employability skills. Then he or she examined the list and added and subtracted concepts as he or she thought about them again in relation to the learners' needs. Finally, the instructor generated the hierarchy of concepts (in outline format) shown in Figure 6-2.

**FIGURE 6-2. A Concept Outline Used to Organize Instruction**

---

**EMPLOYABILITY SKILLS**

I. What are employability skills?
   A. Academic skills
   B. Personal management skills
   C. Teamwork skills

II. Why are employability skills needed?
   A. Changes in the workplace
   B. Changes in the home
   C. Preparing workers for the future

III. How are employability skills acquired?

IV. The portfolio — Documenting employability skills

Using a concept outline or framework, then, can help to clarify the important ideas to be communicated to a group of learners and to organize the ideas into some meaningful flow. Of course, as instructional planning proceeds, you may decide to rearrange the outline. For example, you may decide to start with item "III" to get at the issues of concern to a particular group of learners right from the beginning and then move back to definitions and, finally, on to strategies. The point of the concept outline is not to tie you to some rigid structure for presenting information, but to make sure you have covered all of the important topics in some logical way.

## GENERALIZATIONS

Another tool that can be used to help organize instruction is the generalization. A **generalization** is really an expansion of a concept.

To be a generalization, a statement must meet two criteria. The statement must be universally true. That is, a generalization expresses an idea with which everyone throughout the world would agree. Further, most generalizations indicate a relationship between certain concepts. Consider, for example, the following generalization: "Design is the process of organizing the basic elements of line, form, shape, texture, and color." This statement is really an expansion of the concept "design." It tells you something about design that you can incorporate into your own conceptualization of what design is. In this statement, the elements of line, form, shape, texture, and color are related to the concept of design. Thus, the statement above meets all of the criteria of a generalization because it: expresses an underlying truth, has an element of universality, and indicates relationships.

### Levels of Generalizations

Just as with concepts, generalizations can be placed in a hierarchy from first-level generalizations to third-level. Simple ideas precede those that are more complex. This also helps you to organize your instruction logically and to help learners to build from simple to more complex ideas.

The first level of generalizations is usually descriptions, definitions, or analogies. They may also involve identification or classification. For example, "Unity is the oneness of design." This statement is really a definition and so falls within the first level of generalization.

The second level of generalizations shows relationships among ideas. Comparisons are made and include at least two concepts. For example, "A child's physical needs are affected by his or her particular level of development," represents a second-level generalization since it shows the relationship between developmental level and physical needs.

The third-level generalization usually explains, justifies, interprets, or predicts. A third-level generalization may be remote in time or space. It may also suggest a direction for behavior, for example, "Clothing may help the

**FIGURE 6-3.** Criteria for Generalizations

Evaluate generalizations you write to determine if they are:

**Sound**
  —supported by fact that can be substantiated (for example, research, word of a specialist).
  —applicable to similar situations.
  —likely not to become outdated.
  —based upon universally acceptable values.
  —undergirded by sound assumptions.

**Technical**
  —clearly stated.
  —consists of understandable, unambiguous terms.
  —complete statements.

**Instructional**
  —helpful to learners in gaining insights in dealing with realistic problems and new situations.
  —significant enough to influence behavior.
  —able to be developed through reasonable instructional activities.
  —important enough to be worth the learner's time in developing.

individual to make adjustments when changing from one role to another and to attain success in that role."

In Figure 6-3, some of the criteria that can be used in evaluating generalizations are listed. The criteria will help to judge both the soundness and the structure of generalizations.

Sound generalizations are supported by substantiated facts. Research can be cited to support the generalization. Further, generalizations are likely to be *universally* true—true to all people from all environments and backgrounds. They are also likely to be true over time. Sound generalizations do not become outdated.

In addition to actual content of the generalization, certain technical consideration should be taken into account. Generalizations need to be clear, unambiguous statements that all can understand. Simple, complete statements are easier to communicate.

Finally, generalizations need to address content that is valuable or significant. Learners need to recognize that the outcomes pursued are worth the support.

## The Role of Generalizations in Instructional Planning

Generalizations are useful in instruction because they represent the universal truths that you hope learners will be able to express after instruction. Suppose you had just given a seminar on "Efficient (and Inexpensive!) Housing Design" to a group of people expecting to design and build their own log homes.

At the end of one session on utilities, participants are asked to summarize some of the main ideas of the session. One person raises a hand and says, "I guess the most important thing I learned today was that centrally locating the utilities in a dwelling is an economic advantage." You are thrilled! Your learner has just reiterated one of the generalizations toward which you had directed your instruction. Even though you never *said*, "Central location of utilities in a dwelling is an economic advantage," your learners discovered the idea through the learning activities you provided.

Concepts and generalizations work hand in hand. After generating the list of concepts to be taught and organizing them so that related concepts appear together in an outline, then you can generate statements about these concepts and their relationships. These generalizations can then become the outcomes from instruction that you expect—the statements you hope learners will be able to make when the instructional session ends.

## LEARNER OUTCOMES OR OBJECTIVES

Many who serve in a communicator's role are perfectly happy working only with concept outlines and/or generalizations. These tools help them to structure their communication and provide organization for the instruction they want to provide. However, concept outlines and generalizations do not clearly identify the **outcomes** of instruction; that is, the learner behaviors that are expected after instruction occurs.

No matter what kind of teaching you are doing, you will want to know whether your learners are, in fact, learning what you are teaching. You can almost always find out if someone has learned by looking at what he or she can do after the learning episode has occurred. For example, you know immediately whether the learner has mastered the elements of interviewing a potential employee by watching the individual role-play an interview. You can easily tell if a learner has mastered the art of diapering a baby by watching him or her diaper an infant. You can ask test questions and look at the responses to determine whether or not learners have learned certain facts and ideas.

Thus, if you can describe before you begin teaching what it is you want students to be able to do, you can quickly decide whether your instruction was effective by watching your learners in action. Descriptions of what the learner will be able to do after participating in some kind of learning experience are called learner *outcomes* or *objectives*.

## SPECIFICITY OF LEARNER OUTCOMES

Learner outcomes can be stated very broadly or very specifically—and at all points in between. **Broadly stated learner outcomes** are sometimes called **goals**. Goals describe global learner outcomes. You might, for example, describe the goals for a parenting course in the following way: "After completing this course, the learner will be able to demonstrate effective parenting techniques." This global statement is useful in describing the course and what learners will be able to do after taking it.

Broadly stated learner outcomes are less helpful in the daily planning for the course. In planning for day-to-day instruction, **specifically stated learner outcomes** are more helpful. For example, an extension specialist might plan a presentation on restoring wet carpeting for a community that regularly experiences flooding. The specialist would want to develop a number of specific objectives for that presentation. One of the specific learner outcomes for this session might be: "After attending the session, the learner will be able to identify a strategy for removing excess water from carpeting."

The relationship between the purpose or use of the learner outcome statements in instruction and how general or specific they need to be is shown in Figure 6-4. Each outcome relates to the others, but varies in specificity depending upon the instructional element of the program to which it relates.

## WRITING SPECIFIC LEARNER OUTCOMES

You have probably experienced the "aha" phenomenon sometime in your life—that moment when something that has not been clear before, all of a sudden, makes sense. You say, "*Now* I get it!" or "Aha!" Almost magically, you *know* what you didn't know before.

The "aha" phenomenon is satisfying for the learner, but frequently is not seen by the instructor. How does an instructor know if a learner has learned something? The instructor looks for a behavior that can be seen to judge

**FIGURE 6-4. Level of Specifying of Outcomes**

| NATURE OF OUTCOME | INSTRUCTIONAL ELEMENT | OUTCOME |
|---|---|---|
| General | Program | Program Goal: Learner will use life management skills in everyday living. |
| | Course/Session | Session Outcome: Students will demonstrate effective consumer behaviors. |
| | Unit | Unit Goal: Students will effectively balance personal income and expenditures. |
| Specific | Lesson/Presentation | Specific Learner Outcomes: Students will correctly balance a personal checkbook. |

whether the learner has learned. A good example of this is the common test. The learner reads questions and marks answers (a behavior). The instructor can then look at the marks to determine whether the learner is performing as intended. Of course, the questions must be carefully designed to measure the desired behavior.

Learners may demonstrate behavior in more direct ways, too. For example, a client might remove stains from a fabric while the professional watches to see if the process is being done correctly.

It is up to the instructor to decide what observable behaviors constitute "knowing" in the learner. They must be observable and measurable behaviors. Listed in Figure 6-5 are examples of nonbehavioral (nonmeasurable) and behavioral (measurable) verbs. You can clearly *see* a learner write or recite or demonstrate. These verbs describe behaviors that can be observed and evaluated. You cannot see whether a learner knows or understands a concept. There are *behaviors* that show learners know or understand, but they are best communicated using explicit behavioral verbs.

Specific objectives become the basis for every other instructional decision you'll make. Objectives drive instruction. In fact, a road map is a perfect analogy. The **objective** is your destination; instructional techniques or the materials or resources you choose are merely routes. While selecting the best route is important, it is meaningless without a destination — like riding around in circles on an air-conditioned bus. You and your learners must know the destination or objectives before you're able to make meaningful decisions about instruction.

## FIGURE 6-5. Behavioral and Nonbehavioral Verbs

| Behavioral Verbs | Nonbehavioral Verbs |
| --- | --- |
| write | know |
| recite | understand |
| identify | really understand |
| differentiate | appreciate |
| solve | fully appreciate |
| construct | grasp the significance of |
| list | enjoy |
| compare | believe |
| classify | learn |

## Elements of Learner Outcomes

No matter how general or specific a learner outcome is, a meaningful objective has certain pieces or components. It may be helpful to think of these components as the *ABCs of Objectives*.

**Audience.** The "A" component is the audience. Objectives that have meaning define the audience or learner. For example, in the objective, "Seventh grade nutrition students will develop a day's meal plan using the Food Guide Pyramid," *seventh grade students* are the learners or audience. Clearly, the audience is important in deciding learner outcomes and writing objectives since, for example, what is appropriate for seventh grade students may not be appropriate for the disadvantaged homemaker.

**Behavior.** The "B" in the ABCs of objective writing is behavior. What should learners be able to do as a result of instruction? What measurable and observable behavior is anticipated? In the objective, "Given appropriate materials and tools, employees will demonstrate window caulking," the intended outcome is being able to caulk a window.

**Condition.** "Given the appropriate materials," is an example of the "C" component of the objective — the condition. The condition refers to the criteria by which, or the situations under which, the learner's performance will be assessed. It may describe the resources used (given a recipe), limitations imposed (within 20 minutes), or when and where the learner will perform (in his or her own home).

Meaningful objectives include all three of the ABCs or elements described here. Examples of complete and incomplete objectives are given in Figure 6-6.

---

**FIGURE 6-6. Examples of Complete and Incomplete Objectives**

**Complete Objectives**

Given various pictures of food, the preschoolers will sort healthy foods from junk foods.
  *(condition)*                    *(audience)*        *(behavior)*

Based on the principles discussed in class, students will be able to select the most
  *(condition)*                              *(audience)*                    *(behavior)*
appropriate housing for a described family.

After reviewing some sample policies, senior citizens will be able to discriminate
  *(condition)*                              *(audience)*                    *(behavior)*
between valid and exaggerated insurance claims.

**Incomplete Objectives**

The students will identify home safety hazards. *(Under what conditions?)*

Demonstrate CPR using Resusci-Annie. *(Who is the audience?)*

The teenage parents will be given a list of toys appropriate for developmental level. *(What is the expected behavior?)*

# Writing Objectives Learners Will Understand

Objectives actually provide a common understanding between learner and instructor about what will be learned, so it is important to write good objectives. Good objectives should be clear, workable, and fluent.

**Clarity.** First of all, it must be clear what the learner is supposed to be able to do. State the objective as clearly and simply as possible and include only *one* expected behavior. Action verbs should be used to identify the behavior. Use verbs that have common meanings. Both learners and instructors understand terms like *label, collect, inspect, make up, choose,* and *alter.* For instance, if told that after instruction, the learner will be able to identify potentially harmful mixtures of household cleaning products, the learners know what to expect. You know what to look for to determine whether or not learning took place.

**Workability.** Objectives also need to be workable: something that can realistically be achieved through instruction. "Teens will make good spending decisions" may be pretty hard to guarantee, even as a result of your best efforts. You may, however, be able to measure whether they can identify types of consumer fraud, advertising appeals, or various sales techniques, and describe how they are designed to influence consumer spending.

**Fluency.** Finally, is the objective fluent? Does it make sense to you and the learner? Does the wording flow smoothly? What you intend as an outcome needs to be stated clearly, concisely, and in terms that make sense to the learner. Ask yourself this: As a result of my planned instruction, what will the learner be able to do? You need to be able to state this in words that make sense to your learners.

See Figure 6-7 for good and poor examples of each of the elements discussed. Objectives may need to be written several times before they become clear, workable, and fluent.

---

## FIGURE 6-7. Examples of Good and Poor Objectives

| | |
|---|---|
| **Not Clear:** | Students will decide what to do. |
| **Clear:** | Given a case study that involves making a decision, the student will state his or her decision and defend it. |
| **Not Workable:** | Learners will select a career wardrobe. |
| **Workable:** | Given a description of a work environment and a prescribed budget, learners will identify, from catalogs, appropriate clothing for a career wardrobe. |
| **Not Fluent:** | Based on the principles discussed, the learner will, with 100% accuracy, in the context of his or her own buying decisions in the market place, select toys that are developmentally appropriate and safe for his or her child(ren). |
| **Fluent:** | After a lesson on toy selection, learners will identify toys that are unsafe for children. |

# TYPES OF OBJECTIVES

As you think about the kinds of outcomes you might plan, it becomes clear that there are different types of objectives that might be achieved. Sometimes, the purpose of instruction is to develop a particular skill. Other times, you hope to modify the attitudes or opinions of learners. Many objectives have to do with imparting new information, and having learners be able to apply that information. These various types of learning that involve acting, feeling, or thinking, can be classified into three learning domains: cognitive, affective, and psychomotor (Bloom, 1956).

The **cognitive domain** emphasizes thinking. Objectives in the cognitive domain have to do with learners' knowing, understanding, or comprehending. Labeling the parts of the reproductive system, interpreting a tax form, or formulating a response to a family crisis are all outcomes in the cognitive domain.

The **affective domain** emphasizes feelings. Objectives in the affective domain deal with how a learner feels about something, for example, his or her degree of acceptance or rejection of something. Some behavioral objectives in the affective domain would include enjoying time spent with young children, recognizing contributions of older family members, or listening empathetically to others. You will note that even though the verbs used here describe feelings, it is easy to recognize evidence that would indicate whether or not these outcomes have been achieved.

The third domain of learning, the **psychomotor domain**, has to do with acting and is concerned with how learners control or move their bodies. The psychomotor domain relates to skill development, for example, applying a first-aid bandage, operating a convection oven, or diapering a baby.

Some educators have suggested a fourth domain. The **perceptual domain** (Moore, 1970 & Hooker, 1980) has recently been applied to family and consumer sciences (Hausafus & Williams, 1987). Perception involves the use of cognitive and affective skills to create meaning from stimuli received through the senses. The perceptual domain emphasizes the process of receiving stimuli or information through the senses, interpreting those stimuli, and finally, responding to the stimuli.

The perceptual domain, as modified by Hausafus and Williams (1987), includes first sensation, then figure perception, symbol perception, perception of meaning, and perception of performance. To illustrate the process, the learner might detect problems in a child's verbal skills (sensation), recognize verbal problems such as stuttering (figure perception), discriminate between stimuli or events that prompt stuttering and nonstuttering responses (symbol perception), determine the factors that stimulate a stuttering response (perception of meaning), and make decisions about altering the factors that stimulate the stuttering response (perceptive performance). Although this domain has not been widely applied, it may have significance for those communicating family and consumer sciences content.

## Levels of Objectives

Even within any one domain of learning, not all objectives are created equal. For example, one outcome might be to "remember" the information, while another stated outcome would be to "apply the information." This illustrates that within any domain of learning, there are various levels. The lower levels require less ability, and are prerequisite to the higher levels of learning.

An example within the cognitive domain illustrates how the levels of learning relate to one another. Suppose one outcome identified for learners in a family financial management session is to "create a budget." That implies a pretty high level of learning. It suggests that the learner has to apply some

---

**FIGURE 6-8. The Cognitive Domain and Levels of Learning**

**COGNITIVE DOMAIN**
**(Emphasis on Thinking)**

| Level | Description | Sample Behaviors |
|---|---|---|
| 1. Knowledge | Recalling, remembering, and recognizing | Define terms<br>Recall facts<br>Name parts |
| 2. Comprehension | Understanding and explaining | Describe<br>Give examples of<br>Explain how to<br>Construct a model |
| 3. Application | Using ideas | Demonstrate in a laboratory<br>Prepare a sample |
| 4. Analysis | Reasoning | Analyze the problem<br>Distinguish between<br>Point out the advantages |
| 5. Synthesis | Creating | Combine two or more<br>Integrate your ideas with<br>Modify the plan |
| 6. Evaluation | Making a judgment | Assess the problem<br>Weigh the consequences |

Bloom, B.S. (1956). *Taxonomy of education objectives, Handbook I: Cognitive domain.* New York: David McKay.

---

information in a new way to restructure, reorganize, and synthesize. It is easy to see that before this outcome can be met, there have to be some lower level objectives achieved. For example, learners would need to be able to identify various marketing strategies in order to understand advantages of each and to select appropriate strategies for specific target audiences. While these would be classified as lower level objectives, they are clearly necessary in order to be able to function at the higher level. These objectives might be classified as prerequisite knowledge for the session's objective—to create a budget. Figures 6-8, 6-9, and 6-10 illustrate the domains and the levels within the domains.

**FIGURE 6-9. The Affective Domain and Levels of Learning**

**AFFECTIVE DOMAIN**
**(Emphasis on Feeling)**

| Level | Description | Sample Behaviors |
|---|---|---|
| 1. Receiving | Becoming aware | Paying attention to<br>Tolerating<br>Acknowledging differences |
| 2. Responding | Doing something about phenomenon | Agreeing to try<br>Volunteering for<br>Obeying the guidelines |
| 3. Valuing | Developing attitudes | Initiating a plan<br>Showing concern by<br>Assuming responsibility for |
| 4. Organization | Arranging personal values | Adjusting lifestyle<br>Disclosing information about<br>Adapting to |
| 5. Characterization | Internalize a value | Showing devotion<br>Influencing others<br>Exemplifying |

Bloom, B.S., & Kratwohl, D.R. (1956). *Taxonomy of educational objectives, Handbook II, Affective domain.* New York: Longmans/Green.

**FIGURE 6-10.** The Psychomotor Domain and Levels of Learning

| PSYCHOMOTOR DOMAIN (Emphasis on Action) | | |
|---|---|---|
| Level | Description | Sample Behaviors |
| 1. Perception | Detecting sensory cues | Tasting<br>Listening<br>Detecting |
| 2. Set | Ready to act | Placing hand<br>Positioned at |
| 3. Guided Response | Imitating or practicing | Achieving an expression<br>Copying<br>Repeating<br>Imitating |
| 4. Mechanism | Increasing efficiency | Demonstrating<br>Producing<br>Conducting |
| 5. Complex<br>  Overt Response | Performing automatically | Controlling<br>Proceeding<br>Guiding |
| 6. Adapting | Modifying skill | Adjusting<br>Altering<br>Varying |
| 7. Origination | Creating new movements | Designing<br>Constructing<br>Originating |

Simpson, E. (1967). The classification of educational objectives, psychomotor domain. *Illinois Teacher, 10,* 110-145.

## Using the Domains in Planning Instruction

As you plan for instruction, try to include objectives from all three domains. For example, in a unit dealing with the care of young children, you would probably plan for outcomes in each of the three domains. Most authorities would agree that effective parenting involves knowledge (cognitive domain), technical skills (psychomotor domain), and healthy attitudes (affective domain).

Many objectives will overlap into more than one domain, though they are characterized by their primary emphasis. For instance, "altering a pattern" is a psychomotor objective even though the actual skill requires some cognitive knowledge in order to perform.

Planning for instruction also includes writing objectives for different levels of learning. As has been shown, you can't apply information without first having known and understood the information. Similarly, in the affective domain, the learner can't come to value a particular behavior or phenomenon until he or she has had an opportunity to receive and respond to the behavior or phenomenon. Finally, within the psychomotor domain, learners cannot complete the complex skill, (swimming, for example) until they can accomplish simpler skills (floating).

## SUMMARY

Deciding what to teach is a critical step on the path to effective communication of family and consumer sciences content. It involves assessing the body of knowledge in a particular area and your philosophy about that body of knowledge, specifying concepts or generalizations to be covered, and identifying specific learning objectives.

Your philosophy strongly influences the nature of instruction you provide. Whether you hold a humanistic, academic, technical, or social reconstructionist philosophy will determine the "slant" of your communications.

A variety of tools can be used to assist in organizing the content you want to communicate. Concepts are particularly useful in organizing ideas into coherent, organized patterns. Generalizations help in identifying the universal truths that are embedded in the information presented. Both concepts and generalizations can be organized by level of complexity.

Objectives describe what you expect the learner or client to be able to do after instruction, whether the instruction is provided over weeks or over only hours or minutes. In either case, objectives must be written so that they are measurable and tell both the learner and instructor what is expected as the result of instruction.

Meaningful objectives describe the audience, behavior, and the conditions under which this behavior will be performed. This behavior can be described as primarily cognitive, affective, or psychomotor. Within any one of these domains there are levels, and to achieve higher levels of learning within each domain, it is necessary to first accomplish lower level objectives. Well thought out objectives become the basis for all other decisions about instruction.

## REFERENCES AND RESOURCES

Bloom, B. (1956). *Taxonomy of educational objectives, handbook I: Cognitive domain*. New York: David McKay.

Bloom, B.S., & Kratwohl, D.R. (1956). *Taxonomy of educational objectives, handbook II: Affective domain*. New York: Longmans/Green.

Hausafus, C.O., & Williams, S.K. (1987). *Perceptual learning in home economics: Classification of skills in the perceptual domain*. Ames, IA: Iowa State University.

Hooker, E. (1980). Application of the perceptual domain to home economics education. *Illinois Teacher, 23,* 166-172.

Mager, R. (1962). *Preparing instructional objectives.* Palo Alto, CA: Fearon.

McAshen, H.H. (1979). *Competency-based education and behavioral objectives.* Englewood Cliffs, NJ: Educational Technology Publications.

McNeil, J. (1977). *Curriculum: A comprehensive introduction.* Boston: Little, Brown & Co.

Moore, M.R. (1970). The perceptual domain and a proposed taxonomy of perception. *A V Communication Review, 18,* 379-413.

Pasch, M., Sparks-Langer, G., Gardner, T.A., Starko, A.J., & Moody, C.D. (1991). *Teaching as Decision Making: Instructional Practices for the Successful Teacher.* White Plains, NY: Longman.

Simpson, E. (1967). The classification of educational objectives, psychomotor domain. *Illinois Teacher, 10,* 110-145.

# 7

# SETTING THE STAGE

The theatrical reference "setting the stage" is consistent with what many instructors have experienced in working with groups. Instructors are often concerned about the "audience" — how they will maintain audience interest and judge audience reaction. More than one teacher has commented on the need to entertain learners. This chapter, however, will focus more on the physical setting and how it impacts effective instruction. This includes the physical conditions that are most likely to facilitate learning and the technical factors that enhance instruction.

## PHYSICAL ARRANGEMENTS

Although instruction can probably take place just about anywhere, it is more likely to happen and to happen as planned if it occurs in an appropriate physical environment. The physical setting that most often comes to mind is a stark classroom with rows of desks and attached chairs. In fact, this sometimes is an appropriate environment. However, all of the following factors should be kept in mind so that physical arrangements are matched to instruction.

## ROOM ARRANGEMENT

As simple a concept as it seems, the actual arrangement of the room has a very important impact on the success of any family and consumer sciences professional. If you think back to one of the least successful meetings you have attended, you can probably point to some aspect of the room arrangement that detracted from the message you had come to hear. When planning room arrangement, match it to the instructional activities and to the learners who are likely to attend.

## Matching Room Arrangement to Instruction

Think carefully about the nature of the instruction that will occur. If a group is expected to discuss, then the physical environment should accommodate participants by having chairs or desks that can be arranged in a circle so that people can see and talk to one another. As Bowers (1986) found, students are more likely to be anxious about participation when there are rows of seats (as opposed to circles, random arrangements, or tables). The circular arrangement also eliminates the classroom **action zone** of eager respondents, identified by Adams and Biddle (1970), that results when students select their own seats in a room of rows of seats, Figure 7-1. When a responding action zone has established itself, it takes considerable instructor effort to involve all learners in a discussion. If the instructor intends to lecture and to use the chalkboard or projection screen, however, rows of desks are a reasonable arrangement so that each learner can see the front of the room.

Room shape should match the nature of the presentation. A common shape for conferences is a long narrow room with only a few chairs across and a narrow aisle. Obviously, this shape is not the most desirable. Be sure such a room, at a minimum, has a public address system that works well, or those in the back may be unable to hear.

## Matching Room Arrangement to Learner Activities

Activities in which the learners are involved also suggest specific physical arrangements. If learners are expected to take notes, they will need desks or conference tables; if they are only to listen, then "theater" seating is acceptable. If learners are working on projects, space will be required to move around and to spread out materials. Facilities to allow clean up should be available.

**FIGURE 7-1. The "Action Zone"**

THE "ACTION ZONE"

Research in elementary and secondary classrooms indicates that when students are allowed to select their own seats, those who are willing to respond will sit in the center front of the classroom and in a line directly up the center of the room. These are, as well, the students most likely to be called upon by an instructor (Adams & Biddle, 1970).

INSTRUCTOR

| X | X | X | X | X |
|---|---|---|---|---|
| X | X | X | X | X |
| X | X | X | X | X |
| X | X | X | X | X |

Learners who are expected to work in small groups or teams need seating and space that will accommodate several tables or chair groupings so that participants can break off into their groups. Conversely, if you do not wish participants to function as a small group (talking apart from the whole group or working cooperatively), do not place them at small tables. Family and consumer sciences teachers are often assigned to teach in rooms equipped with several small tables. These teachers know how difficult it is to maintain attention to the front of the room or to get students to work independently. The physical arrangement can in part be blamed for these difficulties.

## Matching Room Arrangement to Learners

The needs of participants should also be carefully considered in planning adequately for space. If setting up a room for an adult audience, for example, place seats farther apart to allow more "elbow room" and rows farther apart to allow more leg room. Young children should be seated so that they have plenty of "squirm" space on either side.

It is best to match room size to audience size; too small a room creates a feeling of crowding and discomfort. On the other hand, a room too large also causes discomfort. As Brooks (1988) notes, "a room that is too large can create a space barrier . . . which makes eye contact impossible and allows for distractions from other sources" (p. 91). If using a room too large for the audience, consider stacking extra chairs or roping off back rows (Bodenhamer, 1984).

# MATCHING INSTRUCTOR PLACEMENT TO INSTRUCTION

Another consideration related to instruction and room arrangement is where the instructor should stand in relation to the participants. By staying behind a desk, counter, or lectern, the instructor separates himself or herself from the learners. There are times when this separation is undesirable; for example, when working with a client who may be particularly sensitive or defensive. When the goal of your instruction involves discussion and learner participation, avoid staying behind a desk or lectern. Sit down with a client or small group to help break down the barrier between learner and instructor.

Standing to lecture or discuss is a more formal posture than sitting, but sitting may affect some learners' ability to see and hear what is going on. Think about the kind of instruction that will take place before deciding on room arrangement and instructor placement.

# OTHER PHYSICAL CONSIDERATIONS

The room arrangement and instructor placement are just two physical conditions to be considered. Dunn's (1977) research on learning styles supports the notion that conditions such as temperature and light influence how individuals learn. Consider some of the following factors in arranging the physical conditions of instruction.

It is probably impossible to make everyone physically comfortable, but learners are more likely to be alert and attentive in a room that is a little too cool rather than a room that is too warm. Simply opening a few windows may be helpful in adjusting room temperature. In windowless rooms, adjust the thermostat. When giving a presentation in such a setting, arrive early enough to check out the temperature. This will give you time to locate the person responsible for adjusting room climate. There is nothing more distracting to the instructor or the participants than a room that is uncomfortably warm or cool.

The room lighting should be matched to the instructional activity. Project work, note taking, or demonstrations call for good lighting. Check the lighting in rooms where films or videotapes will be shown to make sure that they can be adequately dimmed. Find out ahead of time how to dim the lights and, if necessary, designate someone to dim the lights at the proper time.

## EQUIPMENT AND SUPPORT MATERIALS

Several other types of arrangements need to be made prior to meeting with learners. Considering equipment and support materials that will help meet learner needs well in advance of your presentation should help to make the learner more comfortable and ready to learn.

## LEARNER NEEDS

You can anticipate the needs of the learners prior to instruction and add to the success of your lesson. For example, if it is desirable for learners to get to know each other in a short period of time, provide name tags for participants. These may be prepared ahead of time or provided for learners to complete. Make sure that tags and markers allow individuals to write their names large enough to actually be read by someone facing them. It is a good idea for the instructor to wear a name tag, too. In some instructional settings you may ask learners not only to provide their names on the name tags, but something else about themselves that will help others get to know them. This might be where they are from, a group they are in, or a particular interest they have.

Consider developing an agenda to share with learners, Figure 7-2. Adult learners particularly appreciate agendas, and they are recommended even for college students (McKeachie, 1986). An agenda can be fairly simple, such as the listing of the two or three major activities planned. It might be somewhat more detailed with short explanations of the planned instructional activities and approximate times. Agendas can be written on a chalkboard, posted, or duplicated and handed out to participants.

One item that may be noted on your agenda is a scheduled break. Consider whether or not a break in instruction is appropriate. Sessions lasting 60 minutes or less probably do not require a break. Think about whether a break is advisable when working with an audience that may be hard to settle down, or

**FIGURE 7-2.** Sample Single-Session Presentation Agenda

| | |
|---|---|
| SAMPLE SINGLE-SESSION PRESENTATION AGENDA | |
| AGENDA | |
| September 15, 19____ | |
| "Can We Talk . . . ?" | |
| 6:00-6:30 | **Registration** |
| 6:30-6:45 | **Welcome and Introductions** |
| | Lydia Hellman, Women's Wellness Center |
| | Coordinator |
| 6:45-7:00 | **Physical Changes of Women** |
| | Dr. Cindy Johnson, Family Practitioner |
| 7:00-7:15 | **Break for Refreshments** |
| 7:15-8:00 | **Emotional Changes of Women** |
| | Dr. Edith House, Psychologist |
| | Community Mental Health Center |
| 8:00-8:30 | **Time for Individual Questions** |

a group so large that it will be difficult to reorganize and get back to the instructional plan.

Carefully consider the audience when deciding on a break. Some groups may particularly need an opportunity to walk around, leave the classroom, or to get refreshments. If you decide a break is appropriate, make sure you provide specific details on how long the break will last, what amenities are provided during the break, and when the instructional session will resume.

## INSTRUCTOR NEEDS

Setting the stage to meet instructor needs requires consideration of everything from what support materials will be needed — and when — to whether or not the required materials are working properly. This is truly a case where, "An ounce of prevention is worth a pound of cure!"

Prior to instruction, the instructor should determine what kinds of equipment or support materials will be needed, for how long, and at what point in instruction. (See Chapter 12 for additional considerations.) Instructors should make a list of all the equipment and resources needed during an instructional episode, from chalk to video recorders. Consider making notes in the margins of your instructional plans to denote the use of particular equipment or materials. This may seem like a trite activity, but many experienced instructors have been unable to present as strong a presentation as planned merely because they have forgotten to bring a marker to write on an overhead transparency or chalk to write on the chalkboard. For the classroom teacher with a well-stocked desk and a room phone, this level of pre-planning may be less critical than it is for the instructor making a presentation in an unfamiliar setting. Still, pre-planning of instructional materials and resources is important since items like audiovisual equipment most often need to be ordered and delivered to the classroom. It is important to note when they are needed, too, so they are in place prior to beginning your presentation. Nothing interrupts a talk more quickly than the ill-timed delivery of additional equipment.

All equipment and resources should be checked before instruction begins to assure that they are in working order and that the instructor knows how they are to be used. Check to make sure the pages of the flipchart *will* flip to the back and stay put; that the light on the overhead projector *is* working; that you know *which* button to push to make the VCR play, and that you *can* reach the pull-down screen when it is needed. All of these small considerations assure smoother instructional delivery.

## DEALING WITH DISTRACTIONS

Distractions that can quickly destroy the "stage" you have set include both visual distractions and uncontrolled noises. **Visual distractions** range from people entering or leaving the room to waiters and waitresses clearing the tables to people taking flash pictures. If at all possible, eliminate visual distractions. When that is not possible, wait to begin speaking until distractions terminate.

Noises that can be controlled in advance include such things as loud room conditioning systems, public address systems that hiss or provide "feedback." Such noises can be eliminated by checking the room well in advance and requesting technical assistance from building coordinators.

**Uncontrolled noises** and **distractions** can present more of a challenge. Brooks (1988) suggests avoiding overreacting or using humor. In either case, put yourself in the position of the audience. If the distraction is annoying them, deal with it quickly and directly. If it is not bothersome to them, ignore it.

## SUMMARY

Carefully planning the physical arrangements in which instruction will be provided helps to "set the stage" for effective instruction. "Setting the stage" requires consideration of the comfort and convenience needs of the instructor and the learners. Carefully planning the physical arrangements in which instruction will be provided helps to set the stage for effective instruction. Physical arrangements include the selection of space, the arrangement of seating, and the maintenance of a comfortable temperature. The selection of appropriate instructional space facilitates the implementation of learning activities. When instructional planning includes consideration of the relationship of the physical environment to instruction, effective communication of family and consumer sciences content is more likely to occur.

# REFERENCES

Adams, R.S., & Biddle, B.J. (1970). *Realities of teaching: Explorations with videotape.* New York: Holt, Rinehart, Winston.

Bodenhamer, S. (1984). *Communications: Checklist for planning a successful meeting.* Columbia, Missouri: University of Columbia Extension Information.

Bowers, J.W., & 36C:099. (1986). Classroom communication apprehension: A survey. *Communication Education, 35,* 372-378.

Brooks, W.T. (1988). *High impact public speaking.* Englewood Cliffs, NJ: Prentice Hall.

Dunn, R. (1979). *Learning: A matter of style.* Alexandria, VA: Association for Supervision and Curriculum Development.

McKeachie, W. (1986). *Teaching tips* (8th ed.). Lexington, MA: D. C. Heath.

# 8

# INSTRUCTIONAL PLANNING

Thus far, several important considerations for organizing instruction so that it leads to identified learner outcomes have been outlined. All of these considerations can be compiled into a coherent instructional plan. A tremendous amount of thought and effort goes into creating a good instructional plan. Elements that help to assure that the instructional plan works as intended include writing the plan down and managing instruction.

## WRITING AN INSTRUCTIONAL PLAN

Many professionals have good ideas for organizing instruction, but fail to carry out their plans because they do not write them down. Without a written plan, midway through the session, the instructor may not remember what comes next, or the fantastic closure that was planned is lost. Sometimes an instructional activity has not gone as planned, and there is no time remaining to reinforce critical learning outcomes. Without a written instructional plan, it is difficult to make last minute adjustments.

A written instructional plan is important for good instruction to occur. All good plans must contain these essential elements:
- Clearly stated learner outcomes and/or concepts and generalizations to be covered.
- A review of relevant past instruction.
- An overview of the learner outcomes and expectations for the session.
- Clear descriptions of both instructor and learner activities.
- A closure.
- Announcements.

As noted in previous chapters, instruction can be organized in a number of different ways. Some instructors are more comfortable thinking about the topics (or concepts) to be covered first. Others find it easier to begin with the conclusions (or generalizations) that learners are expected to reach. Still others find it easiest to think of instruction as change in learner behavior and to begin by clearly stating the desired learner behaviors (or outcomes). Whatever triggers the organization for a learning session for the instructor, each of these elements must eventually be incorporated in the written plan.

**FIGURE 8-1. Sample Instructional Plan**

| | |
|---|---|
| **TOPIC:** | Setting Limits: Using Positive Guidance Techniques |
| **DATE:** | 9-15-9x<br>Revised: 9-20-9x |
| **AUDIENCE:** | Parents of preschool children |
| **PRESENTER:** | Meredith McKenzie |
| **LEARNER OUTCOMES:** | After completing this session, parents will be able to:<br>1. identify the developmental characteristics of two-, three-, and four-year-olds.<br>2. list and describe appropriate ways of setting limits for two-, three-, and four-year-old children.<br>3. role-play given situations using the appropriate guidance methods identified.<br><br>**Resources:** Name tags<br>Transparencies/developmental characteristics<br>Handout: Chart with "strategies" column<br>Case study cards<br>Reading and community resources list |
| **REVIEW:**<br>10 minutes | Round Robin introductions/name, sex, and ages of children, one thing you would like to learn today |
| **OVERVIEW:**<br>5 minutes | Summarize participant learning requests. Overview objectives and methods planned for achieving objectives. Acknowledge which concepts will be emphasized, ways in which other learning needs might be met.<br><br>**Introduction:** Read case study, "Disruptive Lisa." Ask for *brief* examples of other disciplinary problems parents are encountering.<br><br>**Establishment of set:** Everyone encounters times when children "act out" like Lisa, but deciding the best way to help the child work through the problem relates to that child's developmental age and stage. Today, we will review developmental characteristics of preschool children ages 3 to 5 and identify some strategies that can work for each. |

*(continued)*

# INTRODUCTORY INFORMATION

One method of organizing an instructional plan is shown in Figure 8-1. The introductory information includes the topic, date presented, intended audience, and the presenter. The topic gives the overriding concept for the material contained in the plan. Writing the concept at the top of the plan makes the plan easier to retrieve at a later date. For instance, it is easier to remember and to scan for a plan that has to do with "Child Guidance" than it is to read the entire plan to determine its content.

**FIGURE 8-1.** *Continued.*

| | |
|---|---|
| **PRESENTATION/ EXERCISES:** 15 minutes (Transparencies—leave columns covered until discussed) | Summary of developmental characteristics of two-, three-, and four-year-olds. Solicit examples from participants. Tie examples of undesirable behaviors to developmental characteristics. Check: Are developmental characteristics clear? Do you understand why undesirable behaviors result from these developmental characteristics? |
| 15 minutes | **Handout: Chart of transparency with last column blank.** Reveal last column on transparency chart showing strategies for dealing with undesirable behaviors at each developmental stage. Participants may fill in notes in the last column as you discuss. Tie positive guidance methods to developmental characteristics of child and child's ability to respond to guidance techniques. Encourage participants to share examples of times when they used any of these strategies and found them successful. Check: Are strategies and when to use them clear? Are there any questions? |
| 15 minutes | **Case Study Cards.** This is an opportunity to apply what you have learned. As I read each case study, try to identify at least one strategy that would work in this situation. Role-play what you would say/do in this situation. |
| **CLOSURE:** 10 minutes | Today we have: 1. overviewed developmental characteristics. 2. identified strategies. 3. role-played responses to cases. Can you identify at least one strategy that you will try with your child/ren? **Handout: Resource List.** Note that this shows some additional reading that can be done to help identify better ways of dealing with children. Community agencies that also work with parents/children are listed with phone numbers provided so you can make contact. |
| **ANNOUNCEMENTS:** | Thank you for coming! Note that there are additional sessions of interest planned for the future. |

Although the topic of this plan might seem to indicate the intended audience (parents), it is a good idea to indicate the audience on the plan. This session could have been organized for a child study club that wanted some ideas for guiding children or for a group of adolescents exploring the parenting styles within their own families. Since good instructional plans require so much time and effort to devise, it seems wise to clearly label them. At a later date, you can quickly find them and know, at a glance, the nature of the plan.

Depending upon how the written plan is to be used, it may be a good idea to indicate who was responsible for writing and/or presenting the plan. In school settings, plans are often kept in the principal's office or must be filed in an agreed-upon place for use by substitute teachers. Again, indicating the author/presenter of the plan may make it easier to retrieve. Even in cases where the written plan will be seen by no one other than the instructor, it is wise to indicate the author/presenter of the plan at the top of the plan. Good instructors should take credit for the excellent instructional plans they create.

## LEARNER OUTCOMES

The next section of the instructional plan lists the learner outcomes. When writing a plan, it is often helpful to refer back to the learner outcomes that you specified originally. If these outcomes are clearly written at the beginning of the plan, it is easier to "stay on track" and to design instruction that leads to the specified learner outcomes. It may happen that, as the instructional plan is being developed, the outcomes are modified; nevertheless, writing them down initially will help you to know when you are making a conscious decision to modify learner outcomes.

## INSTRUCTIONAL RESOURCES

The instructional resources needed for implementing the plan should be included next. Detailed information about audiovisual aids used should be included. Any films, videotapes, filmstrips, slides, or recordings should be listed. Include titles, length, and source. If handouts are to be used, they should be clearly titled and a copy attached that could be used for duplication. Transparencies or the originals from which they were made should be attached, too.

This section is very useful if a plan is to be used again at a later date. There is nothing more frustrating than being unable to remember the title or source of the great videotape you showed last time.

### REVIEW

The next element in the instructional plan is the review. The review section of the plan can be used to determine what experiences the audience and the presenter bring to the session and what expectations they both have for the session. Icebreaker activities might serve this purpose. In essence, icebreaker activities that ask participants to identify why they have come to the session or what they want to learn provide a "review" of previous knowledge and experience relevant to the instruction.

When an instructional plan is a "stand alone" plan, there will be nothing that needs to be reviewed from previous plans. However, in cases where the instructional plan being written is part of a sequence of instructional plans, the review section should clearly reiterate previous concepts learned and the place of this plan's intended learner outcomes in the instructional schema. Further, the review can help to clear up any previous misunderstandings, questions, or concerns about the instruction provided so far.

## OVERVIEW

An overview of instruction should appear next. The overview introduces the topic and the expected learner outcomes to the audience. As Robert Mager noted in *Preparing Instructional Objectives* (1984), "...if you're not sure where you're going, you're liable to end up somewhere else." A clear statement about "where the instruction is going" helps to orient learners. As a part of the overview, instructors clearly identify the topic(s) for the session. They also help learners *establish set* (that is, understand the topic and how it relates to previously learned information and ideas). The overview can also stimulate interest in the topic and help learners to see why the topic is important to them.

## PRESENTATION/EXERCISES

There are a number of ways to write the main section of the plan. One method for writing what is going to happen during the instructional session is shown in Figure 8-1. In the example, under "presentation/exercises" details about what both the instructor and the learners will be doing during instruction are provided.

Some choose to write a detailed overview for this section of the plan. Others find a list of activities easier to follow. This section should include your content outline or any lecture or discussion notes. No matter how you write it, it ought to be sufficiently detailed so that someone else could pick up the plan and proceed with the instruction without any difficulty.

## CLOSURE

The final element of the instructional plan is the closure. Some presenters may find it tempting to eliminate this section of the plan. After all, the learners have completed the learning activities; surely they have accomplished the learning outcomes and have a clear understanding of what has been covered! Unfortunately, this is not always the case.

The closure of an instructional plan allows the instructor time to pull loose ends together, to reiterate major concepts and to evaluate student learning. Often, a series of questions that are related to the learner outcomes are used.

If there is time, this might even be a written exercise. Learners can be asked to summarize findings, draw conclusions, or state generalizations. For both the learner and the instructor, the closure is a valuable element of the instructional plan.

## ANNOUNCEMENTS

In some settings, it is appropriate to include a section in the instructional plan for announcements. Information about what will be coming in the next instructional session can be reviewed. Homework that should be done can be summarized. If students are to bring materials for the next session, these can be noted. Sometimes plans must be made for future field trips or other special instructional opportunities. If time is not provided for this type of activity, the instructor may be faced with providing such information after the session has ended to only a few learners who remain behind.

## INSTRUCTIONAL MANAGEMENT

The best laid instructional plan can easily go awry if the instructor does not manage the instructional session. Management includes estimating and controlling instructional time and varying activities and pace. It also includes taking audience size into consideration.

## ESTIMATING INSTRUCTIONAL TIME

A first step in managing instruction is determining the length of the instructional session. Once you have determined available instructional time, estimate the required time for every planned component of your instructional plan. List every activity you plan to include during the instructional session and assign an estimated time for completion of the activity. Include activities such as introductions, icebreaker activities, lecture, discussion, games, questions, breaks, wrap-up, completion of evaluation forms, etc. Many of these activities (like introductions) may seem insignificant, but when they are not planned, they consume instructional time.

Next, examine your instructional plan to determine whether timelines are realistic. Icebreaker activities, for example, can consume a great deal of instructional time. Likewise, instructors need to estimate the time required to deliver a lecture, conduct a demonstration, or discuss a case study. In many cases, this will mean practicing and timing the activity. For the instructor not used to lecturing, it may be impossible to really estimate how much time it will take to "talk through" an outline or to demonstrate a particular procedure without actual practice. Making good estimates of the time needed for discussion, questions, and games is sometimes difficult for experienced as well as inexperienced instructors, but some careful thinking and planning help create more realistic timelines.

# STRATEGIES FOR MANAGING INSTRUCTIONAL TIME

Throughout instruction, the instructor has responsibility of either controlling the time required for an activity ("we have time for one more question," or "we have only two minutes to complete this activity") or modifying the plan. Keep in mind that setting time limits and guidelines *prior* to an activity will be less frustrating to learners than interrupting or cutting short an activity. It is better to tell learners that they have just 15 minutes for a group discussion than to wait and warn them with only one minute left. The best procedure is probably to do both; to announce the limits (or call attention to their agenda) and then to announce periodically the time remaining.

Think about an activity where learners are organized in a circle. The instructor begins by throwing a beach ball to one of the learners who catches the ball and tells others one new idea, habit, or attitude he or she hopes to "catch" in the coming year. The intention is that each learner has an opportunity to share with the group this type of information. Although the instructor has allocated 10 minutes for this icebreaker activity, after 10 minutes only 4 of the 10 participants have had an opportunity to participate. The instructor must now modify other aspects of the plan or cut short this activity. The consequences of either decision are likely to be negative. Instead, the instructor should have created guidelines to make sure the activity only lasted 10 minutes (for instance, "When you get the ball, you have exactly one minute to give us your ideas. The timer will sound when your 60 seconds are up.") or plan more time for the activity.

Even with established limits, there are bound to be times when learners clamor for additional time to finish a task or more time to work on a particular activity. The instructor is responsible for making judgments on a case-by-case basis as to whether there is value in modifying the plan or if the original plan should be followed.

## Beginning on Time

Assume the session will begin at the scheduled time. Although this assumption may not hold true when working with few clients who are scheduled to visit your office, classroom teachers and group instructors should commence instruction at the scheduled time, barring any major complications. Generally, the beginning of a session should not be delayed for latecomers unless there are a significant number of learners involved or if there is an obvious and justifiable reason for the delay. These circumstances might include inclement weather, a late-arriving bus, or another session or class that held participants beyond the expected time. Delaying instruction for latecomers penalizes those who have arrived on time, as well as reducing available instructional time, and should be avoided.

## Filling Instructional Time

Always have a contingency plan in case the planned activities require less time than anticipated. This may include planning some additional discussion questions, having prepared examples, problems, or questions that can be used for additional practice or reinforcement, or including more practice than planned (a second turn, practicing an alternate procedure, practicing a procedure under different conditions, etc.).

The following are all techniques for filling instructional time.

- Some classroom teachers keep word searches or puzzles handy. These activities can fill time but should be tied to the learner outcomes. (Filling time with a crossword puzzle that has to do with personal hygiene when the topic for the day was using elements of design in planning an aesthetic environment is inappropriate.)
- Group leaders can ask a learner to repeat the demonstration just conducted.
- Having talked about a particular case study, an instructor might ask participants to now write one that illustrates the points just described.
- Instructors of young children may keep on hand art supplies so that youngsters can make a poster, mobile, collage, or banner that illustrates the concepts for the day.
- Related computer programs, video tapes, or audio tapes may be appropriate resources for individual learners who complete assignments or activities ahead of the group.
- Early completers can also be asked to assist the instructor in some way to prepare for the next scheduled activity.
- If a presentation to a large group ends ahead of schedule, the presenter can ask for questions or give a more relaxed summation.

It is important to remember that the filler activity selected should match the content of the instructional session and have a meaningful role in reinforcing or enhancing learner outcomes. Showing a filmstrip on cookie making to fill a session on meal planning is inadequate and inappropriate. Instead, pose a new problem for practice: "Using the principles we have discussed and used to plan your own food intake for tomorrow, plan tomorrow's meals with: foods that could all be packed picnic style; foods available at very low cost; foods you've never tried; regional foods from another part of the U.S." These are examples of additional practice exercises that make use of learners' time and newly acquired knowledge—yet exercises that could be assigned to fill the extra 5-15 minutes that can occasionally occur, even with a well thought out instructional plan.

## When You've Planned Too Much . . .

Having too much planned may be more of a problem than having too little content to cover. If you are forced to leave out major points or to eliminate pieces of the content due to time constraints, you need to make reference to these points. You may be able to refer them to the next session: "Tomorrow we'll finish our discussion by talking about two additional types of credit."

Where that is not possible (with group presentations where you will not be able to meet again), you need to explain the relationship of the missing content to what you have covered. "The two criteria in selecting a child care provider that we will not have time to discuss involve safety and space. Making sure that the child care facility is physically safe, that providers follow safety precautions and procedures, and that the facility provides adequate space for children and their activities are just as important as the three other factors we've discussed today." Presenters may even offer to cover missed material in future sessions or may refer learners to sources where they can learn about the content not covered.

In some cases, you will realize you do not have adequate time to get through your instructional plan, but modifications can be made that will not significantly damage the plan. Quickly scan your plan. Can you shorten a discussion? Provide less time for a game? Eliminate one or two examples? Assign a short writing assignment for after the session rather than during the session? These changes will probably go undetected.

Even when time is short, instructors should take time to summarize what has happened during the instructional session. Instructors should not interrupt themselves mid-sentence to say, "I see we've run out of time." The effective instructor should always provide some wrap-up by highlighting key points, summarizing major concepts, and again, if appropriate, providing some general information about content that was eliminated if it is critical to understanding. It may or may not be appropriate to acknowledge that you have run out of time and apologize for not covering all the information. Some instructors may indicate that they are sorry there was not enough time to discuss content in more detail or to cover additional material. In other cases, you need not call attention to the fact that you underestimated the time required to work through your instructional plan. No one else will know!

## VARIATION IN ACTIVITIES

After generating the list of activities and approximate times, go back and review the list to determine whether or not the instructional plan is balanced and interesting. For example, is a variety of instructional activities planned? A minimum of three different activities within an hour-long instructional session is recommended to maintain interest and to cater to various learning styles. These three activities may include such combinations as lecture, discussion, and written assignment; film, discussion, and small group project; demonstration, discussion, and reading assignment; game, small group discussion, and slide show. The combinations are endless, and each represent variation in the ways content is presented and reinforced.

## VARYING INSTRUCTIONAL PACE

Think about organizing the instructional session so that the pace of instruction shifts. For example, a lecture (listening) time might be followed by a game, then followed by a reading assignment. This change or shift in activities also represents a change in types of learner participation and pace of instruction. Review the instructional plan to make sure such variety exists.

Some attention needs to be given to the balance of these various activities and their position in the schedule. In a 55-minute instructional period, for example, the well-meaning instructor may plan for a discussion, game, and film. The film, however, runs 45 minutes. Shown at the end of the period, there is no time for a discussion. Shown at the beginning of the period, there is no time to prepare learners for the experience and to guide their viewing. The instructor needs to determine whether or not the film is worth the required time, and, if so, how other necessary instructional activities can be scheduled to best accommodate the film. Some preparation could be done in a previous session; learners could do some reading and preparation before the session; only part of the film could be used during the session, and part in a subsequent session; only the most valuable portion of the film might be used at all. There are a number of options that need to be considered in sequencing instructional activities within a session and determining whether or not the time requirements of the activities justify their use.

## AUDIENCE SIZE

A factor that has considerable influence when planning for instruction is the size of the audience. In many cases, the instructor will have little influence on the size of the group; a class will be assigned, a session must be staffed; or the program model dictates a certain number of learners be served. If the instructor, however, does have some opportunity to determine class size, consider the following.

Ideally, the purpose of instruction should drive audience size. If, for example, the purpose of instruction is simply to disseminate some information to individuals and lecture is the method of choice, then one may serve a large group easily and economically. If, instead, instruction requires some practice and application, or if the contributions of the participants are important for learning, then the instructor should work with a small group of learners.

What are the advantages and disadvantages related to audience size? Many of these seem obvious. Large groups allow you to provide information to many people at one time and to provide consistent information. Having multiple sessions or multiple instructors for a group may mean that not everyone will obtain the same information or obtain it in exactly the same way. Having one presenter for the entire group assures a uniform message. The large group, however, does restrict involvement. There are opportunities for fewer learners to participate, and the types of instructional strategies that can be successfully used are limited. For example, demonstrations, discussion, simulation, or games all become more difficult in large groups. Even the use of audiovisual resources may be restricted. For example, while 100 people may be able to see the screen for an overhead transparency, how about all 500 learners or all 2000 learners?

## Strategies for Working with Large Groups

In working with large groups, some modifications can be made so that techniques other than lecture can be used. Many instructors divide their large group into smaller groups for discussion, games, or role-playing. Video monitors placed throughout the room can allow the broadcast of demonstrations from the front of the room throughout the auditorium. Handouts can replace overhead transparencies. Instructors can provide students with "True/False" or A,B,C,D cards that can be raised in unison to respond to a question.

Besides the problem of choosing and varying instructional activities with large groups, instructors face the challenge of working with learners who may, in the large group, feel anonymous. Feeling nameless or faceless in the crowd may lead to feelings of diminished personal responsibility, which damages morale and may decrease motivation for learning (McKeachie, 1986). Instructors who frequently work with large groups have learned a few strategies that may lessen some of these feelings.

If you anticipate a large group, arrive in time to meet and speak with at least some of the learners. This establishes some personal contact. Also, you may wait after the session to talk with learners. During the presentation, instructors may need to leave the security of the podium and walk into the audience so that learners have an opportunity to see and hear the presenter from closer range. Again, circulating among the learners heightens personal contact. If you are working with a large group over a period of time (a university class, for example), you may adopt some additional practices. Some instructors use a seating chart so that they get to know at least some students. A seating chart with pictures (provided by learners) may speed up the process!

You may also arrange to meet specific learners. For example, invite 10 learners to meet before the next session to help plan activities, or invite some learners to meet after class for a follow-up discussion or coffee. The degree to which these types of activities will be successful may depend on the personality and attitude of the instructor, but some specific attempts should be made to reduce learner feelings of anonymity.

## SUMMARY

The number of factors that must be considered when planning and managing instruction may seem overwhelming to the new professional. Using the summary in Figure 8-2 may help in sorting out some of the details. Managing instruction includes creating a good instructional plan, developing a reasonable timeline for the plan, and matching the timeline and plan to the size of the audience. With practice, many of the suggestions for communicating content effectively, as outlined in this chapter, will become second-nature to you.

**FIGURE 8-2. Considerations in Instructional Management**

---

**ESTIMATING AND CONTROLLING INSTRUCTIONAL TIME**

- Determine how long the session should be.
- Begin at the scheduled time.
- Estimate the time for each activity.
- Use techniques to shorten or lengthen times as necessary.

**FILLING INSTRUCTIONAL TIME**

- Use activities related to the objectives.
- Ask participants to apply the content to a new situation.

**SHORTENING THE PRESENTATION**

- Eliminate activities or examples that are not critical to the objective.
- Summarize points that can't be covered in detail.
- Divide a presentation into several parts.

**VARYING INSTRUCTIONAL ACTIVITIES/PACE**

- Use at least three different activities.

**AUDIENCE SIZE**

- Match audience size to the purpose of instruction, if possible.
- Use techniques designed to increase interaction with large audiences.

---

# REFERENCES AND RESOURCES

Bodenhamer, S. (1984). *Communications: Checklist for planning a successful meeting*. Columbia, MO: University of Columbia Extension Information.

Erickson, S.C. (1984). *The essence of good teaching*. San Francisco: Jossey-Bass.

Mager, R.F. (1984). *Preparing instructional objectives*. California: Fearon.

McKeachie, W. (1986). *Teaching tips* (8th ed.). Lexington, MA: D.C. Heath.

# 9

# TALKING TO LEARNERS

One of the most common forms of relating information is for an individual to talk to a group of people. In fact, lecturing is probably the oldest method of communicating to groups. It existed long before print became a popular communication mode. In recent years, there has been occasional criticism of lecturing. "It's so boring to just sit and listen; I fall asleep!" is not an uncommon comment in university settings where lecture continues to be used to a great extent. Why, then, has lecture persisted? Despite numerous technological innovations in delivering information (television, interactive computer programs, and even video disc), the lecture remains a common method of instruction in a wide variety of settings.

## DECIDING WHEN TO USE A LECTURE

Many studies over the years have compared lecturing to other methods of teaching in a number of different subject matter areas (Spence, 1928; Remmers, 1933; Lifson et al., 1956; Beach, 1960; Solomon et al., 1964; Barnard, 1942; Detert, 1978; Blake, 1990; Odubunmi, 1991). When knowledge is measured, the lecture is as efficient in delivering information as any other method. However, discussion is more successful when application, problem solving, attitude change, motivation for further learning, and transfer of knowledge to new situations are desired.

Despite the limitations of lecture, there are situations in which talking to learners makes sense. Obviously, printed materials can provide the same information to a group of people as the lecture can. However, printed materials tend to become dated almost before they actually reach the page. The lecture allows for the most current information to be presented. Even if learners have read something before coming to the lecture, the lecturer has an opportunity to update that information, compare it with other sources, help the learner organize the information read, and synthesize it with other sources of information. The good lecture provides a structure into which the learner can insert information; a "cognitive map" to be embellished as new information becomes available. It can focus on the important points and areas of controversy relating to a particular subject matter. Further, good lecturers can generate enthusiasm about the area of study with their own enthusiasm and interest.

There are other factors in a learning situation that also dictate the need for lecturing. When there is one "expert" who will be providing information and a large number of learners, discussion is difficult at best. Further, if there is a lot of information to be given in a limited time, the lecture is an efficient method of providing that information. Finally, if it is critical that everyone have the same information—and that they interpret it in the same way—the lecture provides a good base of information to learners.

The key to using the lecture appropriately is first to determine whether or not the situation requires the lecture be used. Since the lecture is not the ideal format for all kinds of learning outcomes, you should carefully consider whether it is the instructional method of choice. The checklist in Figure 9-1 can be used to judge whether the lecture format is appropriate in a particular situation.

## ORGANIZING A LECTURE

The well-planned lecture includes an introduction, body, and conclusion. These are all part of an outline that is the basis of the lecture.

---

**FIGURE 9-1. Determining if a Lecture is the Appropriate Method**

**Content considerations:**

Do the outcomes specified call for:
- update of printed materials already read by learners?
- presentation of the most current information (especially in fields where there is rapid information change)?
- synthesis of materials from a number of sources?
- organization of diverse materials into a structure or cognitive map?
- delineation of important points in materials already presented?
- delineation of issues and debate related to specific subject matter?

**Contextual considerations:**

Does the context of the presentation call for:
- a large number of learners to hear the *same* information?
- a single "expert" presenting information?
- a large amount of information to be presented in a limited period of time?

## Lecture Introduction

The introduction should immediately capture the attention of the members of the audience and help them focus on the subject of the lecture. This is often accomplished by posing provocative questions or presenting an interesting story or anecdote that points to the gap between what learners already know and why they need to know the material to be presented in the lecture. This helps establish the relevance of the lecture. Besides capturing attention, establishing the relevance of the lecture, and helping learners focus on the topic, the introduction may inform learners of important points on which to focus during the lecture. One way to address these points is to include a specific statement of the intended learning outcomes of the presentation.

## Body

Probably the most common error in organizing the body of a lecture is planning to include too much. Beginning lecturers tend to rush through material, while more experienced lecturers include fewer points and more development of those points. A study of outstanding lecturers revealed that they used a simple plan, but many examples (Davis, 1976). No matter how much information is included, it should never merely repeat what learners have already read in a text or other resources. The lecture should be designed to expand on those points that lead to relevant learner outcomes.

The body of the lecture may be organized in a number of ways. Goyer (1966) identified several methodologies in his research on organizing ideas. Two of these organizational strategies were sequential relationships and component (part-whole) relationships.

For some content, there may be an obvious **sequential relationship**. For example, a procedure is generally described starting with the first step and moving through the remaining steps. Historical accounts generally start with the event most distant in time. Sequential organization may also include working step-by-step through a problem-solving or decision-making model.

Using the **component (part-whole) relationships method** of organizing material illustrates to listeners that the large idea or topic is made up of several smaller ideas or sub-points. It may include stating the major relevant principles or aspects of an issue, and then providing information and examples under each of these headings so that listeners come to see the relationship between each subtopic and its explanation, as well as the relationship between each of the major topics. This has been called **classification hierarchy** (Bligh, 1972). For example, a lecture on the development of two-year-olds would include discussion of their social, emotional, physical, and intellectual development. Under each of these major topics would be examples and information about each domain of development.

No matter which of these organizational schemes is used, effective lecturers include in their explanations the **rule-example-rule technique** (Rosenshine, 1971). This means sequencing explanations so that the principle, rule, or main point is stated and explained, illustrated by example, and restated.

No matter which structure is chosen in developing the body of the lecture, it works best if learners understand the organization of the lecture and if they are given cues throughout for indicating the logical order of the lecture. Structured notes or open outlines are good tools for helping students process and organize what is being said. These materials are prepared ahead of time by the lecturer and given to students for reference during the lecture. There may be headings, questions, or even blanks to be completed as the instructor proceeds through the lecture. The example in Figure 9-2 shows the structured notes that might have been used if the beginning of this chapter had been delivered as a lecture. The words in parentheses under each line show what the learner would be expected to fill in as the lecture proceeds.

Another effective strategy for helping learners organize and process information is periodic summaries within the lecture. This gives learners an opportunity to catch up on material, confirm their own understanding, and possibly facilitates transitions from one part of the lecture to the next.

## Conclusion

The conclusion is often a neglected part of the lecture. Good lectures don't just trail to an end or stop when the session time is up, but are "wrapped up" in a way that helps students organize and process what they have just heard. The conclusion allows the instructor to once again emphasize the major points of the lecture. It is a good time to encourage learners to ask questions or for the instructor to ask questions to stimulate further thinking and to check understanding of the material covered.

A good lecture involves substantial preliminary preparation. The steps presented in Figure 9-3 provide a guide for preparing a good presentation.

## ENCOURAGING AUDIENCE ATTENTION

A well-organized, purposeful lecture can only be effective if it is received and understood by the learner. How can the instructor assure that learners will focus on what is being said? Much depends on the way the lecture is delivered. The effective lecture is lively and stimulates continuing interest.

### Voice and Gestures

First, the instructor must speak in a voice loud enough to be heard by all of the learners. This may require the use of a microphone in some settings, and the instructor should experiment with its use before the lecture or presentation. Microphones that can be attached to the lecturer's clothing often allow movement away from the podium and free the hands.

Interesting speakers vary the volume and pace of their speeches. The voice may be raised for emphasis, or lowered to capture attention. The lecturer may speak more slowly when emphasizing a major point, but perhaps talk at a more conversational pace when recalling an example. The variation in pace and volume fends off the monotony that lulls listeners to boredom.

**FIGURE 9-2. Example of an Open Outline**

## SO YOU HAVE TO/WANT TO GIVE A LECTURE

**INTRODUCTION**

Capture _____
(audience attention)*

Focus on _____
(topic/important points to be learned)

How?
1. Story or anecdote

2. _____ to the audience
(Importance)

3. What will be learned

**BODY**

Develop a few good _____
(points)

Use a simple _____
(outline)

Organize:
Big ideas first; then specifics or

_____ first;
(specific examples)

then _____
(general/big ideas)

Consider using _____
(structured notes)

Periodic summaries

**CONCLUSION**

Emphasize _____
(important points just made)

Allow for _____
(questions/clarification)

*(Words in parentheses indicate what would be filled in the blank as the lecturer proceeds with the lecture.)*

---

Gestures and movement provide visual stimulation for learners. Movement, too, can help the lecturer hold the attention of learners. At least one study (Fifer, 1986) has linked teacher mobility in classrooms to a decline in inappropriate behavior among learners. As the instructor moves about, learners focus their attention on the instructor and are less likely to be distracted. Gestures and movements must, however, be used judiciously so that they do not create distraction rather than interest. Gesturing wildly, rattling change in pockets,

## FIGURE 9-3. Preparing to Present

**Preliminary preparation:**

In preparing for your presentation, have you:
- clearly identified the characteristics of your audience?
- written precise learner outcomes for the presentation? (If not, see Chapter 10: Talking With Learners.)
- prepared a list of concepts or a complete concept outline?

**Introduction:**

Have you decided upon an introduction that will:
- capture audience attention?
- establish the relevance of the lecture?
- help learners focus on the topic?
- review the learner outcomes of the lecture to help learners focus on important points?

**Body:**

In planning the body of the lecture, have you:
- developed a *simple* plan that does not contain too much information?
- identified examples for each important point?
- sequenced materials appropriately for the material being presented (step-by-step for sequential topics, general to specific or specific to general)?
- prepared structured outlines or notes (if appropriate) or other methods of helping learners follow the presentation?
- developed periodic summaries throughout the lecture at appropriate points?

**Conclusion:**

Have you planned a conclusion that:
- will be able to be presented in the time you have available?
- allows you to emphasize major points of the lecture?
- encourages learners to ask questions?
- allows you to present questions that check learner understanding?
- allows you to ask questions to stimulate learner thinking?

pacing, or other nervous habits actually draw attention from what is being said. Many instructors find it helpful at times to videotape a lecture and then review their performance for signs of distracting or annoying mannerisms in speech or gesture.

## Eye Contact

Eye contact is an important element in maintaining the attention of learners. Eye contact makes the message more personal to the learner. Learners are less likely to be distracted from a lecture that seems directed toward them. Communication is a two-way street, and learners who are addressed orally and visually are more likely to participate in the communication process.

Eye contact also provides the instructor with feedback (the other half of the communication loop). The instructor who is really looking at the faces of individual learners is more likely to read signs of confusion, boredom, or interest than the instructor who chooses a sight line above the heads of learners or stays focused on the written lecture outline. For that reason (and others), the reading of lectures is never recommended. Lecturers whose hands are riveted to the sides of the lectern and whose eyes are glued to the typed page, are less likely to stimulate interest than lecturers who move and speak with animation and visually "connect" with learners.

## Humor

One strategy for creating interest throughout the lecture is using humor. Some studies (Kaplan & Pasco, 1977; Powell & Andersen, 1985) suggest that humor actually increases retention. Learners who recall humorous episodes find that these memories trigger memory of the context of the humorous event, or the content or information of the lecture.

Humor also creates a feeling of well-being among learners that enhances the atmosphere for learning. Learners who are comfortable and enjoying the learning experience are more receptive to learning than listeners who are bored and listless.

You don't have to be a comedian to use humor. Some simple ideas for incorporating humor into a presentation include:

- Making overhead transparencies of cartoon or comic strips from magazines or newspapers that illustrate a point or the theme of a lecture.
- Sharing a humorous personal anecdote as an example of a point or principle.
- Telling a relevant joke or funny story to introduce a topic.
- Using children's materials. A child's poem or story used with learners of other age groups is often memorable and fun.
- Finding unusual props. Unusual props can help to "fix" a point in the memories of learners as they associate the humorous prop with the material to which it was linked.
- Using costumes, impersonations, and role-playing to "create" a character, depict an era, or demonstrate a relevant point.

Humor should be used in conjunction with the topic being presented, however. Irrelevant humor (the introductory joke that has nothing to do with the topic, for example) or unrelated props are distracting and should not be used. Irrelevant humor can carry learners away from the topic at hand and create confusion about exactly what the important points of the lecture are.

## ENVIRONMENTAL CONTROL

Well-planned lectures are more likely to be well received by alert, attentive listeners. Learners will be more attentive in environments that are conducive to listening and observing. The learning environment should be physically comfortable. It is likely that learners will remain more alert in a room too cool rather than too warm. All learners should be able to easily see the instructor. Avoid seating arrangements where learners have their backs to the lecturer or have to shift in their seats for a view. Visual and audible distractions should be kept to a minimum. This may mean closing doors or windows to diminish noise or adjusting blinds to minimize visual distractions. Check sight lines to blackboards, flipcharts, or a projection screen that may be used during the lecture. Learners need an environment that facilitates listening and observing.

Many of the points noted above require you to be aware of the appropriate techniques and to practice them. Videotaping your performance regularly and evaluating the videotape using the checklist in Figure 9-4 can also help.

## STRATEGIES THAT ENHANCE A LECTURE

Effective lecturers use a variety of strategies to clarify their messages and to aid student understanding throughout the lecture. These strategies enhance the spoken message and help engage the learner in the lecture. There are several instructional tools that can be used to help present information.

**FIGURE 9-4. Talking So Learners Will Listen**

**Physical environment:**

Before beginning a lecture or talk, have you:
- checked the physical environment to be sure it is a comfortable temperature?
- arranged seating so that learners are not crowded and are facing the lecturer?
- checked sightlines to be sure learners can see all visuals?
- checked equipment such as overhead projectors to be sure they are working?
- checked the acoustics of the room to determine whether a microphone is necessary?
- selected a microphone that allows you to move about when lecturing (as appropriate)?
- checked the microhone to be sure it is working properly and that the volume is appropriately adjusted?

**Voice volume:**

When speaking before a group, do you:
- speak clearly and distinctly so that all learners can hear?
- raise and lower your voice to emphasize points and create interest?

**Pace:**

When speaking before a group, do you:
- vary the pace of the lecture to capture interest?
- slow down when covering important and complex points?

**Gestures/movement:**

When speaking before a group, do you:
- use gestures to emphasize points?
- avoid distracting, repetitive gestures?
- move about slowly as you lecture, if the microphone will allow you to do so?

**Eye contact:**

When speaking before a group, do you:
- look at the learners as you speak?
- refer to your lecture notes only as necessary, and avoid reading the lecture?

**Humor:**

When speaking before a group, do you:
- use humor to ''liven'' the lecture?
- select *relevant* cartoons, jokes, etc.?

## Chalkboard

The most basic of instructional tools is the **chalkboard**. Although the "blackboard" (the traditional type made of black slate) or chalkboard is an old standby, it is often misused or underused. There are a few basic principles that can make its use more effective.

In general, chalkboards should be used to emphasize key points or concepts or to present assignments, announcements, definitions, or problems to be solved. If a large volume of material needs to be presented, it should be prepared in the form of a handout, rather than being written on the board.

The chalkboard can also be used for illustrations, including models, graphs, charts, or other types of visual messages. When any type of complex illustration is to be used, it should be put on the chalkboard before the learners arrive and should be covered until needed. Sheets of paper, window shades, or a cloth curtain are all useful covers for the chalkboard.

Writing on chalkboards can best be seen if the chalkboard has recently been cleaned with a damp cloth. Do not prop papers and other items in the chalkboard tray as they distract from the visual on the board. Chalk needs to provide good contrast so that learners can actually see what is written. Glare can be eliminated from the board by pulling drapes or redirecting spotlights. Printed letters are preferable to cursive letters. Lettering must be large enough to be read. Use the chart in Figure 9-5 as a guide.

When using the chalkboard, avoid blocking the view of students. The lecturer should stand to one side, writing only a few words at a time and then moving so that note takers can see what has been written. Avoid, too, the mistake of "talking to the chalkboard." Lecturers frequently talk as they write, ignoring the learners who are trying to see and hear.

Some specialized techniques can be used to maximize the use of the chalkboard. For example, complex drawings can be transferred to a chalkboard by using an opaque projector. This can be particularly useful when you want to show changes in the illustration by erasing and redrawing.

## Overhead Transparency Projector

The **overhead transparency projector** has many of the same advantages and uses as the chalkboard. It is superior to the chalkboard in a number of ways. For example, it can be used without turning your back to the students. In

**FIGURE 9-5. Readability of Letters at Various Viewing Distances**

| Letter Height | Viewing Distance |
|---|---|
| 1/4 inch | 7 1/2 feet |
| 1/2 inch | 15 feet |
| 1 inch | 32 feet |
| 2 inches | 64 feet |
| 3 inches | 90 feet |

addition, overhead materials can be planned and prepared ahead of time, or can be developed as the lecturer jots down key concepts or outline points during the lecture. Whereas the chalkboard message generally disappears at the end of the session, overhead materials can be saved and stored for use again.

Another advantage of the overhead projector over the chalkboard is that by using masks over a transparency or attaching overlays, complex concepts can be presented in simple parts. For example, a lecturer may prepare a single transparency, perhaps the lecture outline, and cover or "mask" (using an opaque sheet of paper) all but the point being discussed. As each point is discussed, the lecturer can reveal another point on the outline.

The overlay technique can also be used to present complex concepts sequentially or in parts. With the overlay technique, additional transparencies are hinged to the original transparency. A series of transparencies are prepared so that each contains a portion of the whole. As each step or aspect is discussed, another transparency is laid on top of the previous transparencies.

Color may contribute significantly to the message on an overhead transparency. If color is important to the message, it can be added to the transparency with pens (both water-soluble and permanent are available) or by using transparencies that develop in different colors. Color can be used very effectively to help students organize information (for example, by writing all actions the learners are expected to take in red), to clarify information (by coloring something the color it really is), or just to add interest to the overhead. Random use of color, however, can be confusing if used in an outline, so carefully consider color choice.

## Flipchart

Another instructional tool that can enhance a lecture and help to involve the learners in the lecture is the **flipchart**. Flipcharts are large, consumable paper pads that may be mounted on a wall or hung like a picture. They are often propped on an easel. The flipchart is particularly useful when a chalkboard or overhead projector are not available (for example, when a lecture takes place in a workplace rather than in a classroom setting).

The flipchart is used in much the same way as the overhead transparency projector or the chalkboard. It can be used with the *chalkboard technique* (where the lecturer makes notes as he/she lectures) or the *revelation method* (where materials have already been developed on the pages of the flipchart and are revealed at appropriate points in the lecture). The revelation technique works particularly well with the multi-paged flipchart, so that several steps or sequential points can be revealed.

Many of the same guidelines that guide the use of the chalkboard and the overhead transparency direct the use of the flipchart. The marking pens or grease pencils used on the flipchart pages need to provide good contrast so that learners can easily see the message or illustration. Using a variety of pen or pencil colors add contrast and interest to the chart. The message or drawing must be large enough to be easily read and, again, the lecturer needs to stand clear of the chart so it is visible to students. Lecturers should always face the audience, referring to the flipchart at appropriate points, and never "talk to the flipchart." Lengthy material should be prepared in advance. As with the transparency, the flipchart pages can be stored for later use.

The chalkboard, overhead transparency, and flipchart are the instructional devices most commonly used to enhance a lecture. If they are carefully thought out and appropriately incorporated into the lecture, they can contribute a great deal to learner interest and involvement in learning. Without appropriate preparation for use, however, they will become a distraction.

The checklist in Figure 9-6 should be used as you plan a lecture that incorporates the chalkboard, overhead transparency, or flipchart. Clearly, each of these instructional aids can be improved upon by technological innovations discussed in Chapter 13. Nevertheless, these aids continue to be inexpensive and effective ways to enhance a lecture if technology is unavailable.

## USING QUESTIONING TO INVOLVE LEARNERS IN A LECTURE

The use of instructional devices such as the overhead transparency or flipchart can help clarify or expand lecture material and can create interest in the lecture. Another technique, **questioning**, can keep learners focused on the

---

**FIGURE 9-6. Using the Chalkboard, Overhead, or Flipchart**

**Appropriateness of method:**

Are you using the chalkboard, overhead, or flipchart to:
- emphasize key points or concepts, illustrate points by using diagrams, or present assignments, announcements, definitions, or problems?

**Preparation:**

Before using the chalkboard, overhead, or flipchart have you:
- defined learner outcomes and thought about how these instructional devices will contribute to outcomes? (If not, see Chapter 10: Talking with Learners.)
- determined whether the volume or complexity of material to be presented dictates use of a handout rather than one of these instructional devices?
- carefully planned exactly what will be written?
- checked sightlines to the visual?
- printed words large enough to be seen?
- used color appropriately to enhance the visual?

**Delivery:**

When presenting to an audience using the chalkboard, overhead transparency, or flipchart, do you:
- present a reasonable amount of material with each visual?
- talk to the audience rather than the visual?
- stand to one side so that all learners can see?
- use the writing surface efficiently so that the material was:
  □ well organized?
  □ uncluttered?
  □ appropriately sequenced?

lecture material and involved in "processing" the message so that it is not only received, but retained.

Oral questioning is an effective way to stimulate student interest and participation. Questions can be used to introduce a lecture, clarify points in the lecture, and check for student understanding. They can also be used to summarize a lecture and encourage students to use the ideas expressed in the lecture. While questions can take considerable time and may sometimes move the instructor slightly off the point of the lecture, questioning is still a valuable aid in the lecture.

There are levels of questions that correspond to the domains and levels of knowledge (See Chapter 10: Talking with Learners.). **Knowledge-level questions** require students simply to recall information or recognize the correct response. Knowledge-level questions should require the student to respond with more than a simple yes or no answer. Yes/no questions include too much information in the question and should be avoided. Although a knowledge-level question is frequently considered "low-level," it is important to include during the course of the lecture to determine whether learners are retaining important pieces of information.

**Comprehension questions** challenge the learner to translate, interpret, or extrapolate information from the lecture. Comprehension questions check student understanding of the lecture material and help the lecturer to determine whether learners grasp major concepts.

**Application questions** require students to use the lecture material in a specific context or to solve a particular problem. Application questions allow students to practice what they have just heard by applying it.

 **Analysis questions** require the learner to break down an issue or problem and determine the relationship between the parts. Analysis questions would most likely come toward the end of the lecture when students have the concepts, generalizations, and principles needed to problem solve.

Likewise, synthesis and evaluation questions involve higher- level thinking. **Synthesis questions** require learners to organize information in a new way. **Evaluation questions** require learners to make judgments based on specific criteria. These higher-level questions may be used to summarize a lecture.

Generally, a lecturer should begin questioning by asking a question of the entire audience. It is important to give learners time to process the question and formulate an answer. Relax during the pause and indicate by your attitude that there is time for learners to think about the question before having to respond. **Wait time** is an important element in increasing the number of persons who may respond, complexity of responses, and number of student questions (Tobin, 1980; Tobin & Campie, 1982). The question may, after a time, be directed to a specific learner or be reworded if it becomes clear that learners are uncertain about the appropriate response. The lecturer should avoid answering the question. Additional questions should be presented in a logical sequence. Lecturers often begin with lower-level questions ("How do you define complete protein?") and move to higher-level questions ("Given the dietary plan I've just described, how well do you believe it meets recommended daily requirements?"). Examples of different levels of questions used to involve learners are shown in Figure 9-7.

Correct answers need to be reinforced. When the lecturer responds favorably to an answer, other learners are encouraged to participate. Partially correct responses should be recognized, too. The correct part of the response should be acknowledged ("There is research to support your answer. . ."), but the incorrect part of the response has to be addressed, too. Try redirecting that part of the question or asking another student to expand on it (". . .but there may be others in the audience who would disagree with your conclusion. Is there someone who has a different interpretation of that data?").

Questioning is an ideal way to stimulate student motivation and participation in the learning process. Developing good questioning techniques requires practice and evaluation of how well the questioning in a lecture accomplished these goals. The checklist in Figure 9-8 can be used to help you evaluate your use of questioning in the lecture situation.

## FIGURE 9-7. Examples of Questions at Various Levels

**KNOWLEDGE**
- What are the three primary colors?
- What nutrient is most needed for growth of muscle?

**COMPREHENSION**
- What is protein?
- What does the graph show to be the point of diminishing returns?
- What trends in the job market can you see for professionals in family and consumer sciences in the next decade?

**APPLICATION**
- Describe how to create the secondary colors using the color wheel.
- How would you apply the "principles of discipline" given in your text to the situation shown in the film?

**ANALYSIS**
- Which of the statements in the article on cholesterol are inconsistent?
- Analyze the case study using the paradigm presented in the reading.

**SYNTHESIS**
- What educational plan will meet the needs identified in the community survey?
- Describe a comprehensive strategy for influencing a piece of legislation.

**EVALUATION**
- Given the following criteria, judge the displays.
- Evaluate the fund-raising plan presented by the committee.

## FIGURE 9-8. Effective Questioning Techniques

**Using questions for an appropriate purpose:**

Are you using questions to:

• introduce the topic for the lecture, summarize the lecture, clarify points, check for student understanding, or encourage learners to use the ideas in the lecture?

**Knowledge questions:**

Do the knowledge questions used:

• require the student to respond with the appropriate knowledge?

• avoid a simple "YES" or "NO" response?

• help you to determine whether learners are remembering important pieces of information?

**Comprehension questions:**

Do the comprehension questions used:

• challenge the learner to translate, interpret, or extrapolate information from the lecture?

• help you to determine whether learners grasp major concepts?

**Analysis questions:**

Do the analysis questions used:

• require the learner to break down an issue or problem and determine the relationship between the parts?

• appear primarily near the end of the lecture (after students have concepts, generalizations, and principles needed to problem solve)?

**Synthesis and evaluation questions:**

Do the synthesis and evaluation questions used:

• require learners to organize information in a new way and/or make judgments about that information?

• appear in the closure portion of the lecture?

**Questioning technique:**

In incorporating questions in the lecture, did you:

• ask clear, definite questions?

• allow sufficient time for learners to consider a question before calling on someone?

• ask questions clearly relevant to the topic being covered in the lecture?

• ask questions in an orderly sequence?

• ask questions from a number of different taxonomic levels?

• reinforce correct answers?

• reinforce the correct portion of partially correct answers?

# DEMONSTRATION

**Demonstration** combines the best of lecturing — explaining — with showing. Demonstrations can be used whenever the learner can best learn by not only being told, but by being shown something. A demonstration shows how something is done, how it works, how it is made, or how it is used. It may be used to illustrate hard-to-describe terms and processes. Not only is the demonstration a valuable strategy for effective learning, it also may set a standard for a product or process. Desirable work habits can also be displayed.

An effective demonstration has three parts. It begins with a good introduction that motivates learners to watch and listen. The introduction can be short, but it should help learners understand the *what* and *why* of the action that will be demonstrated. The introduction is the ideal place to point out how what is being demonstrated correlates with what has already been learned by the audience and how it will fit in with future activities.

The body is where the instructor *tells how* and *shows how*. Besides showing how to do something, the instructor should be explaining what is being done, how it is being done, and why it is being done.

The demonstration must have a closure. This ties together what the learners saw and heard and emphasizes the main points or procedures. The closure may also provide learners with an opportunity to ask questions. The closure of the demonstration should review the key points. It may include how the procedure just demonstrated differs from the way it is done in "real life." If the end product does not look or perform as it should, an explanation should be given. The closure does not necessarily have to be an oral presentation of the demonstration. For example, it may be accomplished by asking the viewers a series of questions that lead to generalizations and conclusions. Figure 9-9 outlines some questions to ask as you prepare a demonstration.

The good demonstration begins with careful planning. When possible, complete time-consuming steps in advance. For example, the instructor demonstrating application of wallpaper may have already prepared the wall for adhesive. The baby to be diapered may have been undressed before the demonstration began. However, the procedure and the physical setting in which it is performed should be as close to actual conditions as possible.

Before beginning the demonstration, all necessary tools, materials, supplies, and visuals should be organized and at hand where the instructor will need them. Items that are not being used should be placed to one side, or, if possible, out of the view of the learners altogether.

Some instructors prepare demonstration trays that contain premeasured ingredients or prepared materials. As each tray is needed, it is brought into the demonstration space. When the action involving a tray is complete, items are reloaded onto the tray and it is placed out of view. The demonstrator is then ready to bring out the next tray. If a demonstration is likely to be repeated regularly, you may wish to prepare index cards describing exactly what is to be placed on each tray. Numbering the cards and trays can help to organize the presentation quickly each time it is to be used.

## FIGURE 9-9.  Guidelines for Demonstration

**Appropriateness of method:**

Are you using the demonstration to:

- illustrate hard-to-describe terms or processes and/or demonstrate a standard for performance?

**Preparation:**

Prior to beginning the demonstration, did you:

- ensure that the physical environment was comfortable?
- check to be sure all learners could hear and see?
- collect all necessary tools, materials, supplies, and visuals?
- make sure all tools, materials, supplies, and visuals were in good condition?
- organize materials so that they could be easily found and reached?
- complete time-consuming steps in advance?
- sequence the demonstration logically?
- practice the entire demonstration?
- check to be sure you were in appropriate attire for the task (work apron on, jewelry removed, etc.)?

**Introduction:**

In introducing the demonstration, did you:

- tell what you were going to demonstrate?
- explain why this demonstration would be important to the audience?
- point out how what will be learned fits with what the audience already knows?

**Body:**

During the body of the demonstration, did you:

- proceed in an organized manner?
- slowly and carefully explain each step?
- ask questions to be sure learners understood each key point?
- keep only essential materials in the demonstration space?
- work toward the audience?
- talk to the audience and not the materials?
- speak loudly enough for all to hear?
- use demonstration mirrors, videotape, illustrations, or models to project hard-to-see procedures?
- perform the operations with ease and confidence?
- avoid long spaces of silence?

**Conclusion:**

In concluding the demonstration, did you:

- review the key points of the demonstration?
- point out variations in the demonstration compared to "real life"?
- explain why if a product or procedure did not go as planned?
- allow opportunity for audience questions?
- motivate the learners to try the procedure themselves?

The prepared instructor has not only gathered necessary materials, but has also sequenced the demonstration. **Sequencing** involves thinking through the most logical way to demonstrate the procedure. It is usually wise to sequence the demonstration in the same way the action is completed in "real life." It is critical that the steps be completed in logical order if they are to make sense to the audience. Occasionally, you may wish to show the finished product at the beginning of the demonstration to set the context for the steps or to generate enthusiasm for learning.

Along with the visual presentation must come the oral explanation. Each step must be explained, including key points and specific techniques essential to performing each step. It is important to present the steps slowly enough that learners do not miss any information. The instructor may need to ask questions throughout the demonstration to ensure that the learners understand what is being demonstrated.

Explanations should coincide with the action being performed. In cases where a step takes a little longer than the explanation, the demonstrator should be prepared to present additional relevant information so that there is no long pause in the oral presentation. For example, the person demonstrating bathing and dressing an infant might spend the long time it takes to dry a baby, talking about the consequences that may result from not drying the soft skin folds thoroughly.

It is important that, during the demonstration process, learners be able to both see and hear. The audience should be gathered around the demonstration area in such a way that they have a sight line to the demonstration area. As the instructor demonstrates, he or she should work as much as possible toward the audience. Instructors may also use tilted mirrors or video monitors to project hard-to-see procedures.

Since maintaining learner interest is important, the instructor needs to present the material with ease and enthusiasm. Good pacing and self-confidence usually come with practice. In fact, practice is critical if the demonstration is to be a success. Learners are more likely to be motivated to complete a procedure themselves if the demonstrator is successful.

Finally, the instructor should select clothing that is appropriate for the procedure. The audience will not object to more informal dress if that is what makes sense. For example, it would be perfectly appropriate to wear blue jeans and a leather work apron when demonstrating the construction of a toy box. Instructors should avoid jewelry and bright nail polish. These may distract the audience. Long sleeves, or clothing that constricts movement, and some types of jewelry should also be avoided for safety reasons and to allow for ease of movement.

## SUMMARY

The lecture can be an exciting and dynamic method for reaching learners and clients. When carefully chosen and developed, this method can lead to successful learning. Often, attention to simple aspects of pace, voice, or gestures helps to make a dull lecture "come alive." Humor, questioning, and eye contact can help as well. Visual aids are often chosen to help the audience follow the lecture.

Demonstration combines telling with showing. It is especially useful to show how something is done, how it works, or how it is made or used. Just as with a lecture, the demonstration has an introduction, body, and closing; and, as with successful lectures, it is planned and practiced in advance of presentation to an audience.

## REFERENCES AND RESOURCES

Barnard, J.D. (1942). The lecture demonstration vs. the problem-solving method of teaching a college science course. *Science Education, 26*, 121-132.

Beach, L.R. (1960). Sociability and academic achievement in various types of learning situations. *Journal of Educational Psychology, 51*, 208-212.

Blake, C.G. (1990). Effects of instructional strategies on the learning of organizational behavior by a large university class. *Journal of Instructional Psychology, 17*, 59-64.

Bligh, D.A. (1972). *What's the use of lectures?* (2nd ed.). Harmondsworth, England: Penguin.

Davis, J.R. (1976). *Teaching strategies for the college classroom.* Boulder, CO: Westview Press, 1976.

Detert, R.A. (1978). *A comparison of two methods of instruction on learning and retention of ninth grade health education students.* Eugene, OR: Microform Publications, College of Health, Physical Education and Recreation, University of Oregon.

Fifer, F. (1986). Teacher mobility and classroom management. *Academic Therapy, 21*, 401-410.

Goyer, R.S. (1966). *A test to measure the ability to organize ideas.* Special Report #9. Athens, OH: Center for Communication Studies, Ohio University.

Hunkins, F.P. (1972). *Questioning strategies and techniques.* Boston: Allyn and Bacon.

Kaplan, R.M., & Pasco, G.C. (1977). Humorous lectures and humorous examples: Some effects upon comprehension and retention. *Journal of Educational Psychology, 69*, 61-65.

Lifson, N., Rempel, P., & Johnson, J.A. (1956). A comparison between lecture and conference methods of teaching psychology. *Journal of Medical Education, 31*, 376-382.

Odubunmi, O. (1991). The effect of laboratory and lecture teaching methods on cognitive achievement in integrated science. *Journal of Research in Science Teaching, 28*, 213-224.

Powell, J.P., & Andresen, L.W. (1985). Humour and teaching in higher education. *Studies in Higher Education, 10*, 79-90.

Remmers, H.H. (1933). Learning, effort, and attitudes as affected by three methods of instruction in elementary psychology. *Purdue University Studies in Higher Education, 21*.

Rosenshine, B.V. (1971). Objectively measured behavioral predictors of effectiveness in explaining. In Westbury, I., & Bellack, A.A. (Eds.), *Research into Classroom Process*. New York: Teachers College Press.

Solomon, D., Rosenberg, L., Bezdek, W. E. (1964). Teacher behavior and student learning. *Journal of Educational Psychology, 55*, 23-30.

Spence, R.B. (1928). Lecture and class discussion in teaching educational psychology. *Journal of Educational Psychology, 19*, 454-462.

Tobin, K. (1980). The effect of extended teacher wait time on science achievement. *Journal of Research in Science Teaching, 17*, 469-475.

Tobin, K., & Campie, W. (1982). Relationships between classroom process variables and middle-school science achievement. *Journal of Educational Psychology, 74*, 441-454.

# 10

# TALKING WITH LEARNERS

Talking to learners is an effective way to disseminate information. There are other strategies that are primarily instructor- or leader-centered that require the attention of learners, but not their full participation. Talking *with* learners involves learners as full participants in the instructional process. Learners are required not only to receive information and seek to understand it, but are called upon to verbally articulate their ability to understand, apply, synthesize, and evaluate. They become involved, too, in the teaching and learning process as contributors. As reported by Soloman, Rosenberg, and Bezdek (1964), this leads to gains in student comprehension.

The ideas and expertise contributed by learners influence both the instructor and the other learners in the environment. Sometimes talking with learners serves as a basis for instruction; as the instructor talks with learners through the interview process, for example, new instructional needs emerge. Talking with learners creates motivation and interest because learners are an active part of the learning process. Although most good instructional strategies are learner-centered, strategies involving talking with learners most clearly involve them as partners in the learning process. The methods of talking with learners addressed in this chapter include discussion, interview, and questioning.

## DISCUSSION

Most people inside and outside educational arenas think they understand the process of discussion. Discussion is perceived as the interaction between people on a particular topic. This, in fact, describes a *conversation* rather than a discussion. The primary difference between a conversation and a discussion is that a *discussion* is goal-directed. That is, in a discussion, which is planned and implemented for instructional purposes, there is a goal or purpose rather than the aimless interaction that occurs between people that is better classified as conversation. A discussion leads to some conclusion.

## INSTRUCTIONAL GOALS OF DISCUSSION

There are several types of instructional goals that are best reached through discussion. One common goal of an educational discussion is problem solving. An instructor may use the discussion technique as a method for getting learners to reach a common solution to a problem or as a mechanism for getting learners to look at a number of perspectives and alternatives to any given problem. As learners state their opinions, add their perspectives or share individual knowledge, other participants have an opportunity to consider their own points of view in light of the perspectives of others. Sometimes the debate and interactions lead to consensus on a particular issue or problem. At other times, discussion assists individuals in clarifying why they have taken a particular position or brings learners to an understanding of why others have opposing points of view.

This suggests a second possible goal of discussion: to assist each learner in articulating the logic of his or her own point of view. As learners create arguments or formulate statements about what they think, they come to understand their own viewpoints better. Learners have an opportunity to evaluate their own points of view, as well as the positions of others.

A third possible goal of discussion is to allow learners to apply principles or generalizations. This type of discussion is based on some shared knowledge or content in a group. Learners might be asked, for example, to consider the relationship between elder care issues and child care issues. This discussion would require that learners come equipped with some prerequisite knowledge.

Discussions may also be organized in order to use the resources of learners. Through discussion, learners with expertise in areas have a forum for sharing their knowledge and information. Discussions also stimulate interest and serve to motivate learners.

## PLANNING FOR DISCUSSION

The instructor planning and managing a discussion has a number of important roles throughout the process. The first is to plan the discussion. The instructor needs to determine the purpose of the discussion. Is the intent to problem solve? To share diverse points of view? To develop motivation? To call on the resources of members of the group? To allow learners to apply principles? To help learners develop and express the logic and validity of their own arguments?

Once the purpose has been defined, the instructor must next determine how to begin the discussion. A number of strategies for beginning a discussion are possible, from using a controversial question to describing a common experience that will serve as the basis for the discussion.

Many good discussions begin with an intriguing question that stimulates learners to think about their own positions, causes them to develop a rationale for their viewpoints, or creates interest in sharing ideas. What types of questions are best used for discussion starters? First, the questions should not be those that can be answered simply "yes" or "no." The question should stimulate learners to develop or construct a response. Dillon (1982) found that the structure of the question is critical to a valuable discussion. Inappropriately stated questions can foil discussion. In fact, there is some evidence that a degree of surprise, uncertainty or controversy can serve as a motive for learning (Berlyne, 1960). The best questions are those that have no right or wrong answers, but instead require the learner to state a position and defend that position based on his or her own knowledge, standards, or values.

The starter question may build upon a common experience of the learners (a video they've just seen, a cartoon shared by the instructor, or a case study or vignette provided). Prerequisite knowledge acquired through a reading assignment, a laboratory experience, a field trip, or some interaction with media provide a basis for a successful discussion. Questions following a shared experience might ask learners to put themselves in a particular role. "What would you do next if you were the young woman in the film?" "What other ways might you have responded if you were the elderly man in the cartoon?" "What might the parent have done to have avoided the conflict?" "How would you improve upon the methods you observed?" "Based on your readings, which of the theories seemed most applicable with the clients with whom you'll work?" These are questions that require a common knowledge if a good discussion is to occur.

Other discussion starters may build upon shared knowledge or experience rather than a common instructional experience. For example, "How do you handle a screaming two-year-old in the grocery store?" or "How do you decide on a major purchase when you really don't know much about the product?" or "Do protesters with strong moral convictions have the right to stand in the way of the rights of others?" All of these are questions that might begin discussions.

Some discussions begin with the statement of a problem that needs to be addressed. Learners may be asked to come up with three alternatives to a problem or to identify relevant questions. Each of these tasks requires discussion among learners.

## Brainstorming

One type of discussion—brainstorming—begins with a problem to be solved. In a brainstorming discussion, participants are asked to generate as many ideas as possible on a particular topic or problem. No ideas are evaluated or judged, and each idea is recorded. The brainstorming process usually evolves with one participant building on the idea of another, and so on. The best ideas are said to come after the first 25! Most learners enjoy a free-wheeling, brainstorming session where all ideas are accepted and creativity is celebrated and encouraged.

Brainstorming is a good mechanism for getting past narrow thinking and opening a discussion to broader ideas. Examples of questions that might be used in brainstorming include such questions as: "How should the community solve the landfill problem described?" or "What can Tyler and Sandra do to solve their financial problems?" or "What can be done with the remnants from this renovation?"

## CONSIDERATIONS IN FACILITATING DISCUSSION

One of the first considerations in facilitating discussion is the physical arrangement of the room. The instructor is most likely to facilitate discussion by positioning learners so that they can talk with one another. Rows of desks or theater style seating is least desirable because learners face the instructor rather than each other. This tends to direct comments to the instructor rather than other learners. Since discussion is intended to be interaction between learners, learners need to be positioned so that they can easily see one another, and watch the cues and messages of others. Seating in a circle, semi-circle, or even a double circle is preferred over traditional classroom-style seating.

As interaction occurs and learners begin to talk with one another, the instructor may note some troublesome styles of individual members. These styles may involve behaviors that lead to dominating the discussion, bullying the discussion, or being excluded from the discussion. Sometimes ground rules established by the instructor help to address these behaviors. For example, one rule of discussion might be no "put downs." This means that during the discussion, no person may demean another group member. It is one thing to criticize the ideas of others, but quite another to ridicule the person who states the idea. Another rule that may be proposed is that the group give each person a chance to state his or her point of view without interruption. This is a rule that may require some enforcement. The instructor may, from time to time, need to remind someone that there is no interrupting. In the case of a domineering group member, it may be necessary to wait for an opening and then indicate that it is time to give someone else a chance to speak. Occasionally, the instructor or group leader may need to encourage reticent members to speak by making statements like, "How about some of you who haven't spoken yet, what do you think?" or "Let's give someone a chance who hasn't spoken yet", or "I'd like to hear from some of the mothers/fathers/experienced persons on this issue"—thereby encouraging the underrepresented group to enter the discussion.

When issues are controversial or emotional, participants may have strong feelings and express these in ways that create tension or anger. The leader or instructor may need to divert the discussion to a more neutral area or even lighten the atmosphere through the careful use of humor. It may be necessary at times to actually quiet the discussants.

Another responsibility of the leader or instructor is to summarize the discussion from time to time. In a goal-directed discussion, it is important for learners to understand where they are in the discussion and how they are progressing.

Sometimes the summary is really a recapitulation of what has been said using some active listening language. For example, the instructor might say, "So far I've heard three alternative options for handling this. One..." Another form of summary requires the instructor to integrate or synthesize the discussion to that point, helping learners to see relationships. This type of summary might begin like this: "You've been talking about solutions. As I've listened, it sounds as if you're suggesting two categories. Many of your solutions have dealt with changes in the individual. Other suggestions have dealt with changes in the environment. Are those the only areas in which possible solutions might occur?"

Finally, the instructor is responsible for ending the discussion when the objective or goal has been reached, or at the point where it appears the discussants have contributed what they can or are willing to contribute to the discussion. If a discussion goes beyond the point where learners are enthusiastic, interest begins to wane and learning is less likely to take place. It is important to carefully observe the learners for these signs so that the discussion can be redirected through questions, a summary, or be ended by the instructor.

## EVALUATING DISCUSSION

The success of a discussion can be evaluated in two areas; first, how did the group perform in terms of content? Second, how did the group perform in terms of process? **Content** refers to the intended outcome of the discussion. Good group discussions are productive. The group works hard to understand the assignment and to cover the material or meet the objective. There should be evidence that the material discussed was understood. There should also be strong communication of ideas. If the group discussion has been effective, learners will have listened to each others' positions and used the comments of others as a basis for building additional arguments or as a point for making a competitive argument.

The discussion should also be evaluated in terms of **process**. Participants should be sensitive to the needs of other group members and give others a chance to speak. The individuality of members and their points of view should be respected. Finally, there should be evidence of the positive communication of feelings. During a discussion, feelings should be shared and accepted. Figure 10-1 summarizes the major points made regarding discussion.

## DISCUSSION METHOD VARIATIONS

A number of variations of the discussion method exist, and these are useful with groups of varying sizes. Some of these variations help meet certain instructional outcomes.

### Small Group Discussions

**Buzz groups** or small group discussions occur when the instructor breaks the larger group into smaller cells and assigns each group the task of discussing a certain topic or question. A group leader assumes the role described for

## FIGURE 10-1. Using Discussion as an Instructional Strategy

**Goals of a Discussion:**
- Problem solving
  - Reaching a common solution
  - Examining views of others and self
  - Developing consensus
- Developing a logical point of view
- Applying principles or generalizations
- Sharing learner expertise

**Planning for a Discussion:**
- Determine purpose
- Establish method for beginning discussion
  - Intriguing question
  - Shared experience
  - Shared knowledge
  - Statement of a problem

**Facilitating a Discussion:**
- Seat learners facing each other
- Redirect inappropriate behaviors of discussants
- Regularly summarize points made
- Draw discussion to a close

**Evaluating a Discussion:**
- Content learned
- Process used

the instructor. With small group discussions, participants need to clearly understand what the outcome should be at the end of their discussion time. This outcome might be in the form of a written summary, a "solution," a list of ideas, or questions.

Small group discussions can be used as part of a larger process. Group members first discuss an issue in a small group. Then groups merge and continue to discuss an issue. This works very well when the goal is problem solving or generating many ideas on an issue or a problem.

## Cooperative Learning Groups

One of the most promising forms of small group discussion and small group work is the **cooperative learning group**. The instructor has a particular goal or task in mind. Small groups of learners are matched for the purpose of completing the task or goal, and each person in the group is assigned a role. The success of the group is measured not only in terms of corporate outcome, but in the successful performance of each member in his or her role.

Including cooperative learning as a "talking with learners" strategy may unduly limit consideration of this method as just another type of discussion group. It should not, because uses of cooperative learning extend well beyond facilitating discussion or interaction between learners. Still, most researchers and practitioners in the area of cooperative learning agree that strong discussion and interpersonal communication skills are critical for successful cooperative learning. Consider the ways in which it serves as both a strategy for talking with learners and as a strategy for action-oriented learning.

Proponents of cooperative learning usually cite two strengths of this strategy. First, cooperative methods have generally been linked to higher academic achievement in students (Slavin, 1989). While most of the research has been on youth and adolescents, some positive effects have also been shown among college-aged learners (Fraser, 1977). Second, cooperative learning has consistently been shown to have positive effects on intergroup relations. Studies indicate that learners gain in respect for one another and that the cooperative learning experience improves social acceptance (Johnson, et al., 1983). This may be particularly important in nonformal education where climate has a significant effect on the motivation of learners.

There are several advantages of cooperative learning groups. First, learners learn to work corporately toward a group goal. If individuals remain in their roles (for example, one member may be the recorder, another the researcher, another the designer, and another the reporter), each is dependent upon the other for the outcome. The value of each contributor is affirmed as learners work toward their goal. Another advantage is that participants learn from each other. The strengths of each learner can be used as participants work together on a common project.

Instructors who want to organize learning activities around a cooperative learning model have a variety of options. Proponents of structured cooperative learning have identified multiple structures with different functions or outcomes in mind. One team-building strategy, the round-robin, has each learner in turn share something with his or her teammates. This expression of ideas or opinions is intended to assure equal participation and allows participants to become acquainted with those on their team.

The three-step interview is intended to facilitate concept development. Learners interview one another in pairs, first one way and then the other. They then share with the whole group information they learned. This strategy might be used, for example, in a training session where employees are considering the advantages of a new product line. The idea is to share reactions or understandings, thus developing or expanding concepts. This structure also improves participation and listening skills. One final example is the "numbered heads together," intended to promote mastery of content. The instructor poses a question, and learners consult with one another to assure that each learner knows the answer. Only after the consultation does one group member share his or her team answer with the instructor. This method of talking with learners serves a tutoring function and allows all learners to review and check for knowledge and understanding within a small group. These three examples represent only a small number of possible ways in which learners can effectively learn in cooperative groups (Kagan, 1990).

At least two significant guidelines for organizing and managing cooperative learning groups comes out of the research on its success. First, it is important that the learning groups have to *work together* in order to achieve the outcome, whether it is a product, a reward, or recognition. Interdependence must be required in order to obtain a group goal. This takes careful planning so that the group interaction component is not seen as just a waste of time, but an experience that is of mutual benefit to all learners on the team. Another essential element is individual accountability. The success of the group must depend upon individual performance. Learners might be responsible for developing individual sections of a proposal, for example, or a plan or product (Slavin, 1989). The instructor may find this strategy particularly helpful in talking with learners, and perhaps more importantly, in helping them talk and work with one another. Cooperative learning has been found not only to increase learners' enjoyment of the subject being learned (Slavin, 1989), but also in increasing the ability to work effectively with others (Sharan, 1984).

No matter what organizational strategy is chosen, groups should be mixed in terms of abilities and talents so that there are opportunities to learn from one another. Also, as groups work together over time, the roles should be rotated so that everyone has an opportunity to practice and develop different skills.

The interaction of peers in a cooperative learning group creates a unique type of mentoring or tutoring relationship. This relationship grows out of the goal of getting the project or task done. While cooperative learning groups may involve more than just group discussion, discussion is always part of the process by which cooperative learning groups function.

## Inner and Outer Circles

Sometimes one group of learners may listen and watch another group of learners participate in a discussion. An "inner circle" of learners talk while an "outer circle" listen. At the end of the experience all learners may react to the experience.

## Symposium

Occasionally, learners listen to an outside group of persons in a discussion and interact by asking questions. One format for this type of viewed discussion is a symposium. In a symposium, several "experts" speak on a particular issue or topic, usually from different points of view. Learners have an opportunity to interact with the speakers through questioning.

## Panel Discussion

Another type of discussion—the panel discussion—occurs when a group of experts have a discussion for an audience. Learners "overhear" the discussion.

A chairperson or moderator often manages the flow of this discussion and makes sure that panel members have equal opportunities for participation. This has become a popular "talk show" format.

## INTERVIEW

Another way in which we talk "with" learners is through the interview process. Generally, the purpose of the interview is to elicit information, rather than deliver information or content. While information-gathering is its primary use, nonformal educators, such as those in human service agencies, frequently provide information to learners on a one-to-one basis through the interview process.

## PURPOSES OF THE INTERVIEW

One of the primary purposes of the interview is as a tool for needs assessment with individual learners. Dietitians, for example, who interview clients about diet and eating patterns often do so as a type of needs assessment. What are the current dietary patterns of the client? What is he or she doing that may be harmful or unwise given his or her particular circumstances? What is he or she doing that contributes to overall health? Although these questions are not asked directly of the client, they become the framework for a needs assessment that is conducted through interview with a client. When these broad questions have been answered, the dietitian has a picture of the educational needs of the client. The gaps between what the client knows and what he or she needs to know can be defined as an educational need. This form of needs assessment is conducted regularly by professionals in health care, in human services, in business, and in formal education. By talking with the learner, the interviewer learns what the client knows and practices. The professional uses that information as a basis for planning what the learner needs to know.

The interview may also provide information on what the learner *wants* to know or learn. This is also a type of needs assessment, but the emphasis is on learner interest vs. gaps in the learner's knowledge. An instructor in a community service agency, for example, may determine that parents are interested in learning more about effective discipline of children, or finding ways to help children with homework and school. The instructor might argue that these areas not only represent learner interest, but also real educational needs. The delineation may appear to be an artificial one. It is an important delineation, however, as discussed in planning instruction. Learners may only pursue learning in a nonformal setting if it is of interest to them; educational need alone may not motivate them to move toward a learning episode. Simply put, in nonformal education, learners come because they are interested in learning, not just because someone else determines that they need to know certain information. Often, interest is sparked by the recognition of a need, but not necessarily. The growth in enrichment programs in community education substantiates interest or curiosity as a strong motivation for learning. Thus, the interview is an important strategy in working with learners. Talking with learners, using an interview technique, often clarifies learning needs and interests. Sometimes these are the same. Sometimes they are not.

Interviewing also can be used to actually provide content to learners. The job interview, for example, illustrates how an interview can also be used to share information. The job interview is primarily structured to learn more about the candidates. Applicants have an opportunity to explain why they are suited for the job and to support their qualifications for the position. The interview also allows the potential employer to share something about the position and the organization. Thus there is some communicating of information to the candidates as well as gathering information about the candidates.

Another example of this type of exchange of information in an interview might take place in an economic crisis center. While the human service worker gathers information about the immediate economic needs of the client, he or she is also providing information about resources, policies, and procedures.

## PLANNING FOR INTERVIEWS

Productive interviews occur in environments where the interviewee feels safe and comfortable. Since clients in these environments are frequently asked to share confidential information, the first critical condition is privacy. Complete privacy may not be possible, but the participant needs to feel a sense of privacy. This may be achieved through an appropriate seating arrangement, the use of screens or dividers, or closing a door.

Beyond privacy, the interviewee needs to feel comfortable with the interviewer. This requires developing a sense of rapport between the participants. **Rapport** refers to building an initial relationship with the interviewee that puts him or her at ease in the situation. It allows the interviewee to feel that he or she will be listened to in a fair and nonjudgmental manner.

Rapport-building may begin by asking the client what he or she prefers to be called. The use of first names does not automatically assure comfort for many groups of clients. Older clients particularly may prefer to be addressed by their last names. For others, the use of their professional title is important (Pastor, Doctor, Dean, etc.).

The interviewer may also want to ask some introductory questions to put the learner at ease. Rather than just small talk, these questions need to indicate a sincere interest in the interviewee and provide a chance to talk briefly about nonsensitive issues. During this time of discussion it is important that the interviewer convey an accepting and friendly attitude toward the client. Smiling and maintaining eye contact are important. Body language is also important. Folded arms, a raised eyebrow, or a look of shock all convey judgments about what is being said. The instructor needs rather to convey an open, accepting manner. This includes allowing the interviewee to talk. While it may be necessary to steer the speaker back to the topic of discussion, it is important to avoid interrupting the interviewee during the process. The client needs to feel that what he or she is saying is important and is being heard. Interruptions on the part of the interviewer, such as phone calls, messengers, or distracting behaviors, need to be avoided as well.

## INTERVIEW STRUCTURE

The person preparing to use the interview as a strategy for talking with clients will need to prepare three parts: the opening, the middle phase, and the closing of the interview.

The purpose of the opening is to develop rapport and establish the purpose of the interview. During the middle phase, the interviewer both gathers and provides information. The closing provides a summary of the interview, identifies next steps, and defines the end of the interaction.

The opening of the interview allows the interviewer to establish a relationship with those being interviewed. Introductions begin this phase. They should include names and position so that the client knows by whom he or she is being interviewed. This may be followed by a brief discussion about information that is already known. For example, the interviewer might indicate that he or she knows that the client's children participate in one of the youth programs of the agency, or that the client has been referred by another agency or service. The discussion might also include talk about topics that are of mutual interest and knowledge to both. This may include subjects like local events or issues, topics from the news, or even sports. This part of the opening is really intended to develop rapport between the client and interviewer.

As part of the opening, the purpose of the interview needs to be established. Depending upon the circumstance, either the client or the interviewer will establish and state that purpose. The interviewer, for example, may indicate that the reason for this interview is to establish the particular needs of the client's family so that appropriate referrals can be made. If the client sought the interview, however, he or she will need to indicate the purpose. It may be to describe health needs of a child for the purpose of seeking additional health care or advice, to describe a home management problem to elicit assistance or instruction, or to learn about the services of a particular business or agency from which the client may benefit. Both parties need to be clear on the purpose of the interaction, however, before proceeding to the middle phase of the interview.

The middle phase of the interview is when questioning occurs. Good interviews usually involve planned and prepared questions in order to efficiently and effectively elicit needed information. Planning also assures that information is provided in a systematic and logical way. Not every interview will follow a strict format, but it is wise to have a plan that can be appropriately adapted. Questioning techniques will be discussed in the next section.

As the interview progresses toward its close, the interviewer needs to bring the formal part of the interview process to an end. This can be communicated in a number of ways. The interviewer may summarize the purpose of the interview, or ask the client if he or she has any questions. Arrangements may be made for future contacts or action to be taken. If the instructor or interviewer needs to take specific follow-up action, this should be indicated during the interview closing. Figure 10-2 summarizes strategies for using the interview effectively.

## QUESTIONING AS A STRATEGY FOR DISCUSSION AND INTERVIEW

Questioning provides more than just an opportunity for learners to speak. Questioning is a strategy for obtaining feedback from learners, providing feedback to learners, and stimulating higher order thinking skills.

## QUESTIONING IN DISCUSSION

Questioning is not an isolated strategy for talking with learners, but a strategy used in conjunction with other methods. A successful interview is impossible without good questioning skills. Questioning is also an integral part of discussion. The progress of a good discussion is often dependent upon good questions asked at the appropriate time. These questions allow opportunities for participants to compare ideas, evaluate their own thinking and the thinking of others, and to test their application of the principles and generalizations they have learned.

---

**FIGURE 10-2. Using the Interview Effectively**

**Purposes of an Interview:**
- Needs assessment
- Assessment of learner interest
- Information exchange

**Planning for an Interview:**
- Establish privacy
- Develop rapport
    - Establish names/titles
    - Ask introductory questions to put interviewee at ease
    - Maintain eye contact
    - Acknowledge you are listening

**Interview Structure:**
- Opening
    - Warm-up
    - Establish interview purpose
- Middle
    - Questioning
    - Opportunity for information exchange
- Close

## The Question

The skills needed to develop good questions at various levels of thinking were discussed in Chapter 9. In that context, questions were used as a way for instructors to interact with learners during the lecture. The same principles of developing good questions apply whether they are used in the lecture, the discussion, or the interview.

Remember that a variety of types of questions should be used to stimulate thinking at different levels. Some questions will prompt recall; others will provide feedback about understanding; still others will stimulate learners to integrate information in new ways. Figure 10-3 groups some sample questions according to desired learner outcomes.

Questions are tools for developing higher order thinking skills in learners. Questions help teachers engage students in genuine practical thinking. Whether working with youth or adults, there are questions that will assist instructors in getting learners to look at issues or problems in a reasonable, logical manner.

There are, of course, issues or problems for which there are no "right" answers. The use of questioning is not necessarily to bring learners to the right answer, but to help them process alternatives in a logical and reasonable manner. Good, scrutinizing questions cause learners to think critically and to examine ideas while maintaining respect for individual differences in values, opinions, and standards. Examples of the types of questions that can be raised with learners to stimulate higher order thinking are shown in Figure 10-4.

Higher order thinking questions need to be tailored to the particular discussion or interaction with learners. Consider the types of questions that might be used in talking with family and consumer sciences professionals in business about marketing practices; adolescents about shoplifting; parents and their use of disposable diapers; retirees and their use of leisure time; teenagers and their use of financial resources. These types of questions take learners beyond, "What can I do?" to "What *should* I do?" These questions extend the traditional decision-making model to stimulate higher order thinking skills.

## The Response

Well-formulated questions are the basis for helping students move toward higher order thinking skills. Even the most carefully formulated questions, however, will not lead students to *thinking* if the instructor's response is inappropriate.

Instructor responses to learner's answers generally fall into two categories: closed and open. **Closed responses** generally bring closure to the learner's thought process. **Open responses** require students to expand on their thinking—to seek ideas and solutions that fit with their thinking rather than those that match the response the instructor "wants."

Closed instructor responses may be classified as either criticizing or praising. A critical response can be revealed through body action as well as words. A raised eyebrow may be sufficiently negative that the learner gets the clear indication that his or her answer is "wrong." The thought process then stops

## FIGURE 10-3. Questions Grouped According to Desired Learner Outcomes

**RECALLING**

When was the last time _____ appeared in the story?
What did he or she do then?
Who was responsible for this event?
What did he or she do to cause it?
What was said about this earlier?
Why is what happened before important now?
Tell in your own words what happened before.
What is the name of the person who _____?
Where did the story take place in the beginning?
Close your eyes and describe _____.

**INFERENCE AND REORGANIZATION**

If _____ is true, what does that mean to _____?
How did _____ affect _____?
How did all of this get started?
Why do you think this happened?
Who is responsible for these events?
What do you think happened before (after) this event?
What could have been done to avoid this problem?
What else do we need to know in order to understand what is happening?
What is missing?
Suppose there were no _____, what could happen?

**PERSONAL INVOLVEMENT AND VIEWPOINT**

What would you do if _____?
How would this look to a _____?
What do you think will happen next?
Explain how you would feel if _____.
Describe your feelings for _____.
What did you like (dislike)?
How would you change it?
Why do you suppose this happened?
How would you handle this?
Your answer was almost correct. Can you tell us how you could improve it?

**OBSERVATIONS AND PERCEPTIONS**

List as many _____ as you can of _____.
What do you think is missing?
What does this look like to you?
What do you think happened?
Why do you think that happened?
List some words that describe what you see.
How will this look tomorrow?
What kinds of sounds would we hear if we were in this situation?

*(continued)*

**FIGURE 10-3.** *Continued.*

---

**CLASSIFYING, ORDERING, GROUPING**

Which things belong together on the basis of weight, color, size, shape, function, value, etc?

What do _____ have in common?

Why wouldn't _____ go in this group?

List these items from:
    smallest to largest
    youngest to oldest
    lightest to darkest
    funniest to saddest

List the above items in the opposite direction (largest to smallest, etc.)

What comes after _____.

What comes before _____.

What appears to be in the middle of the group?

How do members of this group help each other?

Can you think of something you would add to the group?

**COMPARISONS, CONTRASTS, AND FORCED ASSOCIATIONS**

Name the way in which these are alike.

How is _____ similar to _____?

How is _____ different from _____?

What was _____ like before _____ took place?

Why do you (or don't you) agree with this?

What could be done to improve _____?

Why do you think this is important? (not important?)

Who was the most (least) important person in this situation? Why?

What color is a thunderstorm (happiness, love . . .)?

What would your (mother, father, guardian) think of this?

---

GaLante, N. (1990). *Thinking Skills.* Broward County Public Schools.

---

**FIGURE 10-4. Examples of Higher Order Questions**

—What type of claim is being made? Is it a claim about a fact, or is it a claim or statement about value?

—If it is a claim about fact, is it true? How do you know? If it is true, can it be generalized to this situation?

—What is the source of the information? Is this a credible source? What makes this a credible source? Why would you trust this particular source in this context?

—What are the reasons for your decision or conclusion? Are these reasons adequate?

—As you come to a decision or a choice, is this choice workable? Can it really be done? Is it safe? Is it reasonable? Is it legal? Is it acceptable to you and others who are important to you? Do you have the time and/or skills to follow through on this decision or choice?

—Can you defend the choice you've made morally or ethically? How will this choice affect your well-being and the well-being of others? Consider this choice in a bigger context. What would the consequences be if large numbers of people made the same choice? How would you feel if those closest to you made the same choice?

immediately. Words such as, "I don't think so" or "My opinion would be different than that" are strong verbal cues that the learner is on the track to an "incorrect" answer.

Even though much more positive in nature, praising responses may be closed instructor responses as well. By confirming a particular way of thinking (using "Good!" or "I agree," for example), the instructor effectively eliminates expansion on a response and movement toward higher order thinking.

Open instructor responses require students to expand on the initial answer given, to think for themselves, and not to search for the "correct" response. "Tell us more about your thinking on that" and "Describe some of the ideas you have that lead you to that conclusion" are both open responses that encourage additional thinking and examination of a topic.

Learners with extensive learning experiences may resist extending responses at first. They are used to relying on the instructor to confirm their ideas or criticize their thinking. Many experiences with immediate feedback have made them dependent upon the teacher as they learn. They may need encouragement to expand on answers and become comfortable with this "new" learner/instructor interaction.

## QUESTIONING IN INTERVIEWS

Although general questioning techniques apply to interviews, there are some rules specific to the development of interview questions. These rules pertain to questions that are open vs. closed, or neutral vs. leading, and primary vs. secondary. In the interview, the interviewer's response is also critical to maintaining a productive line of questioning.

### Open Questions vs. Closed Questions

Interviewers use various types of questions; some are broad, open questions, while others elicit more detailed information. In almost every case, however, the interviewer will want to use open rather than closed questions.

**Open questions** give the client a chance to frame his or her own answers and to provide broad information. Some examples of open questions include, "How do you decide on family expenditures?" or "How do you usually go about selecting a product to purchase?"

**Closed questions**, in contrast, are restrictive and usually require a much narrower answer. Clients are not free to provide as much information. Examples of closed questions are, "Do you ever spank your children?" or "How many calories do you usually consume in a day?" or "What is your income after taxes?"

Open questions allow clients to provide more information. If only a limited amount or scope of information is needed, however, it is acceptable to construct some closed questions.

## Neutral Questions vs. Leading Questions

As interview questions are posed, they need to be constructed and asked in a neutral way. **Neutral questions** are nonjudgmental, open questions that do not direct the client or learner to a particular answer. In contrast, **leading questions** suggest a "right" answer. A leading question might be, "You don't drink alcohol, do you?" That question could be phrased in a more neutral way by asking, "Please tell me about your typical eating and drinking patterns."

## Primary Questions and Secondary Questions

**Primary questions** introduce a topic, and **secondary questions** elicit more detailed information. Interviews should be structured around a series of primary and secondary questions. For example, a primary question might be, "So you have three children. Tell me a little about your oldest child." A secondary question might be, "How do you usually respond when she acts moody?" In interviewing a volunteer for an agency, the interviewer might ask the primary question, "With what kinds of tasks or roles are you interested in helping?" followed by the secondary question, "What kind of experiences have you had working with children?"

At times, it is important to probe the client for additional information. Sometimes a simple statement like, "I'd like to hear more about that," or "Could you explain that in a little more detail?" are helpful. Other times a nod of the head or even silence will encourage the interviewee to expand on his or her statement.

## Interviewer Response

Just as the questions asked should be neutral and nonjudgmental, so should the response of the interviewer. While it is important for the client or learner to feel accepted, he or she should not feel evaluated. There are several responses to avoid when talking with clients. One response to avoid is an evaluative response. An **evaluative response** indicates that the interviewee has made a good or bad choice.

**Hostile** or **angry responses** also need to be avoided. There are times when a client or learner may elicit real feelings of anger or dismay from the interviewer. There may even be times when interaction between client and interviewer leads to confrontation. These are typically inappropriate responses since they can lead to the client being less likely to respond in an open manner.

Well-meaning responses that provide reassurance, for the most part, need to be avoided. This is true because quite often the interviewer is not in a position to provide this reassurance. Indicating to a client "everything will work out just fine" or "this will be over soon" or "don't worry about a thing" may be very dishonest and misleading responses. It is important to be supportive, but not to misrepresent yourself through an inappropriate response.

The preferred response throughout the interview is understanding. Through the use of active listening skills, the interviewer can reflect back some of the feelings and statements that are made in a way that indicates an interest in

## FIGURE 10-5. Guidelines for Interview Questions

- Use open vs. closed (or yes/no) questions.
- Ask questions in a non-judgmental way.
- Do not suggest a correct answer.
- Use a mix of primary and secondary questions.
- Probe to obtain complete responses.
- Use neutral responses to client answers.
- Avoid hostile or angry responses.
- Indicate interest and understanding.

hearing and really understanding the client's responses. Other nonverbal behaviors signal interest and understanding, too. Probes used as necessary tools to keep the interview on track also suggest that the instructor or interviewer really cares about what is being communicated. Figure 10-5 outlines guidelines for effective interview questions.

## SUMMARY

Talking with learners involves a variety of skills such as questioning, planning and implementing discussion, and interviewing. Discussions and interviews require the instructor to first establish the purpose or goal of the interaction. Once the goal has been determined, the instructor can select a model for interaction that best meets that goal. There are several variations of the discussion model. If a primary purpose of the interaction is to acquire information from learners, then the interview is the most appropriate model. Good interviews and discussions depend on well-developed questions that prompt learners to process information and stimulate higher order thinking. Instructors have the responsibility of developing good questions and matching those questions with appropriate responses. The various types of discussion, cooperative learning groups, and interviews are all learner-centered activities. Learners are often more motivated when they play an active part in the learning process.

## REFERENCES AND RESOURCES

Berlyne, D.E. (1960). *Conflict, arousal and curiosity*. New York: McGraw-Hill.

Carson, L. (1990). Cooperative learning in the home economics classroom. *Journal of Home Economics, 82*(4), 37-41.

*Cooperative learning: A guide to research.* (1991). New York: Garland.

Costa, A.L. (1985). *Developing minds: A resource book for teaching thinking.* Alexandria, VA: Association for Supervision and Curriculum Development.

Dantonio, M. (1990). *How can we create thinkers? Questioning strategies that work for teachers.* Bloomington, IN: National Education Service.

Dillon, J.T. (1982). The effect of questions in education and other enterprises. *Journal of Curriculum Studies, 14*, 127-152.

Dillon, J.T. (1988). *Questioning and teaching: Manual of practice.* New York: Teachers College Press.

Fraser, S.C., Beaman, A.L., Diener, E., & Kelem, R.T. (1977). Two, three, or four heads are better than one: Modification of college performance by peer monitoring. *Journal of Educational Psychology, 69*(2), 101-108.

GaLante, N. (1990). *Thinking skills.* Ft. Lauderdale, FL: Broward County Public Schools.

Hunkins, F.P. (1989). *Teaching thinking through effective questioning.* Boston: Christopher-Gordon.

Johnson, D.W. (1991). *Learning together and alone: Cooperative, competitive, and individualistic learning* (3rd ed.). Englewood Cliffs, NJ: Prentice Hall.

Kagan, S. (1989). *Cooperative learning resources for teachers.* Riverside, CA: University of California, Riverside.

Neff, R.A., & Weimer, M. (Eds.). (1989). *Classroom communication: Collected readings for effective discussion and questioning.* Madison, WI: Magna.

*Questioning and discussion: A multidisciplinary study.* (1988). Norwood, NJ: Ablex Publishing Corp.

Sharan, S., Kussel, P., Hertz-Iazarowitz, R., Bejarano, Y., Raviv, S., & Sharan, Y. (1984). *Cooperative learning in the classroom: Research in desegregated schools.* Hillsdale, NJ: Erlbaum.

Slater, S. (1979). 50 ways to involve students in discussion and classroom activities. *Forecast for Home Economics, 61.*

Slavin, R.E. (1989). Cooperative learning and student achievement. In R.E. Slavin (Ed.), *School and classroom organization.* Hillsdale, NJ: Erlbaum.

Solomon, D., Rosenberg, L., & Bezdek, W.E. (1964). Teacher behavior and student learning. *Journal of Educational Psychology, 55*, 23-30.

# 11

# USING ACTION-ORIENTED LEARNING STRATEGIES

In order for instruction to be successful, it must engage the learner. Strategies that focus on learner participation are likely to increase learner involvement in learning and decrease learner distraction. Ideally, in any instructional setting, there will be a great deal of mental activity occurring such as processing information, formulating questions, and thinking creatively. The earlier chapters that covered the use of questioning and discussion suggest the ways in which instructors can stimulate this type of activity through talking with learners.

Instructors may need to initiate a different type and level of involvement in the classroom. They might select strategies that require students to take responsibility for some aspect of their instruction by playing a major role in the learning process. Five types of such learning activities will be discussed in this chapter: debate, role-plays, games, simulations, and laboratories. These activities can be categorized as **action-oriented learning strategies** because each requires the active participation of learners in order for learning to take place. With each of these learning strategies, learning outcomes depend upon learner involvement.

## ACTION-ORIENTED STRATEGIES

You are probably familiar with the debate as an action-oriented strategy. In a **debate**, two opposing teams present affirmative and negative sides of an issue. The issue must be one that cannot be resolved simply through an examination of facts. In a formal debate, rigid rules are followed that dictate how often, how long, and in what order team members may speak. In informal debates, most of these rules are relaxed.

A **role-play** is a spontaneous acting out of a situation by two or more persons who demonstrate the emotional reactions of the people in the situation as they perceive them. Participants are provided limited information about the roles and how they should be played. There is no script, no rehearsing, and no memorizing of lines. Participants are usually provided the brief description in writing, then given a few moments to think about the role before they begin. A role-play is always followed by a debriefing period when the instructor helps learners analyze what has happened during the role-play.

**Educational games** can be commercially-prepared or teacher-made. They usually involve some element of chance, and since their intent is to educate, the outcome should depend upon the skill or knowledge of the player. Games where the outcomes are totally dependent upon chance are not classified as educational, and are not usually recommended in instructional settings. Educational games are designed to teach, reinforce, or introduce some content, attitude, or skill. They range from puzzles to board games requiring strategy to physical contests. One type of game — the simulation — creates some dimension of reality for students so that they can have a vicarious experience.

The simulation has the characteristics of both a role-play and a game. The **simulation** is a symbolic representation of some life experience. Learners are assigned a role and, within that role, they interact with other systems. There are usually rules or guidelines within which the learner must perform. Throughout the simulation, learners are required to make decisions, and those decisions, in turn, influence the system and their role. Simulations allow learners to experience some of the emotion and feelings of the real life experience in the safety of a simulated environment or relationship.

A **laboratory** is a planned and supervised practice experience. Learners have an opportunity to practice a process or skill, or to apply a principle or investigate a problem under supervision. The instructor acts as a facilitator, and learners are responsible for making decisions about procedures and practices within the laboratory.

## WHY USE ACTION-ORIENTED LEARNING STRATEGIES?

Debates, role-plays, games, simulations, and laboratories all require that learners become actively involved in instruction. Effective instructors have discovered that there are a variety of reasons for including active participation strategies in the learning process.

First, active participation creates interest on the part of learners. Learners are more likely to stay focused on instruction if they are expected or allowed to do something. While passivity may lead to boredom or inattention, activity typically generates interest and attention.

Different types of learning activity may also help accommodate the various learning styles of the audience. Learners who may have difficulty understanding an oral explanation of a type of communication pattern, for instance, may understand it quite easily when it is demonstrated during a role-play. Other learners may need the movement allowed by a game, or enjoy the teamwork (group work) required in the laboratory. Debate may provide additional challenge for some learners. These are just some examples that illustrate how strategies that allow active participation in the classroom may broaden the potential for reaching learners with various styles. As you will see, activities such as games may cater to several styles at the same time.

The use of action-oriented activities also allows learners to view content from different perspectives or points of view. While hearing about or reading about content is one type of experience, working with the content through one of these methods provides another form of learning. Imagine adolescent students who may have difficulty understanding a particular point of view about families, a piece of legislation, or some type of medical technology. Now imagine them debating these issues, perhaps developing a position of support for the "misunderstood" point of view. Likewise, a parent who role-plays the point of view of an adolescent sees issues from a different perspective. These are examples of using active learning to see content from another point of view.

Talking yields one dimension of understanding; doing provides another. This common sense statement about active learning strategies leads to another that may seem obvious. Active learning strategies can be matched to all levels of learner outcomes, and at any of these levels, they reinforce intended learner outcomes. In other words, the right active learning strategy can help learners acquire skills in the cognitive, affective, and psychomotor domains by serving as tools for reinforcement or practice.

One example of a cognitive, active learning strategy is a simulation that encourages young students to learn about the challenges faced by pioneer families who moved West. Students learn by simulating a wagon train trip as it might have occurred. Games too, are frequently used to accomplish cognitive outcomes; learners may practice the recall of facts and information using card games, "bees," or some modification of TV game shows.

The old game of "sewing machine road race" illustrates an active learning strategy that focuses on the psychomotor domain. For years, sewing instructors have required students to sew (with unthreaded sewing machines) over lines or "highways" drawn on paper in order to teach control of the sewing machine. Successful students were often awarded an "operator's license." This simple game was used to teach a low-level psychomotor skill.

Role-plays have been most commonly used in teaching and practicing interpersonal skills. Many affective learner outcomes can be best taught by having students experience the roles or circumstances of others, as done in role-play.

Action-oriented learning strategies that encourage involvement also encourage learners to take some responsibility for their own learning. When learners are expected to "do" rather than just "listen" or "receive," they exercise some level of control over themselves and what is learned. Participants involved in a game of skill where points are awarded by performing a process correctly or where winning is contingent upon figuring out an appropriate strategy must rely on themselves — not an instructor — to be successful. In addition, the degree of success that they achieve is dependent upon themselves. One example might be a stock market simulation where clients in a financial planning seminar are given an assigned amount of money to invest (hypothetically). While the success or failure of the individual or team may in part depend upon conditions beyond their control (like the value of the Japanese yen or the President's health), the success — the learning — depends upon their own initiative and understanding rather than the instructor's ability to lecture. While adult learners need and expect this level of self direction, young students who feel very little control over their learning environment may also appreciate this aspect of active learning. Adolescent learners may enjoy being able to make choices (within the context of the game or role-play) without having specific permission from a teacher or leader.

This independence or responsibility carries with it the capacity of reward for individual initiative or achievement. Games, laboratories, and debates particularly provide an opportunity to recognize and acknowledge the success of participants. Since games and laboratories, for example, allow students to demonstrate a broader range of skills than a paper-pencil test, the most successful participants may or may not be the same learners who regularly score well on tests or written assignments.

Many games, simulations, and role-playing assignments allow learners to exercise their imaginations. One category of games — fantasy games — are especially helpful at encouraging students to create and develop new ideas or strategies. Sometimes these types of games may appear to provide little content, but in fact, may actually be facilitating the types of processes frequently taught in family and consumer sciences. One example is a game where students are given an envelope of seemingly random materials, such as a paper cup, pencil, paper clip, shoestring, and balloon. They are then asked to make a household tool or a toy for an older child using the items. The organization of these materials into a usable item encourages problem solving and creative thinking.

The preceding example leads to one final reason for including active learning strategies in instruction: many are fun and motivating for learners (and for the instructor). Even the schoolmaster in the one-room schoolhouse realized that spelling was more fun if it was turned into a game — the spelling bee. Most experienced instructors have recognized and understood that many tasks that may be required for learning to take place can be made more fun by incorporating these tasks into a game or activity. Flash cards are more fun than a list of facts to memorize; a crossword puzzle is a more interesting route to learning the meaning of terms than simply looking them up in the dictionary; a contest to see which team can earn the most points via correct answers is more exciting than just studying alone. Games, simulations, debates, laboratories, and role-plays are examples of learning activities that involve learners in instruction and make instruction more effective and interesting. Figure 11-1 summarizes the reasons for using action-oriented learning strategies.

**FIGURE 11-1.** Advantages of Action-Oriented Learning Strategies

- Create interest.
- Accommodate different learning styles.
- Allow learners to see content from a different perspective.
- Can be matched to all levels of learner outcomes.
- Encourage learners to take responsibility for learning.
- Allow reward for good performance.
- May encourage use of imagination.
- Add an element of fun.

# SELECTION OF APPROPRIATE
# ACTION-ORIENTED LEARNING STRATEGIES

The principle that should operate in the selection of all instructional activities/strategies can be restated here: The instructional strategy must be consistent with the intended learner outcome. In other words, the appropriate selection of an active learning strategy is determined by the content and level of the intended learner outcome. The slickest, most fun-filled game packaged and sold is NOT appropriate unless it moves learners toward the intended learner outcome. Let's look at a ridiculous example. Imagine the NINTENDO game series, but instead of Luigi and Mario (the famous Mario Brothers) we have saturated fats and monounsaturated fats. Instead of little blue and green monsters we have LDLs and HDLs (cholesterol). Would changing the names of the frantic little characters and their foes justify the use of the game in the classroom? And, if so, for how long? Most readers familiar with this example will by now be shaking their heads, and yet this example should serve to make a more serious point. A game, role-play, simulation, laboratory experience, or debate should only be used as an instructional activity if it conveys appropriate content at an appropriate level. To determine this, the following questions should be asked. What should learners know as a result of instruction? How can that best be achieved?

When should games, role-plays, simulations, laboratories, and debates be used to help learners achieve intended outcomes? The most obvious aspect of this match is content. If the learner outcome describes applying knowledge of window caulking, then the game should be about window caulking — not about energy conservation. A simulation that focuses on food choices is NOT appropriately matched to an objective stating that "learners will identify factors that contribute to the world food shortage." While this seems like an obvious point, temptation often draws us to use something "close" because it is well-packaged, well organized, or just looks like fun. It is important that learners understand the purpose of the activity. This may not be possible if the content of the activity is not well matched to the instructional outcome desired.

Besides a match between the activity content and the content of the learner outcome, the activity should match the level of the learner outcome. Lower level cognitive outcomes require the learner to recall, identify, or define information or facts. This first level of learning is best matched to games that would require learners to label, match, arrange, retell, or memorize. This might include card games where learners match equivalents (lottery-type games), adaptations of TV game shows where learners provide information, or puzzles. Games matched to the application level of learning might include some types of puzzles, the development of mobiles, organizing collections, or role-playing particular content. An example of an application level game is the "baby care Olympics" where learners compete in various aspects of infant care (dressing, bathing, diapering, and bottle preparation) for points and awards.

One common use of the laboratory experience is to require learners to apply some principle or skills in real practice. A higher cognitive level — synthesis — requires learners to produce, predict, plan, or compose. Games that might match this level of learning include those where students are required to invent a product or process, create an original song, story, or jingle, or make predictions. Simulations often require learners to analyze or synthesize information in order to make decisions during the game. Role-plays, too, can be successfully used at this level when the roles require that learners draw together knowledge and ideas from multiple sources in order to respond.

Debates are usually most successful when used to facilitate higher levels of learning. Since they require students to draw together information, develop original presentations, and evaluate using some set of criteria, debates are best suited to reinforcing synthesis and evaluation level outcomes.

The same principle holds true for the matching of activities to outcomes in the psychomotor and affective domains. Instructors should look closely at what they expect learners to be able to do before selecting a game, assigning a laboratory experience, or creating a role-play. The baby Olympic game previously described could reinforce outcomes at the "mechanism" psychomotor level, but would probably not be appropriate if the learner was simply expected to "perceive" (lowest level) how to fold and pin a diaper.

The potential use of role-plays and simulations with affective outcomes is perhaps obvious. The affective domain deals with learning involving feelings, values, and attitudes. Assuming the roles of others or watching as others play these roles is conducive to the changes often described in affective learner outcomes, outcomes that describe responding, valuing, organizing, and characterizing.

While the first criteria for selecting and using these active learning strategies is a match between the strategy and the content and level of the learner outcome, there are still questions related to the efficiency of these methods for achieving the outcomes.

An important question relates to the benefits of the activity. Will the benefits justify the time required? Instructors should analyze the time required to prepare for, explain, monitor, and follow up the game, simulation, role-play, laboratory, or debate. While games or simulations may take very little instructional time, some commercially-developed ones require several weeks playing time! Debates generally require a great deal of preparation time for participants, as well as reporting time. Instructors should carefully consider whether or not the activity provides sufficient value for the time required.

Instructors should also look at the level of sophistication and difficulty of the activity. Even if the content and level appear to match the learner outcomes, it may be that the directions or processes are too complex for the learners. For example, middle school-aged learners could become frustrated and bored during a game that lasts several rounds, particularly if they are required to observe rather than participate. Some games may seem inappropriate, too, for adult learners, even though they are well matched to the learner outcome. Think, for example, of adult learners propped against the walls around a classroom, each being asked to spell a French cooking term. Those who miss are asked to sit down. Whether or not knowing the spelling of these terms is an appropriate learner outcome, the activity seems ill-matched to the learners.

Another consideration is the concomitant learning that may accompany the activity. **Concomitant learnings** are sometimes called the "hidden curriculum" because they refer to what is unintentionally taught, often through the process of instruction. Laboratory activities, for example, may teach teamwork and cooperation as strongly as they reinforce the investigative process. Competition is one possible concomitant learning. Participants may learn that winning is more important than cooperating or that finishing or completing is valued over being thorough. Consider the cost to some students of losing as well. Some instructors complain that learners take the content less seriously when game playing or role-playing. Managing these and other problems in using active learning strategies will be discussed in the next section.

Debates, role-plays, games, simulations, and laboratories are effective active learning strategies if thoughtfully selected. Instructors need to carefully consider whether or not the activity matches the level and content of the intended learner outcomes. Other considerations include how well the activity is matched to the learners and whether or not the activity teaches or reinforces desirable attitudes and behaviors. Figure 11-2 summarizes the factors to consider in selecting appropriate active learning strategies.

---

**FIGURE 11-2. Keys to Selecting Appropriate Action-Oriented Learning Strategies**

- Matches the intended learning outcome in relation to:
  — Content.
  — Domain.
  — Level.
- Benefit to learning justifies the time required.
- Activity is appropriate level of difficulty for the learners.
- Positive concomitant learnings result.

# DEBATE

Debate is sometimes classified as one type of structured discussion, along with the panel discussion and symposium. Quite often, however, these other types of discussions rely on the use of "experts" or outside speakers rather than the learners in the classroom. Debate as an active learning strategy requires learners to serve as members of the debate teams. It becomes the responsibility of the learners to identify the key issues related to the topic, to prepare for an initial presentation or position statement, and to be prepared to respond to the argument of the opposing team.

## USING DEBATE

Since debate requires learners to synthesize ideas from a variety of sources, develop an original argument, and make judgments about the merits of the arguments of others, it is usually used to reinforce higher level learner outcomes. It requires that students have a good deal of prerequisite knowledge and that they are able to do the research and preparation needed to successfully prepare for the actual debate. Since debate presents two sides of a particular issue, it is also an appropriate strategy for some affective learner outcomes involving receiving and responding to different attitudes or opinions.

Besides selecting debate as an instructional strategy for higher level objectives, instructors might consider using debate when dealing with controversial topics or issues for which there is no definitive right or wrong answer. The stated purpose of a debate is for one team to try to persuade the other team to accept their point of view. This requires that a topic be selected that can be successfully argued "pro" and "con," and that neither position can be supported only by data. Examples of such topics might include: "National health insurance should be available to all persons," "Grandparents should have legal access to their grandchildren under any circumstances," or "The U.S. has an obligation to assist the starving nations of the world."

If debate is deemed to be the best learning activity for a particular learner outcome, there are some steps required of the instructor to facilitate the activity. First, make sure that the topic for the debate is an appropriate, debatable issue where positions can be taken and defended. Sometimes topics emerge from class discussions. The instructor should be sensitive to topics that create dissension in the group. During a group discussion with early adolescents, for example, the leader may become aware that the learners hold opposing points of view about household tasks; some see these as a responsibility of a family member, others see them as enforced child labor. A debate could be based on the topic, "Every family member has a responsibility to contribute labor to the household or family." Learners would have an opportunity to coherently present their points of view. The preparation and discussion would probably clarify the thinking of the participants, as well as provide listeners with new perspectives.

Sometimes debate topics are suggested by current events. A newspaper story about prenuptial agreements during a unit on marriage preparation, or a report of a family's experience with interracial adoption while studying childbearing options may generate topics for debate. As indicated, debate topics are generally presented to the teams as statements that must be debated pro or con.

Debate team members should be selected well in advance of the scheduled debate and given adequate time and opportunity to research and prepare their points of view. Depending upon the learning environment, instructors may wish to provide to the teams some resource material, or to make suggestions about where to access materials. Team members may be assigned or allowed to volunteer. Since the debate team is expected to function as a team, it may be important to select members who learn best in that environment, or who are willing to work in that mode. Team members will usually be expected to prepare independent of the supervision of the instructor, so this, too, has implications for the selection of team members.

In formal debates, the debate begins with one member of the team giving reasons (in a prepared statement) why his or her team favors the position or issue. This is followed by a member of the opposing team stating his or her point of view. This continues until each team member has had an opportunity to state his or her position and the reasons and data supporting that position. Team members generally refer to notes during their statements, but they do not read written statements. After each team member has stated his or her point of view (alternating teams), team members have an opportunity to respond to the arguments of their opponents. During this time, team members are not allowed to raise new issues, but they may cite new research material or supporting data. Often, time limits are imposed on statements and rebuttals, with a timekeeper indicating by hand signal or bell when the time is up. Participants are not allowed to interrupt another speaker.

At the conclusion of the debate, the moderator (instructor or student) should briefly summarize the points made, referring only to the highlights. A prepared discussion should follow the debate so that the observers have an opportunity to engage in discussion on the topic. The guidelines outlined for the follow-up and debriefing of role-plays apply to the debate, too. Questions should be prepared that assist learners in making generalizations about the points made and in formulating their own position and rationale for that position. It may be necessary to reemphasize that team members may not hold the particular view of the team on which they served—but were merely presenting the arguments from that perspective.

## ADVANTAGES AND DISADVANTAGES OF DEBATE

The debate allows participants to take responsibility for their own learning through research and preparation of a position on a controversial topic. Through this process, learners have an opportunity to explore in some detail the data and research that supports a particular point of view, and to clarify their own thinking about the issue. Debate as an active learning strategy fosters analysis, synthesis, and evaluation skills, and provides a strong intellectual challenge to some learners.

Listening to the debate is usually an interesting experience since there is variation of speakers, styles, and points of view. Many debates become quite lively as team members refute the points of the opposing team, so the experience may liven up the learning environment.

Those not involved in the actual debate may, however, become passive observers rather than active learners. Another disadvantage is that important or key points may or may not be covered, depending on the skills of the team members. In fact, without thorough research, the debate may consist more of opinion than facts. In some cases, one team may be stronger than another, suggesting that one position is more worthy than the other. Quite often, less capable learners find debate a difficult learning activity.

Another potential disadvantage of debate as a learning strategy involves the ability of the debate monitor. Inexperienced monitors may not be able to successfully integrate or highlight the discussion, or may not adequately help learners explore what happened during the debate.

Some instructors feel that the time spent in preparing for and delivering the debate may not be worth the outcome. This may be a disadvantage of the strategy, depending on the instructional plans of the teacher or leader. Other instructors feel that the strategy may be poorly suited to their group of learners. Since the strategy does create two adversarial groups, it may not be appropriate in instructional settings that resemble or function in part as support groups. Figure 11-3 summarizes some of the key points to be considered in using debate.

## ROLE-PLAY

You can use role-play most effectively if you carefully select situations that lend themselves best to role-play, plan carefully for its use, and follow guidelines that lead to successful role-play.

## WHEN TO USE ROLE-PLAY

Role-play is a technique that increases student involvement and leads to understanding of the reactions of people and possible responses in a situation. It is best used when desired learner outcomes involve students developing insight into human relations, handling difficult emotional situations in a risk-free environment, looking more objectively at their own behavior, and testing alternative ways of working out a solution to a problem.

Oftentimes, role-play is used to help students develop insight into problems in human relations. There are few other techniques that lead to this outcome as successfully. A good example of this type of role-play is one in which three people are selected and given a written description of their roles. The three descriptions direct the students to act like: (1) himself or herself, (2) someone

## FIGURE 11-3. Debate

**Use when:**
- Synthesis of ideas is important.
- Higher level learning outcomes are desired.
- Dealing with controversial issues.

**To prepare:**
- Select a topic appropriate to debate.
- Provide sufficient preparation time.
- Select team members likely to be able to work together.
- Emphasize "roles" being played in the debate.

**During the debate:**
- Allow each team member to present a position statement.
- Alternate presentations from the two teams.
- Allow a specific period of time for rebuttal by each team.
- Enforce agreed-upon rules of conduct for the debate.
- Summarize.
- Re-emphasize the roles that team members "play" in a debate.
- Debrief and discuss using prepared questions.

**Advantages:**
- Allows learners to take responsibility for their own learning.
- Fosters higher level learning.
- Is interesting to those viewing the debate.

**Disadvantages:**
- Viewers of the debate may become passive participants.
- Teams may miss important points.
- Opinions, rather than facts, may predominate.
- Support for a particular point of view may be swayed by personality or presentation skills.
- Debate can be difficult for less capable learners.
- Summary and discussion must be lead by a skilled monitor.
- Time spent may not be worth the outcome.
- Inappropriate when learners function as a support group.

who knows another person in the group is "out to get him or her," and (3) a person who knows that the entire group is "out to get him or her." The other learners are then invited to converse with each role-player one at a time. The audience does not know the roles each player was asked to play and none of the role-players hears the conversations with either of the other two role-players. The audience is to praise the role-players in the conversations. Follow-up focuses on each of the roles that was portrayed and the generalizations that can be made about why people react differently to praise. (Klemmer & Smith, 1975). Such a role-play may lead learners to have more powerful insights than if the same content was delivered in a lecture entitled "Understanding Reactions to Praise."

Very emotional situations that might be embarrassing or too emotionally "charged" to discuss in other contexts are often easily handled in a role-play.

A role-play that fits this description is one in which a male and a female are chosen to play the roles. The female must play the role of a male who is trying to convince a girlfriend to have sexual intercourse with him. The male plays the role of the girlfriend who has decided she is not ready to have sexual intercourse with anyone. Such a role-play asks the players to assume "alternate roles" and leads to clearer understanding of an issue that isn't always explored as thoroughly or unemotionally in the back seat of a car!

When learning outcomes call for students to better understand their own behavior, role-play can often be used. Some simple role-plays that lead to better understanding include real life situations that are regularly encountered such as: (1) the conversation between the mother who will not listen and the daughter who is trying to explain why she is late, (2) the wife (who has a full-time job comparable to her husband's) approaching the husband about sharing housework, (3) a sixteen-year-old approaching a parent about owning a car, (4) the employee suggesting a new way of doing things to his or her employer. The topics for role-play that lead to better understanding of behavior are as endless as the types of interactions that occur between people.

Role-play can be used to test out different ways of handling a particular situation. One way of doing this is to have different groups of role-players play out the same situation. Several different solutions to the situation will probably result. Another successful method of role-playing that leads to alternative solutions to a particular situation is the "replay." Learners play through a role-play spontaneously the first time. After discussion, the role-play is repeated with the players changing their enactment to follow the guidelines developed during discussion.

## USING ROLE-PLAY

The previous section of this chapter highlighted the types of learner outcomes most likely to be accomplished by using role-playing. Once role-play has been determined to be the most effective strategy to be used to accomplish learner outcomes, it works best when the instructor has carefully planned for the role-play situation. Careful planning involves:
- Selecting the role-play situation that most clearly relates to learner outcomes.
- Preparing (in written form) any character or scene descriptions necessary.
- Thinking carefully about possible learners to select for the different roles.
- Planning the questions to be used in the follow-up discussion.

There are many sources of role-play available in teaching technique texts, family relations journals, and even popular magazines. Letters to newspaper and magazine advice columnists may suggest situations and roles appropriate for dramatization. Occasionally, the instructor will find several that relate directly to the learner outcomes he or she has specified. Even when commercially-prepared role-plays are not readily available, they are easily prepared by the teacher. Generally, everyday life experiences are a rich source of role-play. Note ideas for role-plays from your own life experiences on index cards to have a ready source of role-plays for teaching. When a particular learner outcome calls for role-play, scan the ideas you already have, or develop a situation based upon the learner outcome.

Role-play is generally most successful when those who must play the roles are given clear descriptions of the situation or of the behavior they must portray. Although oral descriptions may suffice, players have an easier time if given written descriptions of the role-play that must be carried out. Descriptions should be complete enough to allow the person to play the role, but they should not inhibit spontaneity or "script" the play. The idea is for the learner to depend upon his or her own knowledge or experience in responding.

Participants in the role-play can be selected by volunteer or by assignment. Encourage volunteers since, by volunteering, learners are clearly indicating they feel comfortable with the situation. Plan ahead, however, in case learners do not volunteer to play a role. In advance of the situation in which you wish to use the role-play, identify learners most likely to feel comfortable in the role-play situation. Students who speak out often in class and are not afraid to express an opinion in other situations are generally most comfortable in a role-play. Be wary of assigning learners to a role that is too "close to home" and would cause embarrassment. Consider having several groups do the same role-play in order to involve as many learners as possible.

In contrast to many other types of learning sessions, the role-play session probably does not begin with a clear statement of the concepts to be learned. Role-play is designed to help tease out generalizations about behavior and to make the abstract nature of human relationships more concrete. The discussion that takes place after the role-play is the opportunity for generalizations and ideas to surface. In planning for the role-play, then, the instructor must carefully plan the follow-up discussion. The following guidelines can be used to structure the discussion after any role-play:

- Ask each role-player how he or she felt while playing the role.
- Ask class members to react to the behavior of each role-player.
- Give role-players a chance to indicate how they wish they had played the role.
- Ask the class how they would have acted if they had been the role-players.
- Ask what led to or contributed to the responses or the behavior of the role-players.
- Ask students to summarize what seemed to be operating in the situation (What are the generalizations or conclusions they can draw?).

Even though these are standard questions that can be asked at the end of each role-play, be sure to write them down and be prepared to respond as you would whenever using questions in a learning situation.

During the role-play session, the instructor should introduce the role-play, select the characters, set the scene for the characters, and give them time to get into the role. The instructor signals the beginning and ending of the role-play, debriefs the characters, and leads the discussion.

The introduction to the role-play should indicate the purpose of the role-play, but not give away the generalizations that can be drawn from the action.

The instructor should point out that anyone playing a role is doing just that —
and may not be representing a point of view or kind of behavior that represents
his or her true feelings.

If the instructor has decided to ask for volunteers for the role-play, he or
she should do so after the introduction so that students will be more likely
to volunteer. As in any unfamiliar situation, students may need some time
to decide whether or not they wish to take part in the role-play.

After characters have been selected for the role-play, give the role-players
their written instructions and some time to get into the role (one to three
minutes is usually adequate). Encourage them to think about the age, personality, and pressures on that role and the reactions of that character. The
audience can also hear this introduction as it helps to set the stage for them.
Occasionally, a role-play is designed so that one person has to play himself
or herself while others take on roles.

When students have had an opportunity to think about the situation that
must be played, announce that the role-play will begin. This helps to remind
learners that this is a dramatization and that, even though those playing the
roles may make the characters very real, they are only playing parts.

It is the instructor's duty to end the role-play at the appropriate moment.
Sometimes, it is difficult to know when to end the role-play. Generally, when
the players have demonstrated a series of responses in an attempt to play the
scene and have provided sufficient evidence of behaviors that will be discussed
during the summary session, it is time to stop the role-play. It is often best
to stop the dramatization when it is at a high point, rather than after it has
started to become repetitive and to drag.

The instructor should use good questioning techniques and planned questions in handling the post-role-play discussion (See Chapter 10, "Talking With
Learners."). During the discussion portion of the debriefing or follow-up questioning, it is important to de-role the participants. This simply means purposefully separating the attitudes and opinions expressed on the part of the character
from those of the learner who played the character. This can be easily done
by conscientiously referring to the learner in the role. For example, the instructor may begin by acknowledging the players: "Gary, thank you for playing the role of the abusive father. You did a good job in thinking through
his reactions." Or, "Mrs. Grant, you can step out of the role of the teenager
now while we talk about what just happened." Any references thereafter to
the performances should also acknowledge the role rather than the person,
for instance, "When Gary was playing the abusive father and said that he
thought the child deserved it," or "when the teenager complained." These types
of references should be made rather than referring to what Gary or Mrs. Grant
said, so that learners do not subconsciously assign the portrayed attitudes or
comments to the participants. It may help the audience to differentiate between the role and the person playing the role if the fictitious character's name
is used when discussing the feelings and attitudes portrayed. This is particularly
important when highly controversial issues are being discussed.

The follow-up discussion or de-briefing transforms role-playing from a spectator sport to a learning activity. Unless learners and role-play participants have an opportunity to analyze and synthesize the experience — to develop generalizations — very little learning may actually occur. Instructor preparation for the follow-up discussion is every bit as important as selecting the correct role-play situation, setting up the role-play, and selecting appropriate players.

## ADVANTAGES AND DISADVANTAGES OF ROLE-PLAY

There are a number of advantages to role-play as a learning activity. When carefully planned and implemented, role-play interests both participants and observers. It is a technique where learners are actively involved in learning and exercise some control over the learning situation. Because it is organized around a fictitious story or scene, the role-play may allow participants to express their feelings more openly than they would during a simple discussion about a controversial issue. Even though the learner outcomes specified for the lesson may revolve around particular generalizations, role-play has the added advantage of fostering group cooperation and developing initiative on the part of participants.

Role-play has disadvantages as well, most of which stem from the particular group of learners expected to complete the role-play. In certain groups, able learners may not volunteer or be willing to be assigned to characters for the role-play, and the instructor will be forced to choose less able students to play the roles. Self-conscious students may not be spontaneous in acting out the roles. Students who do not think quickly or express themselves succinctly may lead to an ineffective role-play. Even articulate participants may not get into the spirit of the role-play and play the roles to full advantage. Occasionally, the audience may laugh or make remarks about the people playing the roles and make it difficult to sense the feelings and thoughts of the characters.

In general, the advantages of role-play for allowing learners to practice interpersonal skills and explore sensitive and emotional issues far outweigh the disadvantages. With careful planning, many of the disadvantages of the role-play technique can be avoided. Figure 11-4 summarizes some of the considerations in using role-play as an active learning strategy.

## GAMES

Games, when appropriately chosen, lead to desired learning outcomes, add fun, imagination, creativity, and excitement to learning situations. Games are an important pastime — from the weekend football games to the hours of morning and evening television game shows to the computerized games found in video game parlors. People are involved in games from the infant's simple peek-a-boo to children's hide-and-seek to complicated games of chess. Games fill many hours with thoughtful and challenging activity. When carefully selected, planned for, and used in the learning situation, games have many more advantages than disadvantages.

**FIGURE 11-4. Role-Play**

**Use when:**
- It leads to desired learner outcomes.
- Developing insight into human relations.
- Handling difficult emotional situations in a risk-free environment.
- Developing objectivity in examining behaviors.
- Testing alternative solutions to a problem.

**To prepare:**
- Select the role-play that most clearly relates to learner outcomes.
- Prepare written materials to identify the characters and the situation.
- Select/identify appropriate learners to play the roles.
- Plan the follow-up discussion.

**During the role-play:**
- Introduce the role-play.
- Select the players.
- Set the scene.
- Allow the role-players preparation time.
- Debrief the characters.
- Discuss.

**Advantages:**
- Interesting to observers and players.
- Learners have some control of the learning situation.
- Makes it easier to express opinions.
- Fosters group cooperation.
- Develops initiative.

**Disadvantages:**
- Learners may not participate fully.
- Players may be ineffective.
- Audience may inhibit the role-play.

## USING GAMES

Almost any type of learning can occur through the use of a game. Instructors are more likely to use games, however, when learners need a motivational, fun activity, when a game that matches desired learning outcomes is readily available or easy to make and/or when concomitant learning is important.

The type of game is a critical part of deciding whether the game is appropriate. Abt (1968) developed a classification scheme for educational games that may help in determining the type of game to use. Abt's classification included games of skill, chance, reality, fantasy, and strategy.

In *games of skill*, the outcome depends upon the capabilities of the players. The competitions involved in youth organizations are often games of skill. Students who must compete in demonstrating how to organize a preschool environment, how to prepare a nutritious meal, or how to balance a difficult budget all rely upon their individual capabilities in the competition. Such games of skill reward achievement, encourage individual initiative and responsibility, and discourage passivity.

*Games of chance* are controlled by the environment rather than the learner. Although the games themselves do not lead to learning outcomes, examining the laws of probability or purported systems related to games of chance may contribute to student learning. Such games could be used as a method for selecting students to participate in some other learning activity; for example, the student who gets the number closest to the one that the teacher has in mind is the first student to get to answer a review question and win a point. In general, however, games of chance are only peripherally related to learning.

*Games of reality* help students to experience real-life events in a nonthreatening environment. The relationships, problems, methods, and motives of others can be experienced vicariously through games. Simulations are often games of reality. Such games can be built around common problems or family activities such as communication (or miscommunication) in families, buying a house, or managing crises. Such games are of high interest for adolescent students, but may be too close to reality to be fun for adults.

*Games of fantasy* generally do not lead to significant cognitive outcomes, but they may contribute a great deal to affective learning outcomes. For example, learners might be asked to think of the 10 items they would want to take with them if they had to move to the moon tomorrow. Such a game challenges the imagination, encourages students to abandon conventional perceptions, and may even contribute to decision-making abilities.

*Games of strategy* require the learner to manipulate the environment. One example of a game of strategy is a computerized game that requires students to make decisions about actions they wish to take. Before requesting a particular move or "action" in this game, learners may ask as many questions about the situation as they wish. Games of strategy require learners to use all of the elements of decision making, from defining the problem to evaluating the outcome, and they contribute significantly to higher order learning in the cognitive domain.

As with any strategy in communicating content, the game selected must be carefully matched to intended learner outcomes. As noted previously, it is reasonable, on occasion, to play a game that encourages concomitant learning in addition to other specified learner outcomes. Even then, however, the game chosen must be matched to the types of concomitant learning desired. For example, if group cooperation and solidarity are desirable concomitant learnings as the result of a particular game, games organized so that individuals compete against each other are inappropriate, while cooperative games where the group must work together to solve a common problem are appropriate. Consider whether or not it is wise to allow learners to "choose sides." What learning might result from who is chosen first or last?

The best packaged and most interesting looking game may be unsuccessful if the instructor has not tried the game (preferably with people who are similar to the intended learners), determined how competitors will be chosen/

organized, and generated any back-up material needed to play the game. Trying a game before using it in an instructional setting is critical. The nuances of a game and the kinds of questions that will be asked about how to play the game will surface when trying out a game. A try-out of the game will also help the instructor discover what else must be supplied for the game to be successful. Occasionally, pieces are missing from a game, or the game does not work as expected. A good example is a computerized simulation that needs a particular code in order for learners to "enter" the game—and back-up material that indicates that there is such a code, but that does not reveal it!

Commonly used review games require that instructors generate the questions needed to play the game. These questions must, of course, be matched to intended learner outcomes and should be generated well in advance of the time when the game will be played. Other types of games may also require that material needed to play the game be prepared in advance. When time and effort are put into organizing and planning for a game, the desired learner outcomes are more likely to be achieved.

When using games, there are some simple guidelines that can be followed that help to make any game go more smoothly. Many of the following suggestions can be applied to a variety of games; some will be appropriate only to certain types of games. Even though several of the guidelines note that they are applicable to children—they work for adults, too.

First, obtain the attention of every member of the group of learners before beginning the explanation of the game. It is generally best to have learners seated and the "game pieces" out of sight or, at best, out of reach of the learners. Games tend to stimulate excitement and interest on the part of the learners (which is intended), but the growing excitement prior to the game may distract learners and make it difficult for them to concentrate on the explanation of how the game is played.

It is generally a good idea to organize learners into teams and put them in "starting position" after giving directions. It is a good idea to then give a demonstration of how the game is to be played. The demonstration should give learners a clearer idea of what will happen during the game and will help to generate questions that are more easily answered before the game begins rather than in the thick of competition. Be sure to preface any set of directions with a phrase like, "When I give the signal. . ." so that learners will not start the game before the directions are complete. The demonstration should be given from a position where all learners can see. If the game calls for learners to be organized in a circle, be sure to give the demonstration as a member of the circle. Pause after giving the demonstration and ask for questions.

Have a whistle handy during games that involve a lot of talking or moving about. It is much easier to regain group attention with a whistle than by yelling, "Everybody stop now and listen!" When possible, make corrections in the play of the game without stopping the game. The instructor can play the part of both the coach and the referee during most games.

During competitions that involve scoring, announce the score often. It stimulates interest, excitement, and attention to the game. Most learners participate in the game to win.

With younger learners attempting to play a new game, it is a good idea for the instructor to participate in the game as a player. If there is a need for someone to be the beginning player or "it," the instructor should take that role for the first round of the game.

While the instructor has the attention at the end of one activity, he or she should give the directions for getting the group into formation for the next activity or summarize the results of the game. The summarization at the end of the game can serve to reinforce important learner outcomes.

## ADVANTAGES AND DISADVANTAGES OF GAMES

The specific advantages of different types of games were previously noted. There are advantages to games that apply no matter what type of game is being played. First and foremost, well chosen and carefully planned games motivate learners, help sustain interest in a particular topic and may even serve to increase retention of material. Learners participating in games may learn in spite of themselves! Further, games provide a different context for the material being covered. When learning is disguised as fun in a game, the dull content of a lecture comes alive. Further, games focus on cooperative learning and activity and can help learners develop improved group skills.

Games have several disadvantages, however. Some of these disadvantages may not apply to certain games or may be able to be avoided by careful planning. Games are competitive situations—this is what makes them compelling to learners. At the same time, games can provide an opportunity for able learners to excel while discouraging less able learners. Games are more likely to be vehicles leading to learning if all learners have the possibility of winning.

Games can also be a poor technique to use if learners are eliminated from the game at any point. Learners who are not participating in the game are probably also not learning from it.

The time necessary to play the game may overbalance the learning that takes place. This disadvantage can be overcome if the instructor weighs the potential learning outcomes against the time necessary to play the game. If the instructor tries the game out prior to actually using it in a learning situation, the time necessary to play the game to the end and the potential learning outcomes will be much easier to judge.

Most learners greet games enthusiastically. However, there is some question about whether competition is an appropriate motivation for learning. When winning becomes paramount and the playing of the game secondary, the instructor should consider other methods for achieving desired learning outcomes. Figure 11-5 summarizes the points to consider in using games as active learning strategies.

## FIGURE 11-5. Games

**Use when:**
- Learners need a break from other types of learning activity.
- Game is available that matches desired learning outcomes.
- Concomitant learning is important.

**To prepare:**
- Select games according to the desired learning outcomes related to skill, chance, reality, fantasy, or strategy.
- Try the game with people similar to the intended learners.
- Determine how competitors will be chosen/organized.
- Generate back-up material.

**During the game:**
- Gain full learner attention before introducing the game.
- Do not name the game until finished giving instructions.
- Place learners in the "starting" position.
- Demonstrate the game.
- Answer questions.
- Use a whistle to regain group attention.
- Announce the score often.
- Instructor should participate in the game.
- Summarize at the end of the game.

**Advantages:**
- Motivate learners.
- Sustain interest.
- May encourage retention of material.
- Encourage cooperative learning.

**Disadvantages:**
- Competition may discourage less able learners.
- May be designed so that learners are "out" and not participating.
- Time needed to play the game may not be appropriate in relation to learner outcomes.

# SIMULATION

The simulation has characteristics of both games and role-play. Within a set of guidelines or game-like rules, the learner assumes a role, interacts with some system, and then experiences the consequences of the decisions he or she has made. The learner experiences "first hand" some of the decisions and consequences of a "simulated" life experience.

The simulation is actually a model of a physical or symbolic experience. Sometimes simulations are classified into two categories—*environmental simulations* and *social system simulations.* An environmental simulation creates a simulated physical space. A special needs teacher, for example, might create a simulated supermarket by creating aisles filled with empty food boxes and cans. A social system simulation focuses on interaction with a social system, such as marriage, family, government, the economy, or a banking system.

Here the physical props are unimportant; the emphasis is on the patterns of interaction.

In simulations, learners play a role. Rather than the unscripted, individual role used in role-play, the learner is assigned a role in which he or she interacts with the system. The learner is asked to make a series of decisions that create consequences. The learner experiences these consequences firsthand, but within the safety of the simulated system.

## USING SIMULATION

There are a number of commercially-produced simulations that deal with such topics as marriage and family, poverty, world hunger, and energy conservation. A variety of simulation games has been produced in the form of computer software. One computer simulation, for example, allows students to assume the role of a guest at a party where alcoholic beverages and food are being served. Learners have a chance to select food and drink within a given time period, and then "experience" the resulting blood-alcohol level. Learners must maneuver a car around a course. The computer simulates their level of impairment based on their blood-alcohol level. Learners experience the difficulty of controlling the vehicle while "impaired."

Instructor-developed simulations can be difficult to create, but are well worth the effort in terms of educational outcomes. For instance, many family living instructors utilize family resource management simulations where students, as couples, manage the financial resources of a family.

When preparing learners for the simulation, similar guidelines apply as in preparing them for games and role-plays. The instructor needs to be very clear on the procedures for the simulation and be able to explain them to learners. If the simulation is extremely complex, it may be necessary to create a written set of steps or rules for participants. Learners need to understand their roles and to be clear about what they can and cannot do in the context of their roles.

In environmental simulations, instructors may have to gather a number of objects or materials. For example, a simulation on aging may require a wheelchair, eyeglasses, and walking canes.

During the simulation, the instructor may have an assigned role, or merely act as the facilitator. Make sure learners understand the role of the instructor. Create opportunities for learners to ask for assistance during the simulation, particularly if the simulation goes on for several days or weeks. Simulations may last from two hours to three weeks, depending upon their level of complexity. Be alert to learners who are becoming confused or bored.

The debriefing stage of the simulation is important. Instructors need to be prepared to "de-role" learners, and to talk about how the learners felt and responded during the simulation. This is an excellent time to work on the development of critical thinking skills. Learners can be prompted in being precise in their descriptions and logical in their analysis of events.

# ADVANTAGES AND DISADVANTAGES OF SIMULATIONS

Simulations are highly motivating to students because they require a high level of learner participation. Learners are directly involved in the learning process. At their best, simulations require a significant commitment on the part of learners—one beyond that usually required in other types of learning activities. In order to be truly involved in the simulation, learners have to strongly assume their roles as they make a series of decisions within those roles. The consequences of their decisions modify their circumstances. This, in turn, modifies the conditions under which their next decisions are made.

During the simulation, learners must use a variety of skills. This is an additional advantage to simulations. Further, learners are allowed to practice and experience within a safe environment.

On the down side, simulations generally require a significant amount of time for the game itself, as well as for the preparation and debriefing. Unless the game is well developed and carefully planned, some learners may become bored or lost and drop out. Good follow-up and debriefing is important to make sure that learners have an opportunity to analyze what happened during the simulation.

Simulation is a powerful action-oriented learning strategy. Instructors need to carefully consider when learners are best prepared to participate in simulation and when it is the method that will contribute most to learning. See Figure 11-6.

# THE LABORATORY

Laboratories provide a type of firsthand experience. In laboratories, learners have the opportunity to practice a skill, to apply a principle, and/or to experiment with materials, people, or processes. The uniqueness of a laboratory experience, however, is that it takes place in a controlled, supervised setting. Firsthand experiences like internships or practicums typically take place in the field—a child development center, hospital kitchen, computer center, or client's home—over a specified period of time. Laboratory experiences usually occur in a classroom or other facility that is designed for teaching. When laboratories do occur in the field, they are generally a single instructional incident under the supervision of an instructor or facilitator.

Laboratories, of course, have a long history in family and consumer sciences. The early laboratories emphasized experimentation with cooking, sanitation, food preservation, and garment construction. Although laboratories that teach these types of skills or content still have a place in instruction, the laboratories may have changed forms in recent times. Laboratories almost always involve the use of materials and equipment, but the present emphasis is not necessarily on the development of the manual skills or on the product generated. Instead, laboratories focus more on such things as planning, decision-making,

## FIGURE 11-6. The Simulation

**Use when:**
- Learners need to experience the feelings or emotions of some life experience beyond their personal experience.
- Learners need to explore the consequences of decisions or behaviors of some life experience beyond their current experience.
- Learners need to explore some other point of view, perspective, or problem from the point of view of others.
- Learners need to practice some life skill under "real life" conditions.

**To prepare:**
- Make sure learners have prerequisite knowledge to function within their roles.
- Make sure learners understand their assigned roles.
- Make sure learners understand the rules or guidelines that govern interactions during the simulation.
- Make sure learners know how to access assistance throughout the simulation.
- Make sure all relevant materials, equipment, or resources are gathered for use throughout the simulation.

**During the simulation:**
- Monitor the progress and needs of learners.
- Facilitate action or provide assistance as needed.
- Prepare follow-up activities and discussions so that learners have an opportunity to analyze what happened during the simulation.

**Advantages:**
- Allows learners to take responsibility for their own learning.
- Requires a high level of learner participation.
- Provides simulated experiences to learners beyond their own lives or circumstances.
- May be highly motivating to learners.

**Disadvantages:**
- May be time and resource intensive.
- May lose the interest of some learners if the simulation is too long or too complex.
- May be difficult to develop a level of complexity that really challenges learners.

analysis of results, cooperative learning, and group process. Making the "perfect muffin" is generally not the goal!

The most obvious use of the laboratory is the opportunity to practice a skill or process or to investigate a question or resolve a problem in the safety of a supervised setting. The setting is supervised, and the instructor acts as a resource as learners work toward solutions to problems or practice the application of some learning. Consider, for example, a laboratory where learners experiment with different types of food storage. Learners might test various types of lunch packing techniques combined with different lunch foods and then monitor internal temperatures and bacterial growth. Another laboratory might involve the comparison of different consumer products for noise levels, ease of maintenance, or reliability. Routine health care/monitoring practices, steps in the recycling process, infant care, computerizing inventories, or household repair are opportunities to use a laboratory activity to help students apply and practice learning in a realistic, supervised setting.

## PLANNING AND IMPLEMENTING
## THE LABORATORY EXPERIENCE

Successful outcomes to a laboratory experience depend on a well-planned laboratory activity. The obvious first question is, "Is the learner outcome most appropriately achieved with a laboratory activity?" While laboratories are ideal opportunities for supervised practice, they are generally resource intensive. Laboratories require substantial amounts of planning and instructional time, and often require resources of equipment and materials. If the outcome is best taught with a laboratory experience, then the instructor must carefully plan the experience.

As a first step, both instructor and learner need to understand the purpose or intended outcome of the laboratory. This needs to be communicated clearly so that learners understand why they are participating in the particular activity. The instructor may jointly plan the activity with learners, may state the goal or problem orally, or may make it part of a planning worksheet. However it is clarified, it is important that learners understand the problem or challenge to be undertaken in the laboratory.

Laboratory procedures need to be communicated to learners. These procedures may include the conditions under which the work is to be done, the guidelines for completing the work, and any routines or practices that will help accomplish the laboratory work. For example, a consumer product testing laboratory might require guidelines for computer and material use, a check-out plan for materials, and guidelines for returning the resource area back to its original organization. In the child development laboratory setting, instructors often provide learners with rules for the laboratory, a general routine for the day, and/or a sample planning sheet. Figures 11-7, 11-8, and 11-9 show simple guides that could be used in this setting.

---

**FIGURE 11-7. Sample Laboratory Guidelines**

**YOUR ROLE**

- **You are a teacher as well as a learner.** Make the most of your opportunity to work with and learn from children. At the same time, be sure you remain alert not only to the child(ren) with whom you are working, but also to the larger group.

- **Your presence is important.** Come on time and prepared for your assigned work time. Arrange for a substitute if you must, but inform the office that you will be using a substitute.

- **Be prepared.** Familiarize yourself with the school. Find out where equipment and supplies are stored. Learn the names of children, staff, and other teachers. Know the daily routine.

**DAILY SCHEDULE**

- **Find your name tag.** Pick up your name tag from the bulletin board outside the manager's office. Wear it during the time you are in the school. Return it to the bulletin board as you leave.

*(continued)*

**FIGURE 11-7.** *Continued.*

- **Check the daily lesson plan.** What is the theme for the day? How do the activities contribute to the theme? What activity is your responsibility? Be prepared to carry out your activity for the day, but be flexible enough to switch to a different responsibility if the head teacher asks.

- **Follow the daily schedule.** Be aware of the usual time when activities terminate and new ones begin. Help the children in your activity area make the transition.

- **Participate in clean-up and debriefing.** Clean-up time is usually the time when debriefing occurs. Assess what went well and what could have gone better. Ask for suggestions for improvement.

### THINGS TO KEEP IN MIND

- **Your first few experiences in the laboratory may make you feel uncertain.** Any new "job" is likely to bring with it an initial period when you feel a little lost. This will quickly disappear as you become familiar with the laboratory, the children, and your fellow workers.

- **Dress appropriately.** Think twice before wearing expensive clothes that may be stained with paint and grape juice, or jewelry that is interesting to grab! You will be on the floor a lot, so a short skirt is likely to be uncomfortable. Jeans and slacks are great for the setting, but be sure they look neat and professional. Torn jeans or sweats and tank tops do not look professional.

### GUIDELINES FOR WORKING WITH CHILDREN

- **Talk to a child eye-to-eye.** Go to the child (don't yell across the room) and squat down or sit so you are at the same level as the child. This is generally less threatening and intimidating to the child.

- **Use positive guidance.** Tell the child what he or she *can* do, rather than what he or she cannot do.

- **Place the action verb at the beginning of any guidance direction.** Preschool children are more likely to be able to follow a simple direction that begins with the action desired, for example, "Put the crayons in this box please, Jeremy."

- **Try to give one direction at a time.** Series of directions may be easy for adults, but are often difficult for children.

- **Give direction at the time and place you want the behavior to occur.**

- **Give choices only when you can accept the child's response.** If a child really must stop doing whatever he or she is doing and you ask, "Would you like to move to the reading group?," you are setting yourself up for a response that is really not a choice, "NO!" Use "Would you like to . . ." and "Do you want to . . ." only when the child *has* a choice.

- **Be friendly, firm, and fair.** You need to decide what limits are essential for a particular child in a situation, make them clear to the child, and maintain them.

- **Reinforce desired behavior and ignore undesired behavior as much as possible.** Children really want to please adults most of the time. "Catching them being good" reinforces good behavior. Try phrases like, "George, I like the way you are sitting quietly," rather than "Susie, why can't you sit still?"

- **Be a good role model.** "Monkey see, monkey do" is a statement that seems to apply to children, too!

- **Relax and enjoy the children!**

- **Report any questions or concerns to the Laboratory Manager.** Avoid talking about the children with others *except* in the supervised debriefing session. All information about the children and their families is confidential.

## FIGURE 11-8. Sample Preschool Laboratory Schedule

Tentative schedule for a one-hour class.

Remember to do as much as possible for laboratory set-up prior to 1.55.

| | |
|---|---|
| Pre-class | Arrive at class site.<br>Early parents and children can be seated in the hall. |
| Pre-class | Complete set-up. |
| 5 minutes | Doors open—Begin taking coats, putting on name tags; let children enter play area; set parents in parent chairs. |
| 25 minutes | Free choice of activities at activity centers. |
| 5 minutes | Clean up—(Toys need to be cleaned up three minutes earlier so the area is cleared for snacks.) |
| 10 minutes | Bring children to the snack area. Snacks are served. |
| 5 minutes | Return toys and projects. Help with coats. |
| Post-class | Goodbyes, clean-up, reset-up room. |

## FIGURE 11-9. Sample Planning Sheet

**SAMPLE PLAN SHEET**

NAMES OF TEAM MEMBERS:

ASSIGNMENT:

THEME:

TIME SCHEDULE _____ OKAYED

ACTIVITIES                    PERSON-IN-CHARGE
1.
2.
3.
4.

CHOICES          Physical (motor) development — cutting, painting, markers, crayons, glue, paste, string

Language — reading, puppets

Social emotional — dramatic play, games

MATERIALS NEEDED:

Instructors and learners need to develop appropriate work schedules. Since most laboratory experiences must fit within some time constraints, learners need to learn to plan their work to fit the allotted time. With younger learners, creating an actual time and work schedule may be appropriate. More mature learners may need only to develop a sequence of tasks or an overall plan for their work, rather than tie tasks to specific times.

The instructor is also responsible for the development of any ancillary materials to be used in the laboratory. What types of prerequisite readings or activities are necessary to best prepare learners for the practice experience? What worksheets or logs will they need throughout the laboratory? What types of extended activities or independent study opportunities would help extend the learning of the laboratory activity? These associated activities may make the difference in helping a learner process the information learned from the laboratory.

The instructor can help the learner grasp the critical elements of the laboratory and transfer them to new situations by debriefing following the laboratory experience. Thus, the hands-on experience does not become an end in itself, but rather a vehicle for moving learners toward the desired outcomes. During the debriefing, learners have an opportunity to evaluate the laboratory experience and to engage in thoughtful analysis of the experience. Learners can reflect on what has occurred, analyze the activities of the laboratory, and create meaning or learning from these activities. Instructors should develop questions, discuss applications, and assist learners in formulating generalizations from their experience. These higher order outcomes might not occur automatically as a result of the experience itself. The instructor is responsible for structuring the type of laboratory evaluation that allows students to think about "Why?" "What if..." "How might I have..." "What if next time..."

## ADVANTAGES AND DISADVANTAGES OF THE LABORATORY

Laboratories are excellent learning activities. Creative instructors will think beyond their traditional uses and structure activities in the laboratory to involve appropriate practice in all life skill areas.

Because laboratories involve practice in a realistic situation, they allow learners to exercise decision-making and problem-solving skills. Learners have a chance to see the consequences of their choices. Laboratories may allow learners to objectively apply principles or generalizations they have learned.

Laboratories typically motivate learners because of the high level of learner involvement. They meet the learning style needs of learners who need a "hands-on" experience to best learn. Laboratory experiences have the potential of getting all learners involved in their own learning. An additional advantage of the laboratory is the opportunity for developing and practicing process skills. These may include teamwork skills, leadership skills, and group interaction skills. Learners may also have the opportunity to practice time management, planning and organizational skills. These skills may be the "content" or primary skills learned in the laboratory, or the "process" or secondary skills learned in a laboratory.

Laboratories are, however, generally resource intensive. They tend to require large amounts of planning and instructional time. Also, equipment and material costs may be high. The instructor needs to decide whether or not the learner outcome is best met through this type of resource and labor intensive activity.

Another possible disadvantage of the use of the laboratory experience is that the work load within the laboratory might not be evenly shared. As with any type of group or team activity, instructors need to plan carefully to avoid one or two persons taking all of the responsibility for the group. The principles employed in cooperative learning may be applied to the laboratory activity to avoid this potential disadvantage.

Finally, if laboratories are not carefully planned and their purpose clearly communicated, learners may miss the point of the activity. Consider, for example, a laboratory where learners are expected to observe the effect of heat on protein by applying heat to an egg. Without adequate preparation and a planned closure, the laboratory could become, in the eyes of the learners, merely a lesson on how to fry an egg. Figure 11-10 highlights some of the critical points for using an instructional laboratory.

---

**FIGURE 11-10. The Laboratory**

**Use when:**
- Learners need to practice a set of skills under supervision.
- Learners need to investigate a problem or experiment with alternatives under supervision.
- Learners need to apply processes or principles.

**To prepare:**
- Clearly define the purpose of the laboratory.
- Establish guidelines or procedures for the laboratory.
- Gather materials, equipment, or resources.
- Prepare follow-up activities, ancillary assignments, and debriefing discussion questions.

**During the laboratory:**
- Monitor the progress and needs of learners.
- Provide assistance when requested.

**Advantages:**
- Allows learners to apply or test what they have learned.
- Promotes problem solving and creative thinking.
- Motivates learners through a high degree of learner participation.
- Promotes teamwork and cooperation.

**Disadvantages:**
- Time and resource intensive.
- May not fully involve all learners on a team or in a work group.

# SUMMARY

When learners have the opportunity to actively participate in learning—to manipulate thoughts and ideas given different learning contexts—the amount learned can increase dramatically. Learning strategies such as debates, role-plays, games, simulations, and laboratories give learners responsibility for their own learning and can make learning more meaningful.

All action-oriented learning strategies require the teacher or facilitator to work through three steps. First, the facilitator must plan for and gather appropriate resources for the activity. Next, he or she must facilitate or monitor the activity. Finally, a debriefing or follow-up must occur. Action-oriented strategies are only effective if they truly match the desired learning outcome.

# REFERENCES AND RESOURCES

Abt, C.C. (1968). Games for Learning. In Boocock, S.S., & Schild, E.O. (Eds.), *Simulation games in learning*. Beverly Hills, CA: Sage.

Butler, J.J. (1988). Games and simulations: Creative educational alternatives. *Tech Trends*, *33*, 20-23.

Chamberlain, V.M. (1992). *Creative home economics instruction*. Lake Forest, IL: Glencoe.

Green, C.S., & Klug, H.G. (1990). Teaching critical thinking and writing through debates: An experimental evaluation. *Teaching Sociology*, *18*, 462-471.

Greenblat, C.S., & Duke, R.D. (1981). *Principles and practices of gaming-simulation*. Beverly Hills, CA: Sage.

Greer, P.S. (1990). The one minute clinical instructor: An application of the principles of the One Minute Manager. *Journal of Nursing Education*, *29*, 37-38.

Hall, P.J., Couch, A.S., Underwood, R.A. (1989). *Home economics instruction*. Lubbock, TX: Home Economics Curriculum Center, Texas Tech University.

Hawley, R.C. (1974). *Value exploration through role-playing*. Amherst, MA: ERA Press.

Klemmer, R.H., & Smith, R.M. (1975). *Teaching about family relationships*. Minneapolis: Burgess.

Meier, N.R., Solem, A.R., & Maier, A.A. (1975). *The role-play technique*. LaJolla, CA: University Association.

Spitze, H. (1979). *Choosing techniques for teaching and learning* (2nd ed.). Washington, DC: Home Economics Education Association.

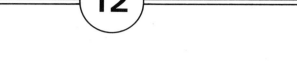

# SELECTING INSTRUCTIONAL MATERIALS

The types of instructional materials available range from the common textbook to a sophisticated, interactive satellite video system; from a simple bulletin board to a computer-activated model. Throughout the years you've spent in school, you have been exposed to a wide range of instructional materials. Nevertheless, when it comes time to design a learning experience, it is easy to forget the variety of materials that might be used. You may be tempted to rely on the kinds of materials that you like best, or that are most readily available. Figure 12-1 outlines the wide variety of aids that can be used to assist you in making a presentation.

## SELECTING INSTRUCTIONAL MATERIALS FOR LEARNERS

With so many types of instructional materials available, how do you decide which to use? When selecting any instructional material, from the commercially-prepared to those developed by product vendors for instructional purposes to those you prepare yourself, there are factors that should be considered. These factors relate to the content of the materials, the "fit" between the materials and the audience, and the usability of the materials as well as congruence with the curriculum design being used.

## CONTENT OF INSTRUCTIONAL MATERIALS

Factors to consider when reviewing the content of instructional materials include: accuracy (including evidence of bias); appropriateness of content to expected learner outcomes; real vs. symbolic requirements; and the need or desire for color, movement, and sound.

**FIGURE 12-1. Types of Instructional Materials**

I. Printed aids

  A. Books
    1. Textbooks
    2. Workbooks
    3. Manuals
    4. Reference books
    5. Fiction
  B. Newspapers
  C. Magazines
  D. Pamphlets/bulletins
  E. Photographs
  F. Charts

II. Audio aids

  A. Tape recordings/records/CDs
  B. Telephone
  C. Radio

III. Audiovisual aids

  A. Films (16 mm, filmstrips)
  B. Television (commercial, public, cable, satellite, videotapes)
  C. Slides
  D. Computers (including video disk systems)

IV. Displays

  A. Exhibits
    1. Maps
    2. Globes
    3. Models or mock-ups
    4. Mobiles
  B. Display boards
    1. Feltboards or flannel board
    2. Magnetic board
    3. Hook and loop board
    4. Pegboard
    5. Bulletin boards
    6. Posters

## Accuracy

The information contained in the instructional materials must be accurate. Just because materials have been professionally produced or elaborately packaged does not guarantee they are accurate.

There are several reasons why information may be inaccurate. Inaccuracies may occur due to the passage of time. Materials may have been produced prior to important research or revision of theories in a particular area. For example, teaching materials developed before the discovery of AIDS might inaccurately convey the life-threatening nature of sexually transmitted diseases.

Materials may suggest inaccurate messages due to the biases of their producers. For example, certain food producers may suggest that their product is "not fattening" based on a calorie count when the food is, in fact, very high in fat, based on the percentage of calories from fat.

Other materials may have key information missing, or be incomplete so that they portray an inaccurate message. A videotape that emphasizes only the advantages of credit might not give an accurate picture of the disadvantages of credit use and potential overuse. It cannot be assumed that commercially produced materials have been developed by content experts. It is necessary to screen all instructional materials for content validity or accuracy.

## Bias

Besides accuracy of content, the instructional materials must be screened for evidence of bias. In recent years most educators have become increasingly aware of the subtle and not-so-subtle forms of sex bias in instructional materials. Instructors should examine materials for evidence of photographs and descriptions of men and women cast in traditional and stereotypical roles: women as passive and docile, men as tough and aggressive; women as homemakers and caregivers of children, men in the paid workforce; women as nurses and teachers, men as doctors and lawyers. The obvious occurrences may be easy to detect, but instructors need to be conscious of balance even in good materials. Instructional materials that imply that women are expected to do household cleaning and that men are the only humans who understand the difference between a fan belt and a dipstick when caring for a car are only two examples of sex-biased materials. Men, women, boys, and girls should be portrayed in about equal numbers with equal status, in equivalent roles.

Sex bias may not be the only type of bias evident in instructional materials. Instructors should also be alert to racial and ethnic bias, as well as age, religious, or political bias. Again, stereotypes may be played out in subtle ways. For example, families in case studies with low socioeconomic status may be consistently given particular ethnic names. Other instructional materials may fail to recognize certain value positions, traditions, or aspects of culture that might influence the content of the material or how the content is received by the audience. Certain ethnic or racial groups may be underrepresented in visual media, or be cast in stereotypical roles. Particular religious and age groups may also be treated in this way. The elderly are vulnerable to this kind of typecasting. Professionals need to be sensitive to these types of bias in instructional materials.

## Usefulness in Achieving Expected Learner Outcomes

After it has been determined that the content is accurate, the usefulness of the instructional resource must be assessed. Materials are only "resources" when they assist in attaining selected learner outcomes. In other words, unless the instructional material is appropriate to the specific instructional objective or outcome, it should not be used. Sometimes instructors decide to use a resource because it appears to be somewhat compatible to the topic. Other times, a good instructional resource may be used to determine a learner outcome.

Neither of these approaches is appropriate for deciding to use an instructional resource.

The selection process should begin by asking, "What should learners be able to do as a result of instruction?" followed by, "What types of experiences and materials will help learners achieve that outcome?" For example, consumer specialists who have determined that learners should be able to develop a budget for their families should resist the temptation to show a videotape on advertising just because it is related to consumer education, or to the problems of his or her learners, or the interests of the learners. Unless the instructional material relates to the learner outcome, it is not an appropriate resource.

## Real vs. Symbolic Representations

There are some additional content considerations relating to the "reality" of the resource. Consider an example of a food science instructor who has been lucky enough to find some models of fats: saturated, unsaturated, and polyunsaturated. The models are actual representations of the molecules that make up these fats. How helpful would these models be in aiding students' understanding of the differences in these fats? One factor to consider is how real vs. symbolic the materials are. In general, the more realistic a representation, the easier it will be for learners to grasp it. The more abstract and symbolic the representation, the more difficult it may be for learners to comprehend it.

One author (Dale, 1969) has classified instructional materials on a type of continuum (in the form of a "cone of experience") from the most concrete to the most symbolic. Materials that rely primarily on verbal communication — on the symbolism of words — are at the top of the cone. Charts and graphs are near the top, too, because they are visual symbols. A model (like the fat models described earlier) is a type of "substitute experience," and while it is still a visual symbol, it makes the concept of different molecular configurations easier to comprehend than a verbal explanation. Pictures, photographs, slides, and videotapes are even more concrete and are near the "real" or bottom of the cone. In selecting instructional resources, instructors should try to select materials that will make the learning as concrete as possible.

## Color, Movement, and Sound Considerations

Other considerations have to do with the color, motion, and sound of instructional materials. You might question whether it is critical that the instructional materials use color vs. black and white representations. For example, it might be difficult to depict the identifying characteristics of various types of meat with a black and white photograph or filmstrip.

Is movement necessary, or is a static representation acceptable? Sometimes watching a procedure in stages through the use of photographs, slides, illustrations or a filmstrip is desirable. Looking at still pictures to review a procedure step-by-step at a slow pace and being able to review certain steps helps to clarify each phase. Other times, however, movement may be desirable. Still photographs or illustrations may not be able to capture the subtleties of movement or the coordination of movements required in certain procedures. It would probably be difficult, for example, to demonstrate cardiopulmonary resuscitation (CPR) without movement.

Another criterion may be the desirability of sound. Is sound necessary, or is the printed word or picture sufficient? Contrasting the different cries of a baby and their meanings might be impossible on the written page, and yet, a description of how to prepare a bottle can be as easily read as heard. In fact, printed instructional materials may be more desirable when learners need to frequently refer to the resource, or when they need to work through materials at their own pace. While an audio or videotape can be reversed and replayed, the written word can be reviewed, read at an individual's own pace, and doesn't require technological support.

At times, however, the instructor may decide that a sound/picture relationship is needed, as provided by videotapes, films, filmstrip/tapes, some computer software, and slide/tapes. In order for the learner to achieve a particular outcome, the instructor may need a resource that both tells and shows the learner. If both sound and picture are needed, the instructor will probably need to select an audiovisual resource over traditional print materials.

## APPROPRIATENESS TO THE AUDIENCE

When selecting instructional materials, it is important to consider the appropriateness of the instructional material for a given audience. Even an accurate, well-developed instructional material will be ineffective if it is not well matched to the audience. Instructors need to review the materials in light of who will use them. Factors to be considered include age, reading level, and size of audience.

### Age

Is the instructional material appropriate for the age of the members of the audience? Adolescent audiences may have difficulty relating to materials that are intended for homemakers or new parents. The examples, photographs, or suggested activities may be irrelevant to the adolescent in the classroom or youth organization. Likewise, families in an agency setting may not be able to effectively relate to materials that have been produced for adolescents or preschool children. There are, of course, some types of materials that are not age-specific. Instructors need to examine resources carefully to determine if there is a specific age for which the materials were designed.

### Reading Level

If the instructional material requires reading, the instructor should be sure to examine the reading level to see if it is appropriate for the intended audience. The instructor may not know the specific reading level of his or her learners, but the learners' educational level is often a clue. Learners with limited formal education or limited English language proficiency can be expected to have

## FIGURE 12-2. Calculating Readability

1. Select samples of the reading material.
   a. Select several random samples.
   b. Begin each sample at the beginning of a paragraph.

2. Count the words.
   a. Count 100 words from each sample.
   b. Count hyphenated words or contractions as one word.
   c. Count numbers and letters as words if separated by spaces. For example, "1,062" and "D.O.A." would each count as one word.

3. Count the number of sentences.
   a. Count complete units of thought. A "sentence" could end with a semicolon or colon as well as a period.
   b. If a sentence contains "but" or "and," count as *one* sentence.

4. Figure the average sentence length.
   a. Use all of the samples selected.
   b. Total the words in all of the samples and divide by the number of sentences.

5. Count the one-syllable words.
   a. Count all of the one-syllable words in all of the samples.
   b. Divide the total number of one-syllable words by the number of samples.

6. Figure the reading ease score.
   a. Find the average sentence length and the average number of one-syllable words per sample on the Flesch Reading Ease Index Table. Look up the reading ease index number.
   b. Use the Flesch Conversion Table to determine the estimated reading grade.

*(continued)*

a lower-than-average reading level. Using materials written for younger learners is rarely the answer since the content, illustrations, and photographs are often inappropriate. If appropriate reading materials cannot be found, alternative types of instructional resources should be used.

There are several methods for quickly assessing the reading level of materials. The Flesch Formula is one method that can be applied (Farr, Jenkins, & Patterson, 1969). Follow the steps outlined in Figure 12-2 to assess the reading level.

## Size of Audience

Some instructional materials work well with large groups, some are better suited for small groups, and others are really best used by an individual. While it might be quite difficult for 300 learners in an auditorium to view the molecular models described previously, this resource would work well in small groups or in a typical secondary classroom. Some materials, such as slides, may work equally well with 10 or 100 learners. Still, other resources can only

FIGURE 12-2. *Continued.*

**FLESCH READING EASE INDEX TABLE**

### Number of One-Syllable Words per Hundred Words

|    | 84 | 82 | 80 | 78 | 76 | 74 | 72 | 70 | 68 | 66 | 64 | 62 | 60 | 58 | 56 | 54 | 52 | 50 | 48 | 46 | 44 | 42 | 40 |
|----|----|----|----|----|----|----|----|----|----|----|----|----|----|----|----|----|----|----|----|----|----|----|----|
| 9  | 94 | 90 | 87 | 84 | 81 | 78 | 74 | 72 | 68 | 65 | 61 | 58 | 56 | 52 | 49 | 45 | 42 | 40 | 36 | 33 | 29 | 27 | 23 |
| 10 | 93 | 89 | 86 | 83 | 80 | 77 | 73 | 71 | 67 | 64 | 60 | 57 | 55 | 51 | 48 | 44 | 41 | 39 | 35 | 32 | 28 | 26 | 22 |
| 11 | 92 | 88 | 85 | 82 | 79 | 76 | 72 | 70 | 66 | 63 | 59 | 56 | 54 | 50 | 47 | 43 | 40 | 38 | 34 | 31 | 27 | 25 | 21 |
| 12 | 91 | 87 | 84 | 81 | 78 | 75 | 71 | 69 | 65 | 62 | 58 | 55 | 53 | 49 | 46 | 42 | 39 | 37 | 33 | 30 | 26 | 24 | 20 |
| 13 | 90 | 86 | 83 | 80 | 77 | 74 | 70 | 68 | 64 | 61 | 57 | 54 | 52 | 48 | 45 | 41 | 38 | 35 | 32 | 29 | 25 | 23 | 19 |
| 14 | 89 | 85 | 82 | 79 | 76 | 72 | 69 | 67 | 63 | 60 | 56 | 53 | 50 | 47 | 44 | 40 | 37 | 34 | 31 | 28 | 24 | 22 | 18 |
| 15 | 88 | 84 | 81 | 78 | 75 | 71 | 68 | 66 | 62 | 59 | 55 | 52 | 49 | 46 | 43 | 39 | 36 | 33 | 30 | 27 | 23 | 21 | 17 |
| 16 | 87 | 83 | 80 | 77 | 74 | 70 | 67 | 65 | 61 | 58 | 54 | 51 | 48 | 45 | 42 | 38 | 35 | 32 | 29 | 26 | 22 | 20 | 16 |
| 17 | 86 | 82 | 79 | 76 | 73 | 69 | 66 | 64 | 60 | 57 | 53 | 50 | 47 | 44 | 41 | 37 | 34 | 31 | 28 | 25 | 21 | 19 | 15 |
| 18 | 85 | 81 | 78 | 75 | 72 | 68 | 65 | 63 | 59 | 56 | 52 | 49 | 46 | 43 | 40 | 36 | 33 | 30 | 27 | 24 | 20 | 18 | 14 |
| 19 | 83 | 80 | 77 | 74 | 71 | 67 | 64 | 61 | 58 | 55 | 51 | 48 | 45 | 42 | 39 | 35 | 32 | 29 | 26 | 23 | 19 | 17 | 13 |
| 20 | 82 | 79 | 76 | 73 | 70 | 66 | 63 | 60 | 57 | 54 | 50 | 47 | 44 | 41 | 38 | 34 | 31 | 28 | 25 | 22 | 18 | 16 | 12 |
| 21 | 81 | 78 | 75 | 72 | 69 | 65 | 62 | 59 | 56 | 53 | 49 | 46 | 43 | 40 | 37 | 33 | 30 | 27 | 24 | 21 | 17 | 15 | 11 |
| 22 | 80 | 77 | 74 | 71 | 68 | 64 | 61 | 58 | 55 | 52 | 48 | 45 | 42 | 39 | 36 | 32 | 29 | 26 | 23 | 20 | 16 | 14 | 10 |
| 23 | 79 | 76 | 73 | 70 | 67 | 63 | 60 | 57 | 54 | 51 | 47 | 44 | 41 | 38 | 35 | 31 | 28 | 25 | 22 | 19 | 15 | 13 | 9  |
| 24 | 78 | 75 | 72 | 69 | 66 | 62 | 59 | 56 | 53 | 50 | 46 | 43 | 40 | 37 | 34 | 30 | 27 | 24 | 21 | 18 | 14 | 12 | 8  |
| 25 | 77 | 74 | 71 | 68 | 65 | 61 | 58 | 55 | 52 | 49 | 45 | 42 | 39 | 36 | 33 | 29 | 26 | 23 | 20 | 17 | 13 | 11 | 7  |
| 26 | 76 | 73 | 70 | 67 | 64 | 60 | 57 | 54 | 51 | 48 | 44 | 41 | 38 | 35 | 32 | 28 | 25 | 22 | 19 | 16 | 12 | 10 | 6  |
| 27 | 75 | 72 | 69 | 66 | 63 | 59 | 56 | 53 | 50 | 47 | 43 | 40 | 37 | 34 | 31 | 27 | 24 | 21 | 18 | 15 | 11 | 9  | 5  |
| 28 | 74 | 71 | 68 | 65 | 62 | 58 | 55 | 52 | 49 | 46 | 42 | 39 | 36 | 33 | 30 | 26 | 23 | 20 | 17 | 13 | 10 | 8  | 4  |
| 29 | 73 | 70 | 67 | 64 | 61 | 57 | 54 | 51 | 48 | 45 | 41 | 38 | 35 | 32 | 29 | 25 | 22 | 19 | 16 | 12 | 9  | 7  | 3  |
| 30 | 72 | 69 | 66 | 63 | 60 | 56 | 53 | 50 | 47 | 44 | 40 | 37 | 34 | 31 | 27 | 24 | 21 | 18 | 15 | 11 | 8  | 6  | 2  |
| 31 | 71 | 68 | 65 | 62 | 59 | 55 | 52 | 49 | 46 | 43 | 39 | 36 | 33 | 30 | 26 | 23 | 20 | 17 | 14 | 10 | 7  | 5  | 1  |
| 32 | 70 | 67 | 64 | 61 | 58 | 54 | 51 | 48 | 45 | 42 | 38 | 35 | 32 | 29 | 25 | 22 | 19 | 16 | 13 | 9  | 6  | 4  |    |
| 33 | 69 | 66 | 63 | 60 | 57 | 53 | 50 | 47 | 44 | 41 | 37 | 34 | 31 | 28 | 24 | 21 | 18 | 15 | 12 | 8  | 5  | 2  |    |
| 34 | 68 | 65 | 61 | 59 | 56 | 52 | 49 | 46 | 43 | 40 | 36 | 33 | 30 | 27 | 23 | 20 | 17 | 14 | 11 | 7  | 4  | 1  |    |
| 35 | 67 | 64 | 60 | 58 | 55 | 51 | 48 | 45 | 42 | 38 | 35 | 32 | 29 | 26 | 22 | 19 | 16 | 13 | 10 | 6  | 3  |    |    |
| 36 | 66 | 63 | 59 | 57 | 54 | 50 | 47 | 44 | 41 | 37 | 34 | 31 | 28 | 25 | 21 | 18 | 15 | 12 | 9  | 5  | 2  |    |    |
| 37 | 65 | 62 | 58 | 56 | 53 | 49 | 46 | 43 | 40 | 36 | 33 | 30 | 27 | 24 | 20 | 17 | 14 | 11 | 8  | 4  | 1  |    |    |
| 38 | 64 | 61 | 57 | 55 | 52 | 48 | 45 | 42 | 39 | 35 | 32 | 29 | 26 | 23 | 19 | 16 | 13 | 10 | 7  | 3  |    |    |    |

**FLESCH CONVERSION TABLE**

| Reading Ease Score | Estimated Reading Grade |
|---|---|
| 90 to 100 | 5th Grade |
| 80 to 90 | 6th Grade |
| 70 to 80 | 7th Grade |
| 60 to 70 | 8th to 9th Grade |
| 50 to 60 | 10th to 12th Grade |
| 30 to 50 | 13th to 16th Grade (College) |
| 0 to 30 | College Graduate |

be used with one or a few learners. A personal computer, for example, may be most appropriate for one to two learners unless a projection device is used so that a group can see an enlarged image of the screen. Instructors should consider the size of the audience before selecting instructional materials to determine whether or not the resource would be an asset in a particular learning situation.

# USABILITY

A final factor to consider in selecting an instructional resource is usability. Usability factors include cost and versatility, preparation and maintenance requirements, time, and documentation.

## Cost and Value

Cost of the material not only refers to the actual dollars spent to purchase the material, but any costs necessary to prepare the material for use, or costs on a per-use basis. Sophisticated or elaborate instructional materials can be quite costly. If the initial purchase price is beyond the budget or uses a disproportionate amount of the budget, you may need to reconsider your purchasing decision.

Besides the initial cost of the resource, a charge may be assessed for use of an instructional material as well. A computer used for data base searches may meet all the other criteria for an excellent instructional resource, but if an instructor is charged $50 per hour or an access fee into the data base, the resource may cease to be affordable.

Another consideration related to cost of an instructional resource has to do with the versatility of the resource to instruction. Materials may not be worth the cost if used only sparingly, under very special circumstances, with a very limited audience, or by only one instructor.

Figuring a cost-per-use is probably well worth the effort required. For example, slides, models, or display boards may have a high initial purchase price, even though the cost-per-use is slight. Having data on cost-per-use would make it easier to differentiate between reasonable and unreasonable purchases.

## Preparation and Maintenance Requirements

To be usable, an instructional resource must be reasonably easy to prepare and maintain. Storage requirements need to be considered. The instructor needs to compare the value received from instruction with the effort needed to use the material. For example, a cow's heart is an excellent instructional material to use in demonstrating the buildup of plaque within the heart valves, but storage and care are important considerations.

Security and environmental conditions may have to be considered. Computer software may provide excellent instruction in many circumstances. However, security for the computers and even the software is an issue. Further, computers do not operate well in adverse environments such as very damp areas or where there is a lot of static electricity.

Maintenance, care, and parts replacement must also be considered. Some materials and equipment require regular cleaning or tune-ups. Some are particularly vulnerable to handling and may be easily damaged or broken.

## Time

Time is another usability factor. How much time does it take to prepare and organize the materials? How much time does it take to get the material set up and ready to use, and then to proceed through it with learners? Some materials, like exhibits and display boards, may be time-intensive in their preparation, but can be used over a long period of time. Manuals and textbooks may require no teacher preparation time, and again, can be used flexibly by learners. Some computer software programs, videotapes, or filmstrips, however, require specific blocks of time for their use. The amount of instructor preparation time and instructional-use time will influence how usable the material is.

## Documentation

Finally, materials must be of high technical quality with good documentation. **Documentation** refers to the directions and ancillary materials that accompany a resource. Computer software programs, for example, usually are packaged with a set of directions that provide detailed information on the program, its objectives, features, equipment requirements, and follow-up activities. This documentation helps the instructor determine how closely the instructional material matches his or her content and audience, and how usable it is in the learning situation—the three primary factors to consider when selecting instructional materials.

Figure 12-3 summarizes the factors that should be considered in selecting instructional materials. Use this summary to assess any materials you might consider using.

**FIGURE 12-3. Criteria for Selection of Instructional Materials**

Are the instructional materials:

### CONTENT CONSIDERATIONS

- up-to-date?
- complete?
- clearly matched to the expected learner outcomes?
- as realistic as possible?
- presented in color (if necessary)?
- designed to show movement (when necessary)?
- presented with sound (if necessary)?
- unbiased with respect to gender, role, ethnic or racial background, and age?

### APPROPRIATENESS TO AUDIENCE

- matched to the age of the audience?
- appropriate for the reading level of the audience?
- appropriate to the size of the audience?

### USABILITY

- worth the "cost-per-use"?
- reasonably easy to use, store, and maintain?
- worth the time necessary to prepare and use?
- an appropriate length for the instructional setting?
- clearly and carefully documented?

# SOURCES OF INSTRUCTIONAL MATERIALS

A previous section of this chapter made it clear just how wide the variety of instructional materials is! All kinds of materials and media are available or can be developed to help learners to learn.

There are many sources of instructional materials. By using the guidelines for selection, even the beginning instructor can successfully identify excellent instructional materials.

## COMMERCIALLY-PREPARED MATERIALS

Commercially-prepared materials are abundant. Companies sell a wide variety of instructional aids that range from chalk to lighted display boards. Some have product lines that address selected content areas specifically.

There are many ways to learn about commercially-prepared materials. New graduates are often bombarded with the catalogs from companies wanting to sell their wares. Advertisements in professional publications provide an overview of a company's product line, and more detailed catalogs are generally available by request.

A visit to the exhibits area of a regional, state, or national professional meeting can help in locating commercially-prepared instructional materials. Vendors use exhibits to make contact with potential customers and to expand their mailing lists. In the case of regional or state meetings, you may also have an opportunity to meet company representatives serving your geographic region. Some company representatives make regular visits to potential customers to make certain you are aware of the latest products available.

Instructors also learn about high quality, usable materials by talking with colleagues about materials they have found particularly useful. A reference librarian can also assist you in finding the names of companies carrying products in which you might be interested. Many states have regional library/media centers available to educators where comprehensive listings are maintained and where there are many materials available on loan.

Commercially-prepared materials have several advantages. They are usually developed by professionals using quality paper, printing, and color. Audiovisual materials may use music and professional actors yielding a high quality commercial production. As such, these materials usually appeal to audiences. In most cases, a content expert has contributed to product development. Finally, cost of commercially-prepared materials may be affordable, although some items will require more of an investment.

There are, however, drawbacks to commercially-prepared materials. In order for a product to appeal to a large number of customers, it may have to include information unrelated to your particular instructional objectives or exclude information that you think is critical. It may also be designed to reach a wide variety of audiences and so lack appeal for your particular audience. Just as with any other instructional materials, commercially-prepared materials can become dated. If the initial cost of a commercially-prepared material is high, instructors may find it tempting to use the material beyond its legitimate "life." Finally, your budget may not allow the purchase of commercially-prepared materials.

## PRODUCT VENDOR/PROMOTIONAL MATERIALS

If you are operating within a limited budget, you may wish to consider materials available from product vendors. Many large companies develop instructional materials related to their product lines. For example, a company that manufactures cleaning products might develop instructional materials on how to clean; a firm selling baby food might provide instruction on infant nutrition.

You can become aware of instructional materials available from product vendors by reading professional publications. Such publications often provide a card where you can request multiple copies of materials from product vendors. Many product vendors are also exhibitors at regional, state, and national meetings and can provide free instructional materials on site or by mail immediately following the meeting.

The chief advantage of instructional materials prepared by product vendors is that they are often inexpensive or free. These instructional materials are often a form of product promotion similar to advertisements. Because they are designed to promote their products or points of view, they are well-produced to attract an audience. Print materials, for example, are usually in full color with attractive illustrations, while audio-visual resources contain music and professional actors just as commercially-prepared materials do.

The potential drawbacks that apply to commercially-prepared materials also apply to materials prepared by product vendors. Such materials may not be directed to your specific audience and may not address the particular instructional objectives you had in mind.

Product promotional materials have some additional instructional drawbacks as well. First, the materials may be narrow in scope. For example, personal hygiene materials might focus on shampoo and soap (products the vendor sells) while ignoring dental hygiene products (which the vendor does not sell).

Second, such materials may not be entirely objective. The strengths and weaknesses of a particular practice or product may not be covered in product vendor materials if pointing out weaknesses may cause a person to think twice before purchasing the product.

In cases where controversy over a product exists, product vendor materials may present a deceptive or biased point of view. For example, materials might cite only research supporting a particular practice rather than research that treats a controversial practice more even-handedly.

Finally, product vendor-prepared materials are subtle (and sometimes not so subtle) forms of advertisement and so frequently feature brand names. Learners may be distracted from important instructional objectives by brand names. An unfortunate example of this would be low-income adults learning to prepare economical meals using instructional materials featuring high-cost, brand name items.

## INSTRUCTOR-PREPARED MATERIALS

If you cannot locate the commercially-prepared materials that you need or you cannot afford them, then you might want to prepare your own materials. Instructor-produced materials and noninstruction-based materials can be quite useful in instruction. With a minimum of equipment (scissors, overhead transparencies, cameras, newspapers, product packages, etc.), instructors can prepare very effective learning materials. In fact, with the right equipment and some know-how, instructors can prepare any one of the types of instructional materials similar to those already identified.

Instructor-produced materials have a number of advantages. First, such materials are prepared with a specific audience and set of instructional objectives in mind. They speak directly to the instruction being provided and are most directly related to the instructional activities planned. Frequently, instructor-produced materials are low- or no-cost. When appropriately done, such materials avoid the pitfalls of commercially-prepared or product vendor-prepared materials.

Disadvantages of instructor-produced materials relate primarily to their preparation. The instructor must have the time, materials, equipment, and expertise to prepare the instructional materials desired. In addition, the final product may not be as polished as professionally-prepared materials.

## NONINSTRUCTION-BASED MATERIALS

A final source of instructional materials are materials not designed for instruction, but products that would assist in meeting instructional objectives. For example, many types of literature can be used to delineate issues for discussion. Films, television programs, music, newspaper articles, short stories, plays, works of art, and cartoons are all examples of noninstructional materials that could be used in instruction.

A concise listing of the criteria to consider in choosing instructional materials from a particular source is provided in Figure 12-4.

## USING INSTRUCTIONAL MATERIALS

Almost everyone has been a victim of misused instructional materials: the software that would not drive the computer, the overhead transparency that could not be read from two feet away, the film that broke in a dozen places, or the model that could not be manipulated correctly. Instructional materials, carefully selected for the audience and perfectly matched to the objective are only as good as their execution or use. Of course, there are unavoidable glitches that cannot be controlled by the instructor (for example, a power outage).

**FIGURE 12-4. Considerations in Selecting Instructional Materials**

Some important considerations in selecting materials from certain sources are listed below. Consider these criteria *in addition to those already identified* in Figure 12.3. Recognize that any material that is not designed for your audience and your objectives is an inappropriate selection no matter how available and technically sophisticated it is.

**Commercially-Prepared Materials**

Are commercially-prepared materials:
- of sufficient technical quality to justify the price?
- available at a "reasonable" cost given their potential "life"?

**Product Vendor Materials**

Are the instructional materials from a product vendor:
- appropriate in scope (do not focus on such a narrow range of ideas/products as to be misleading)?
- objective in their presentation of products?
- objective in their presentation of controversial issues?
- subtle in their use of product/brand names?
- void of unintentional stereotyping or careless wording?

Successful use of instructional materials requires that the instructor: practice using the selected instructional materials; prepare students to participate; use the instructional materials in a way in which they were intended; follow up on use of the material; and evaluate the material after use.

# PRACTICE USING INSTRUCTIONAL MATERIALS

Even under the best circumstances, instructional materials do not always function as intended – the bulb in the projector burns out, the projection screen is stuck (closed!), or the equipment delivered to show the videotape is one format and you need another. However, many disasters can be avoided if you practice using the material and check equipment in advance.

All instructional materials should be read, viewed, or tried well before using them with learners. For example, a computer program should be loaded, executed, and all documentation read prior to use with an audience. Overhead transparencies should be proofread, placed on an overhead projector, and carefully checked from all angles for readability. A videotape should be viewed in its entirety and checked for length, visibility, and content. It is unwise to rely on catalog copy and advertising descriptions of instructional materials.

A review of instructional materials should take place well in advance of the time you actually intend to use the material. There is nothing more frustrating than finding out an hour in advance of a big lecture that the fancy, multi-part overhead transparencies you intended to use are taped together so that they cannot be flipped.

When possible, practice with instructional materials should be conducted in the actual classroom, auditorium, office, or other setting where the instruction will be taking place. An overhead projector may be useless in a room that cannot be darkened; an 18-inch television monitor is not satisfactory in a 100-person auditorium. Plan to arrive at a presentation location at least an hour prior to the time the session is to begin. This allows time to check everything out and to be mentally ready to begin.

Practicing with the actual equipment is helpful. Although most of the principles of running a video cassette recorder are easily applied to many models, there is every chance that you will be given the model with the "hidden" power switch. If actual practice is not possible, at least allow enough time to check that all equipment is present and in working order.

Involving an advisory committee or group of test students when practicing is also helpful. They may see things you don't.

## PREPARING STUDENTS TO PARTICIPATE

The instructor time that goes into selecting and practicing with an instructional material may seem to guarantee its success. However, only the instructor has had the benefit of thinking about and planning for use of the instructional material; only he or she knows how it "fits" into the learning environment unless students are prepared to participate with the material.

The basic tenets of lesson planning should be applied when preparing students to work with instructional materials. Learners should have a clear idea of the purpose of using materials. Learners also need clear directions about how to use the material. When complex activities accompany the use of instructional materials, it is sometimes helpful to go through a "dry run" so learners have an opportunity to ask questions about procedures, expectations, etc. For example, you might plan to use an ergometer in small groups before beginning individual experiments with it.

## FOLLOW-UP

Instructional materials require follow-up. After learners have finished using the instructional material, plan time to answer learner questions, reiterate important points, and reinforce learner outcomes.

## EVALUATE

It is important to evaluate instructional materials as soon after use as possible. One of the best sources of input on the value of instructional materials is the audience. Take a few minutes after using an instructional material to solicit learner opinion—either formally with a brief evaluation sheet, or informally as part of the summary or close of the class. Did the instructional material contribute to attaining learner outcomes? Did learners enjoy using the instructional materials? Did the materials perform as expected? These are all important questions to ask. Since instructional materials are generally

**FIGURE 12-5.** **Using Instructional Materials**

When using instructional materials, the instructor should:
- practice using the materials:
  - well in advance of the time when the materials are to be used with learners.
  - with an advisory committee or volunteer students.
  - in the setting in which they will be used (if possible).
  - with the equipment to be used (if possible).
- prepare students to participate by:
  - introducing the instructional material and tying it to desired learner outcomes.
  - giving clear directions.
  - allowing for student practice with the material (when appropriate).
- follow-up after materials are used by:
  - answering learner questions.
  - reiterating important points.
  - reinforcing learner outcomes.
- evaluate materials by:
  - determining whether learner outcomes were attained.
  - soliciting student opinions regarding the instructional materials.
  - assessing whether the materials performed as expected.

"resource-intensive" (They cost a good deal or require quite a bit of instructor time to prepare.), evaluating their use and refining them is worth the effort.

A checklist to help you plan for and evaluate use of an instructional material is provided in Figure 12-5.

## SUMMARY

Instructional materials are tools for teaching. They can help the instructor achieve his or her instructional goals, but there is nothing magical in the tools themselves. Just as a carpenter carefully selects the right tools for the job, instructors, too, must be deliberate in their choice of instructional resources. Instructors must look beyond just the quality of the resource to how well that resource will work with their learners in their instructional setting with particular objectives. Instructors can choose from a wide variety of materials and sources. Creative instructors soon begin not only to develop skills in matching the right resource to their instruction, but to recognize the value to instruction of all types of materials and media in their environment.

## REFERENCES AND RESOURCES

Dale, E. (1969). *Audiovisual methods in teaching* (3rd ed.). New York: Holt, Rinehart and Winston.

Dickey, J.P., & Hendricks, R.C. (1991). Visual perception qualities of instructional materials. *Clearing House, 64*, 168-170.

Farr, N.J., & Jenkins, J.J. (1969). Simplification of Flesch reading ease formula, *Journal of Applied Psychology, 35*, 333.

Frymier, J.R. (1990). Students' preferences for curriculum materials. *High School Journal, 74*, 123-131.

Olson, J. (1990). Do not use as directed: Corporate materials in the schools. *Educational Leadership, 47*, 79-80.

Powers, L.D. (1988). A conceptual approach for selecting instructional materials. *Agriculture Education Magazine, 61*, 22-23.

# TECHNOLOGY
# FOR INSTRUCTION

Suppose that the year is 2020. An extension professional prepares to attack a problem encountered by residents in rural Alaska. They recently have had several cases of food-borne illness and need to know what is causing the problem. The agent sent food samples to a university for analysis yesterday. A fax of the results came at noon. Apparently, an antibiotic-resistant strain of bacteria is the culprit. An electronic mail message to the extension professional's computer indicated Dr. Drake would be available for consultation at 3:00. The professional turns on a video networking system at 2:55 and prepares to moderate between Dr. Drake at the base university in Maine and rural Alaskans 500 miles from the extension office.

The scenario presented above is possible today and is likely to be a common occurrence by the beginning of the twenty-first century. Existing and emerging technologies will radically change the way people retrieve — and share — information. Today's technology has gone beyond film projectors and microcomputers to all kinds of video distance communications, curriculum management systems, and administrative networks for homes, schools, and communities (Mecklenburger, 1988).

Two technological systems are presently seeing increasingly wide application: computers and communication technologies. The following sections address emerging technologies with particular emphasis on the networking capabilities of computer and video technologies.

## COMPUTERS

Computers as used to communicate content or provide instruction are both the technology of today and tomorrow. While a 1989 study found that nearly

66 percent of surveyed teachers used computers in their classrooms, they also favored increased use (*Education Week*, 1989). Computers already play significant roles in instruction, but as the technology advances and as family and consumer sciences professionals become more adept at using this technology, computers are likely to play an expanded role in the instruction of learners. The possibilities of their use in helping to communicate are abundant.

## ADVANTAGES

One strength of computers is that they allow the instructor to extend learning opportunities. Computer data bases, for example, allow learners to seek and retrieve published and unpublished sources of information not locally available. Learners can research a particular topic through the use of a data base. Computer searching is likely to generate more current information than print indexes, and the search can be done quickly. It allows a much broader search than what could be done manually, and several topics can be searched simultaneously (Brooks & Touliatos, 1989). Through the use of other computer-related technology, like electronic mail, learners may also have the opportunity to use the resources beyond those of the learning environment.

The use of computers also allows instructors to target the individual differences of learners. Different types of software can be selected to meet the specific learning needs or abilities of learners. The cooperative extension agent, for example, may loan learners a computer software program that deals with a topic of specific interest such as investing options, nutritional analysis, or household energy conservation. This same instructor might use a common piece of software to work with individual learners. For instance, the investing options software might be used to work with learners to calculate long-term earnings given different amounts of savings or investments in various options. In the classroom, learners with different abilities may use the same software, but progress through the material at their own pace. Software that branches to levels of increasing difficulty allows learners to work to their own level of achievement.

Computers may allow the classroom instructor or the instructor of non-formal education to aid the slower learner by personalizing experiences, thus avoiding the pressure and frustration that may be experienced from the demands of uniform group instruction. For example, a student may practice calculating sales tax or making recipe conversions as long as necessary to become successful.

The use of the computer also helps reinforce basic computer-use skills and develop confidence in using technology that is bound to be necessary in the lives of the learners. Learners who have the opportunity to use the computer with the help and direction of an instructor may be more likely to access computer technology at work, at the bank, for their grocery shopping, or for home

## FIGURE 13-1. Advantages of Computers in Family and Consumer Sciences Instruction

- Increase access to information (data bases, electronic mail)
- Meet individual learner needs
- Respond to individual learner abilities
- Familiarize students with everyday technologies

record keeping (Shane, 1987). Figure 13-1 summarizes the advantages of computers in communicating family and consumer sciences content.

## USES

Clearly, the computer has many advantages, but in what ways is the computer used as an instructional tool? Computers can be used in instructional settings, both formal and nonformal, in a variety of ways.

A common instructional use of computers, particularly in business settings, is information retrieval. For example, an appliance company may keep detailed product and service information on computers. Customer service representatives can quickly access this information as they respond to individual requests for information.

In its ultimate form, such information can be directly available to consumers via computer networks using hypertext. **Hypertext** allows nonlinear access to information — a user can ask a general question or even indicate "tell me more" to learn about a product or service.

The computer may be used by instructors to develop instructional materials. With the use of the computer, activities can be generated that are appropriate to the instructional objective. Consider, for example, an instructor who is presenting material on automobile insurance. Worksheets can be developed that provide learners with computer graphs and charts listing current local rates, with mathematical problems requiring learners to calculate various costs. The computer can generate the worksheets, complete with answer keys, for the teacher. Additionally, programs are available that allow instructors to create puzzles, games, and other types of displays.

The instructor can also use the computer for recordkeeping, testing, and instructional prescription. Computer-managed instructional packages are available that allow teachers to record, weight, and calculate grades, track students' progress on identified objectives, and generate tests from a question pool. Instructors may also choose to develop their own management systems to maintain records that are specifically appropriate to their own instructional settings.

Computers are also useful in demonstrations and presentations. Traditionally, films and videotapes have been used in lieu of live demonstrations or presentations that were difficult, complicated, expensive, or dangerous to implement. The computer can assist in these types of demonstrations and presentations, and has advantages over the traditional methods. First, while the media mentioned above is linear in nature, the computer has the advantage of being more flexible. Consider, for example, a presentation related to the impact of alcohol consumption on a person's ability to safely operate a motor vehicle. A videotape might depict the possible impact of a specific amount of alcohol on a given person. The computer program, however, would allow learners to vary the level of alcohol consumption, the window of time in which it was consumed, the age, sex, and weight of the drinker, and finally, the various possible consequences.

Through the use of projection equipment attached to the microcomputer, one computer in a classroom can be viewed by a group of learners. As the instructor or learners operate the computer keyboard, learners can view the presentation or demonstration on the projection screen.

Computers can be highly successful instructional tools in conveying content to learners. Through use of the tutorial mode, facts or concepts can be defined, illustrated, and then the learner can be questioned about the information. The process is repeated until the learner demonstrates mastery of the content. Tutorials are typically used in individual instruction, and can be successful with learners of varying abilities.

Drill and practice is another common instructional role of the computer. The computer can provide learners with limitless practice via posed problems or questions and feedback. Items are presented to learners on the computer screen or monitor, and then learners respond by entering their answers into the computer. In some cases, the computer will correct a wrong answer. In others, the computer will simply encourage learners to try again. Correct answers are praised. Some programs allow learners to "branch" to other areas of the program if they demonstrate mastery in certain areas, while others require learners to respond to a set of items until the program is completed.

More and more, computers are being used in instruction for simulations, games, and problem solving. The power and flexibility of the computer allows the learner to set conditions, make decisions, and then realize the consequences of these decisions. Learners can manipulate text, create graphic displays, or control mechanical movement. A computer program, for example, might allow learners to simulate a food science experiment or to test their problem solving skills related to weight loss outcomes due to diet and exercise. Computer games are extremely popular pastimes in the home and at entertainment centers, and attempts are being made to make educational computer games as motivating and entertaining as their arcade counterparts. Many educational games currently exist, but the educational and motivational value of many may be questionable (Bramble & Mason, 1985).

**FIGURE 13-2. Uses of the Computer as an Instructional Tool**

- Development of instructional materials (graphs, charts, worksheets)
- Recordkeeping
- Testing and scoring
- Instructional prescription
- Demonstration
- Tutoring
- Drill and practice
- Simulations, games, problem-solving activities

Figure 13-2 summarizes several of the uses of the computer as an instructional tool. These uses are best served when the software (computer programs that provide the instruction) is well-designed.

## CONSIDERATIONS IN SELECTING SOFTWARE

A variety of computer software exists. As just described, some of this software will support instruction by allowing the instructor to manage records, construct tests and do test analysis, or develop instructional activities. Other software can be used by learners to practice, gain information, do research, practice problem solving, or simulate activities or experiences. While there are family and consumer sciences professionals who have the skills to create their own computer programs, the more common responsibility of the instructor will be to select software that is appropriate to the learner and to the instructional outcome. There are several considerations in selecting software intended for instruction.

First, the instructor must be assured that the program provides accurate information. You cannot assume that the program developer was also an expert in the content area. Check to make sure that the data are correct and up-to-date.

Examine the program, too, to make sure that it presents the content in a balanced manner. Does the program omit any facts that are pertinent to the topic? Is the message consistent with family and consumer sciences philosophy? Consider, for example, a tutorial program on food storage that failed to address the issue of waste created by packaging. This is clearly a biased content presentation. Consider the organization of the content. The program should cover the topics completely, and the topics should flow logically.

The reading level of the materials should be of concern as well. The text should be written at an appropriate reading level for the learners, and the program, in general, needs to be geared to the level of understanding of intended audiences. Consider the examples, graphics, and format used in the program and how well they match the intended audience.

The software should be easy to use. Commands and user inputs should be easy to learn and to remember. Consider what level of computer expertise is required to use the program and whether the program is user friendly.

Any software selected for use in instruction should be of good technical quality. The readability of the print, use of color and graphics, and spacing should contribute to the success of the program. Text that is crowded, small, or difficult to read will discourage learners. Graphics that are difficult to interpret or that fail to represent their purpose may actually detract from instruction.

Finally, instructors need to critically examine whether or not the software is really an efficient use of the medium. Does the software perform a task more accurately, efficiently, rapidly, or creatively than other media? Do illustrations, graphics, and/or sound effects make an important contribution to the software? Consider programs that basically present text to learners on a computer screen. Does it make more sense to have learners scroll through computer screens than flip through the pages of a well-illustrated bulletin?...to spend hours converting a manual recipe file to the computer?...to watch childbirth simulated on the screen of the computer rather than "live" on videotape? While computer technology can enhance instruction, it should be used where it can be used best.

**Documentation** refers to the body of written material that accompanies a software package. The documentation is an important resource since successful use of the program may depend on the instructions and requirements outlined in the documentation. Good software documentation will include several pieces of information.

The documentation should include a description of the requirements for using the program. This will include a list of all the equipment needed for the proper operation of the program, including the type of computer for which the software is intended, computer memory requirements, and required peripherals (extra equipment, such as modem or printer).

The documentation should also include step-by-step directions for using the software. The directions should be complete, precise, and unambiguous.

Documentation may also include explanatory material relating to the content, as well as supplementary worksheets and textual material. Ideally, the documentation is a useful interface between the software and the user and enhances the efficiency with which the audience can use the program (Stone, 1983).

Figure 13-3 summarizes the considerations in selecting software discussed here. The answer to each of the questions portrayed in this figure should be yes.

## VIDEO MEDIA

Video media are forms of technology that are already well-entrenched as instructional tools in most formal and nonformal instructional settings. During the 1980s, the videotape edged out the 16mm film, and the "movies" will

**FIGURE 13-3. Considerations in Selecting Software**

---

**Content**

Does the software under consideration:
- match the instructional objectives?
- provide accurate information?
- provide a balanced presentation of the topic?
- cover the topic completely and logically?
- provide easy-to-use commands? logical instructions?
- have good technical quality?
- make the best use of the computer as an instructional tool?

**Documentation**

Does the written material accompanying the software:
- provide a complete description of what is required to run the program?
  - -type of computer needed?
  - -amount of memory?
  - -required peripherals?
- include step-by-step instructions for operating the software?

---

never be the same again. Although the videodisc is likely to elbow out the videotape, video as an instructional tool is a medium still coming into its own.

Obviously, there are unlimited opportunities to use commercial videotapes in instruction. Every topic from making vegetable garnishes to improving communication with adolescent children to selecting a nursing home is now featured on videotape. The criteria for selecting appropriate video media have been covered in Chapter 12—*Selecting Instructional Materials*. Instructors have responsibility for selecting accurate and appropriate media and for using media in ways that promote optimal learning. As with any instructional tool, the selected videotape should make a direct contribution to accomplishing objectives.

In addition to the pre-prepared videotape, there are other ways in which video technology can be creatively used in formal and nonformal classrooms.

Instructors should take advantage of opportunities to produce their own videotapes. Conferences, guest speakers, resource persons, panels, field trips, or special events can be videotaped and used later as audiovisual resources. Personal videotaping equipment now allows the nonprofessional to do simple editing, so even amateur tapes can be well done. Instructors can also videotape their own demonstrations to be used later in instruction, or to be replayed by learners who need additional assistance.

Learners' projects, demonstrations, laboratories, or other assignments can be videotaped and re-played for evaluation purposes. Not only will the instructor have increased opportunities to observe and evaluate learner performance, but learners, too, may benefit from reviewing their work.

Learners may be involved in developing and producing videotapes as a way to increase involvement in learning. Learners can produce a variety of assignments that are well adapted to this audiovisual medium. Consider student-produced commercials, music videos, role plays, speeches, demonstrations, or reports.

Like the computer, videotape allows learners to experience learning beyond the classroom setting. Learners have the opportunity to review, and in producing their own videos, to express their creativity. Videotape technology expands the instructional opportunities of the teacher and provides variety and high motivation options for learners. Fortunately for educators, new video technology will continue to increase instructional opportunities. Figure 13-4 summarizes some of the common sources and uses of video media.

---

**FIGURE 13-4. Instructional Sources/Uses of Video Technology**

- Commercially-prepared instructional videotapes
- Instructor-prepared videotapes
    - Conferences
    - Guest speakers
    - Field trips
    - Special events
- Evaluative videotapes
    - Learner demonstrations
    - Laboratories
- Learner-prepared videotapes
    - "Commercials"
    - Music videos
    - Role-plays
    - Speeches
    - Demonstrations
- "Popular" entertainment videos with appropriate themes or content

---

## EMERGING TECHNOLOGIES

Technology is changing so rapidly that it is difficult to stay abreast of all the many innovations. Professionals frequently find that a top-of-the-line computer system is out of date by the time it arrives. There are some emerging technologies not being used on a widespread basis today due to cost and other considerations such as the expertise required to use them. However, computer technology has rapidly become both inexpensive and user-friendly. No doubt, many of the technologies described in this chapter as "emerging" will have "emerged" and received widespread use by the time this "old" technology — the printed word — is read.

Many of the emerging technologies are really combinations and permutations of existing technologies that make them more responsive to the needs of users. Many focus on networking capabilities, as well. The following sections outline a few of the emerging technologies that are available now and that are likely to be regularly used by family and consumer sciences professionals of the not-too-distant future.

## INTERACTIVE VIDEO

**Interactive video** is a combination of computer and video technology that provides both "branching" instruction and realistic video images. An interactive video system requires a microcomputer, a videodisc player, and an interface that connects them and allows computer control of the video segments of the lesson (Floyd, 1982). A computer software program provides the instructional "template" for the lesson. Floyd (1982) has described it as a video program in which the user's responses to the material dictate the order and type of messages. For example, a learner might begin an interactive video program by selecting from a computer menu a section of instruction on how to make a home more energy efficient by caulking windows. The computer provides some basic information on tools and supplies needed, the video display shows the techniques, and the computer then quizzes the learner to be sure all of the important points are clear. If the learner wishes to see the video segment again for review, he or she need only request it. In this example, the learner really has the best of both video and computer technologies combined: the computer provides efficient branching, such as the selection and ordering of messages that respond to individual learner needs and learning styles, while the video technology provides realistic close-ups of the techniques being described. Further, the learner has an opportunity to test himself or herself to be sure all is clear before trying to apply what was learned to a real window.

Interactive video programs provide an important avenue for learning. Development of interactive video programs used to require the team effort of instructional designers, audio/video specialists, content experts, and computer programmers. Special software systems are now making it easier for the instructor alone to design interactive lessons (Jarvis, 1984).

## ELECTRONIC MAIL

An emerging technology already being used by large numbers of institutions is the electronic mail (or "e-mail") technology. **Electronic mail** is a combination of computer and telephone technologies that allows individuals to communicate by typing messages into a computer and then sending them (via phone lines) to another designated computer. Suppose an agency-based family and consumer sciences professional wants the latest information from a university-based colleague who is identifying effective methods of parent-newborn interaction. He or she enters a few digits into his or her computer, waits for it to dial a computer network system, and proceeds to send his or her query. The university-based professor receives the query and writes a quick note back that provides several good references. Since the query was not restricted to the single user to whom it was originally sent, other users in the network can provide additional information to the agency-based person as well.

Depending upon the sophistication of the network, other services may be available. Certain systems allow access to users' calendars for purposes of scheduling meetings. Some systems interface between the user and data stored in a mainframe computer.

E-mail allows for immediate and widespread communication networking. A message can as easily be sent overseas as to the office three doors down the hall. It can be sent to a single individual, or to an entire group at once. Like standard postal mail service, it is not intrusive; it can be "opened" at the receiver's pleasure. For the professional interested in communicating family and consumer sciences content, such a system provides a wealth of opportunities for both sending and receiving messages.

## FACSIMILE (FAX) TRANSMISSIONS

While computer-based electronic mail services can transmit documents, their use for this purpose is limited due to the time and effort needed to input printed material. Although overnight mail is speedy, it does not permit *immediate* transmission of hard copy. The **facsimile**, or **fax**, machine has become a relatively common method for sending documents.

The fax is a simple communication system that uses existing telephone lines to transmit messages. All that is needed is a fax terminal, telephone, and an electrical outlet at both sender and receiver locations.

Suppose a teacher has developed a contract with a local business for cooperative work experiences for his or her students. The teacher would like to be sure the contract is acceptable to the school district's attorney, but the attorney's office is 200 miles away. The teacher simply turns on a fax terminal, dials the phone number of the attorney's fax terminal, and feeds in a copy of the contract. The fax terminal in the attorney's office receives the signals sent over the phone line and duplicates a copy of the document for review. Within the hour, the teacher receives another copy of the contract (with additions and corrections) at his or her fax terminal. This kind of communication is rapid and accurate. Can you imagine the time it would take to have accomplished this task on the phone or through the standard mail service?

## DISTANCE LEARNING

**Distance learning** is the broad term used to describe various strategies that involve linking, through technology, the instructor at one location to learners who are in remote locations. It includes the teleconferencing frequently done in business, the video instruction conducted between schools, and the various video or audio broadcasts used in nonformal instruction. The use of distance learning techniques is expected to grow as demands increase for educational and training programs, travel costs continue to rise, and new and less costly technologies develop (Price, 1991).

## Types of Distance Learning Systems

Distance learning systems require telecommunications technology. Some systems are built on fiber optic cable systems that literally move information to its destination on light beams. With fiber optics, information is transmitted by pulses of laser light over hair-thin optically pure filaments of glass (Michigan Bell, 1990). Satellite transmissions have also been used in instruction, although this is an expensive type of delivery system at the present time. Another delivery system is possible through microwave transmissions. Transceivers feed dish antennas or television towers. These systems have the capacity to be completely interactive so that learners and instructors can see and speak with one another (Washor & Couture, 1990). Another type of interactive system, audiographics, allows simultaneous transmission of voices and graphic images across telephone lines. The system uses teleconferencing with speaker phones and computers so that images are displayed in the form of slide presentations or other graphic images (Knapczyk, 1991).

Other types of distance learning systems act as multimedia data bases. Video information systems allow learners or instructors to access information (graphics, illustration, statistics, films, etc.) from a central point via a touch panel. Some of these systems use phone lines. Although they do not necessarily replace an on-site instructor, they allow for the access of instructional resources at a distant location.

Some interactive learning systems combine video, audio, and text and are designed specifically for individual use by learners (no instructor required!). These systems usually need a touch screen monitor, video disc or CD-ROM and a personal computer. Such systems put learning within reach of individuals 24 hours per day, 365 days per year (Brickey & Smith, 1991).

## Instructional Considerations

In general, research over the last 40 years has shown no significant difference in learning when video and traditional instruction are compared. Good teaching can occur through a variety of modes (Price, 1991). As with any good instruction, principles of instructional planning that involve developing appropriate learner outcomes, identifying the content to be conveyed, and selecting appropriate strategies and resources must be practiced when using distance learning.

There are, however, some considerations that are unique to the distance learning context. The professional using distance learning systems will probably be one of an instructional team. Other team members will assist in the actual production and broadcast or transmission of the instructional program. The instructor, however, is responsible for making decisions about the instructional plan and the instructional environment.

First, the instructor needs to consider whether or not the content to be taught is appropriate for distance learning technologies. Teaching that requires the instructor to give significant attention to each individual learner or instruction that involves detailed supervision of projects or activities may not be as manageable through distance learning. In addition, instructional methods may need to be varied. Discussions, games, simulations, or role-plays, for example, may need to be managed on site (rather than by the instructor at a distant location).

Available transmission time and the cost of that transmission time may impact the choice of instructional activities, too. Cost can often only be justified when the number of learners is large.

The available technology may also influence the use and selection of instructional resources. Overhead transparencies, for example, are less useful with some forms of transmission than others.

When video methods are being used to transmit instruction, there are classroom or environmental concerns that must be considered. One of the first concerns is noise. Exterior noise in a viewing room may distract from instruction. The goal in selecting a viewing room should be to find a room that is in a very quiet area of the building. Interior noise caused by ventilation systems, fluorescent lights, or the echo or sound reflections from the video equipment itself are also distracting. Rooms with acoustical ceiling tile, wall coverings, and carpet may reduce some of the interior noises.

Classroom lighting and room arrangements are additional concerns. Television is usually best viewed in normal light, or in a slightly dimmed room. Where two-way video systems are being used, the classroom walls may need to be directly illuminated to improve the image from that room (Price 1991).

The room arrangement needs to be considered, too, in view of the type of technology being used and type of program planned. Theater-style seating is appropriate for teleconferences or lectures with one-way transmission. Theater-style seating does not, however, allow for interaction among participants or easy note-taking. Classroom-style seating may be substituted in one-way transmissions, although it may then be necessary to substitute several monitors for the type of projection system that is frequently used with theater-style arrangements. If two-way video is being used, learners must be seated in relationship to microphones and video cameras.

Whatever arrangement is used, there are some basic considerations relative to viewing distances and the number of persons that can be accommodated with any one monitor. Price (1991) indicates that the general rule is one viewer per diagonal inch of picture width. The monitor should not be placed higher than 30 inches above eye-level of learners. The distance and height of the monitor may be less consequential than the angle to the monitor at which learners sit. Early studies of educational television suggested that learners sitting at far sides of the monitor learned less well than those who were closer to the front of the monitor. Figure 13-5 summarizes the items to be taken into account in preparing to use distance learning.

## SUMMARY

From the traditional classroom to the board room, rapid changes in technology affect the ways family and consumer sciences professionals com-

# FIGURE 13-5. Instructional Considerations in Using Distance Learning

1. **Choose your "network."**
   - Investigate what types of systems are available for your use.
   - Consider the availability of the system, the potential for downlinks, and the cost of using the system.

2. **Determine audience size.**
   - How many potential learners may receive instruction?

3. **Select downlink sites.**
   - The actual sites will be determined by compatibility of distance learning systems, availability of dates, and accessibility for learners.

4. **Reserve uplink time.**
   - Plenty of advance planning is important where systems are particularly busy.

5. **Determine needed seating style.**
   - Seating will be determined by the number of learners, by site, and the level of interaction involved in the distance learning presentation.

6. **Hire downlinkers. Reserve the downlink sites.**
   - Your presentation will be broadcast now to each of these locations.
   - You may need both technical and instructional facilitator at each location, depending upon the type of technology and the type of presentation used.

7. **Plan production.**
   - Remember the general guidelines for good instruction.
   - Avoid planning presentations that consist only of a "talking head."
   - Consider all the ways in which the presentation can be made interactive and that learners can be involved in their location.

8. **Prepare script for presentation.**
   - Most distance learning presentations are carefully scripted because of the importance of timing and presentation style.
   - Have your draft reviewed by persons with experience in telecommunications.

9. **Prepare a set.**
   - Determine the type of set needed for your presentation and make arrangements for that set.

10. **Confirm arrangements at each downlink site.**

11. **Assign facilitator or "captains" at each downlink site.**
    - Assign meeting details to each facilitator.
    - This may include routine activities like arrangements for coffee, determining lunch arrangements, etc.

12. **Mail any technical information to each downlink site.**
    - Provide the detailed agenda and technical information regarding the downlink.

13. **Mail site facilitator directions and any handouts or other materials to be used at each site.**

14. **Check last minute details.**
    - Call each site one last time to make sure someone is assigned and ready for the broadcast.

15. **ACTION.—You're on the air!**

municate content. Increasingly, technology allows professionals to respond to individual learner or client needs for information. Whether computers, video technology, or any of the other technologies described are used, the ability to individualize communication and reach distant learners or clients immediately will revolutionize the instruction professionals can provide.

# REFERENCES AND RESOURCES

J.C. Penney brings CAD to retailing. (1991). *Design Management*, June, 16-18.

Computers in the classroom. (1989, September 13). *Education Week*, p. 3

Bramble, W.J., & Mason, E.J. (1985). *Computers in schools*. New York: McGraw-Hill.

Brickey, J., & Smith, W. (1991). Information on demand, *Adult Learning*, 2(4), 7-8.

Brooks, A., & Touliatos, J. (1989). Computer searches: A guide for practitioners and researchers. *Journal of Home Economics*, *81*(2), 23-26.

Floyd, S., & Floyd, B. (1982). *Handbook of interactive video*. White Plains, NY: Knowledge Industry Publications.

Grunwald, P. (1990). The new generation of information systems. *Phi Delta Kappan*, *72*(2), 113-114.

Jarvis, S. (1984). Videodiscs and computers. *Byte*, 18, 187-203.

Knapczyk, D. (1991). A distance learning approach to inservice training, *T.H.E. Journal*, April.

Macklenburger, J.A. (1988). What the ostrich sees: Technology and the mission of American education. *Phi Delta Kappan*, *70*(1), 18-19.

*Michigan Bell News and Views*. (1990). 1(8).

Price, M. (1991). Designing video classrooms. *Adult Learning*, 2(4), 15-19.

Shane, H.G. (1987). *Teaching and learning in a microelectric age*. Bloomington, IN: Phi Delta Kappa Educational Foundation.

Stone, A. (1983). *Microcomputer software for adult vocational education: Guidelines for evaluation*. Columbus, OH: National Center for Research in Vocational Education, The Ohio State University.

Strickland, M.P., Boschung, M.D., Ludewig, B.H., & Robertson, E.B. (1989). Microcomputers and basic competencies: A model curriculum. *Journal of Home Economics*, *81*(2), 20-22.

Teacher education and technology. (1989). *Journal of Teacher Education, 40*, 2-64.

Watson, B. (1990). The wired classroom: American education goes on-line. *Phi Delta Kappan*, *72*(2), 109-112.

# 14

# MEASURING
# LEARNER OUTCOMES

Measuring learner outcomes sounds like a formidable experience for both the learner and the instructor. For the learner, it suggests a process by which someone else will determine whether he or she meets a standard or "measures up." For the instructor, measuring learner outcomes denotes accountability in instruction. Measurement and its cousin, evaluation, are generally looked upon less than favorably, and yet measurement offers some unique opportunities to both learners and instructors. This chapter will explore some of the uses of measurement in instruction and the methods whereby learner outcomes can be appropriately and efficiently measured.

## MEASUREMENT, EVALUATION, AND GRADING

Measurement and evaluation are not the same. **Measurement** is a data- and information-gathering process (Erickson & Wentling, 1976). In measurement, the instructor attempts to effectively answer the question, "How much?" Instructors can measure the extent to which learners comprehend nutrition content, to what extent they are able to follow the guidelines for disciplining preschool children, how much their attitudes have changed about family therapy, or to what extent they are able to correctly demonstrate how to write a limited endorsement on a check. Through the use of various instruments or tools, instructors are able to gather evidence about what learners think, know, or can do. This is measurement. By contrast, **evaluation** involves judging or placing value on these measurements. Evaluation is concerned with judging the adequacy or worth of what is measured. An instructor may evaluate a learner's performance as above average, his or her attitude as unsatisfactory, or a learner's knowledge as inadequate. Evaluation decisions use measurement data, but evaluation is more than a report of measurements.

A discussion of measurement may seem primarily geared toward instructors who plan to teach in formal settings where testing and grading are expected. Measurement, in fact, has additional uses that need to be understood by all those who communicate family and consumer sciences content. Measurement is used to *determine the level or status of learners.* Instruments can be constructed to "pre-test" learners, to determine their prerequisite skills or to diagnose particular educational needs. If these instruments are constructed and administered properly, they are appropriate in many settings other than in the formal classroom.

Measurement may also provide important data *used in program evaluation.* As will be discussed in the next chapter, program evaluation requires an examination and consideration of data from a variety of sources. Sometimes it is necessary to determine to what extent learners have achieved intended learner outcomes as part of program evaluation. Funding agents, licensing agents, or institutions that supervise various programs may require some type of quantitative data on the progress of learners.

Measurement is also used to *determine student progress.* This is traditionally thought of in conjunction with the evaluation process that leads to **grades.** Instructors may also use measurement, however, to assess the degree to which learners are making progress toward intended outcomes. Youth leaders, in-service education facilitators, and agency trainers might all have use for an instrument that provides formative data on how learners are progressing toward stated outcomes that involve thinking, feeling, or doing.

The practice of assigning grades to learners on the basis of measurement data typifies evaluation. In this case, the classroom teacher determines the different sources and types of data that will be collected. He or she then determines the value of each of those forms — that is, the weight assigned to each source. He or she might determine that 40 percent of the grade will be based on data from performance observations, 40 percent on data from paper-pencil tests, and 20 percent on self-report instruments that ask the learner to determine how much change in attitude or behavior has occurred. The teacher also determines what level of performance (how many points or what percentage) represent each letter grade. What does an "A" mean? What does a "C" mean? Measurement is probably easier to discuss than grading because grading and evaluation require that professional judgments be made about the value or worth of achievement. Measurement involves the objective collection of data.

## VALIDITY AND RELIABILITY

A general goal in collecting measurement data is to give learners an unbiased opportunity to demonstrate what they know, can do, or feel. To do so, all measurement instruments should possess certain characteristics. The first of these is validity. **Validity** refers to the way in which the data from the measurement will be used and the soundness of the use. There are at least two aspects of validity worth noting.

The first is content validity. **Content validity** relates to whether or not the data collected is representative of the tasks they are supposed to represent (Gronlund, 1985). For example, think about the congruence between the following learner outcome and the test item that was designed to measure the outcome.

**Learner Outcome:** The learner will identify the elements of a budget.
**Test Item:** Why should families use a budget?

In this case, the correct response to the test item would not really tell you whether the learner had or had not achieved the intended learner outcome, and to use the data in that way would be to do so with a very low degree of validity. Similarly, to use one test item or limited items to make judgments about a large body of knowledge or to overemphasize some items in relationship to the emphasis given them in instruction would also lead to conclusions with low degrees of validity. The evaluation plan or table of specifications discussed in this chapter helps assure content validity.

**Construct validity** refers to the extent to which the test performance can be interpreted in terms of a particular construct. To use an example from the field, to what extent could you claim that a ten-question true/false test provided data that assured the learner demonstrated an understanding of the principles of interpersonal communication? Construct validity has been a major concern primarily to those in theory building and theory testing, but it does have some practical implications for the use of test results and what people believe or claim they mean.

For data to be interpreted with a high degree of validity, it must be reliable. **Reliability** refers to the consistency of measurement — that is, how consistent results are from one measurement to another. Reliability is primarily a statistical concept with estimates of reliability reported in terms of coefficients — a statistical comparison of two sets of scores. In simple terms, reliability refers to the likelihood that the results of the test would be similar if the test were given again or that the results of part of the test would be similar to the results of a contrasting part of the test. If the same test were given to similar students in first semester family health and second semester family health with a high degree of consistency, the data would be considered highly reliable. If, on the other hand, similar students with similar instruction received vastly different scores because the test was too long to finish, too difficult to interpret, too sloppy to read, or too confusing to understand, it might yield a low degree of reliability. In general, longer tests may yield more reliable data than shorter tests. A test that is too easy or too difficult for the learners may also produce scores of low reliability. The guidelines that follow on constructing test items should be helpful in building tests that yield reliable and valid data.

# LEARNER OUTCOMES AND VALIDITY

As earlier discussed, the learner outcome is, in fact, the basis of all instructional decisions. It serves as a guide to determining what content should be taught, at what level, and perhaps, using what types of learning experiences. It also has a direct relationship to what will be measured and how. Let's look at an example of a learner outcome in order to explore this relationship.

An instructor of an in-hospital, postnatal class has determined the following learner outcome: "Parents will demonstrate the safe bathing of their infant." This stated outcome provides sound, real direction for instructional decisions. The instructor is likely to provide students with information on the steps to bathing a baby, with particular emphasis on those procedures that assure the safety of the infant. Because the outcome indicates that the learners will be able to apply the information ("demonstrate"), the instructor will most likely provide some type of practice; perhaps, first, a demonstration and then an opportunity for parents to try the procedure, themselves, under the watchful eyes of the instructor. In other words, the instructor might provide a laboratory experience for learners. How can the instructor measure whether or not learners have achieved the learner outcome? First, eliminate some of the non-useful measurement techniques. The instructor won't know by asking the parents to explain how bathing is done. All the instructor would know is that the students *understand* or *recall* the process—the instructor won't know whether or not they can apply the knowledge. Asking them to write it down or giving them a paper-pencil test won't help either, since that, too, would only give information about what they know. Similarly, asking them to critique the performance of the instructor would be unsatisfactory. That would give information about what they recognize, not what they can do. The obvious conclusion is that the logical way to measure whether or not they can bathe a baby is to have them bathe the infant, and then determine whether or not they follow the guidelines for safety. The instructor might use a checklist or rating sheet. This is called a performance evaluation—one of many types of measurement that will be discussed in this chapter.

The primary point to be made from this example is that the learner outcome provides the information needed to make decisions about what content should be measured and at what level of performance. For example, if the learner outcome indicates that learners should be able to analyze a diet for nutritional deficiencies, it is not appropriate to measure learner recall of the dietary guidelines. Instead, the instructor must allow learners to demonstrate whether or not they can analyze a diet, and to what extent. An understanding and respect for the relationship of learner outcomes to measurement and evaluation may be the most important factor in developing fair and appropriate measurements of learner outcomes.

# MATCHING LEARNER OUTCOMES
# AND MEASUREMENT TOOLS

As instructors plan instruction, they work toward various types of learner outcomes: cognitive, psychomotor, affective, and perceptual. Each of these types of outcomes calls for its own tools or instruments for measuring results. While there is a growing interest in perception as a separate domain, this chapter will not cover measuring perceptual outcomes. Persons interested in measuring such outcomes should draw from what follows on measuring outcomes in other domains.

## MEASURING COGNITIVE OUTCOMES

Tools for measuring learner performance in the cognitive domain, the domain that deals with knowledge or content, are probably the most highly developed and most precise, and are probably the easiest to prepare. The most familiar are paper-pencil tests. Like all measures of performance, they must be based on the learner outcomes that have served as a basis for instruction.

Instruments or tests used to measure cognitive skills are made up of items that are either recognition items or constructed items. Recognition items are generally statements or questions that require learners to make a judgment (true or false) or provide a response based on recognizing the correctness of provided alternatives (like multiple-choice). Matching items are another type of recognition item. The matching item provides learners with multiple premises and responses, then requires learners to match the two based on some criteria.

Constructed items require learners to construct or develop a response or answer. Short-answer items and essay questions are the best known items in this category.

## MEASURING SKILL DEVELOPMENT
## (PSYCHOMOTOR OUTCOMES)

If the learner outcome involves a type of skill development, instructors may need to consider some method of performance evaluation. Performance measures may include assessment of a complex skill or task that involves more than just psychomotor skills. It may also measure cognitive or perceptual skills needed to perform a task. Skilled performance usually involves a unique combination of skills. Consider, for example, retrofitting a room or dwelling to accommodate an individual with a physical handicap. The outcome measured would depend upon more than just carpentry skills; it would depend on the cognitive understanding of what needed to be done and the ability to apply this understanding. To really measure performance would require that both process and product be examined.

## Process Measurement

**Process measurement** is usually done through the use of some type of observation technique. An instrument is used to rate, check, score, or rank the process observed. The observation may be done by the instructor or by peers, and the instrument serves as a guide for the observer. For example, the professional in business might observe a learner as he or she demonstrates the correct use of a piece of household equipment. Using a checklist, the instructor would check those steps or procedures followed in the use of the equipment. A rating scale could be used to assess the organization of a lesson presented to preschool children. The instructor might use a scale with bipolar adjectives describing the experiences: materials gathered/materials not gathered; presentation sequential/presentation not sequential.

A rating scale can also be used to measure process. For example, an instructor might construct a scale for measuring the extent to which adolescents cleaned a nutrition and foods laboratory after completing an assignment:

1. All cabinets and storage areas were left...

〈 _____ 〉

Orderly / Somewhat orderly / Okay / Not very orderly / Not orderly

2. The supply and work areas were left...

〈 _____ 〉

Orderly / Somewhat orderly / Okay / Not very orderly / Not orderly

## Product Measurement

The same types of instruments — rating sheets, ranking scales, scorecards, checklists — can be used to measure products. Imagine measuring the extent to which a product — a children's book — met the criteria established during instruction. An instructor could use a scorecard as an instrument for measuring this. With a scorecard, different criteria might have different values. For example, if the maximum score were 100 points, the scorecard might look like the one in Figure 14-1.

---

**FIGURE 14-1. Scorecard for Rating a Product**

| | SCORECARD: CHILDREN'S BOOK | |
|---|---|---|
| _____ | Content appropriate for age and stage of child | 20 points |
| _____ | Text (words) appropriate for age and stage of child | 30 points |
| _____ | Illustrations appropriate for age and stage of child | 30 points |
| _____ | Materials selected for construction of book appropriate for age and stage of child. | 10 points |
| _____ | Length of book appropriate for age and stage of child | 10 points |
| _____ | **TOTAL** | |

**FIGURE 14-2.** Rating Scale for Evaluating a Product

---

**RATING SCALE FOR CHILDREN'S BOOK**

1. Is the content appropriate for the age and stage of the child?
   Extremely Appropriate ⟵————————————————⟶ Not Appropriate at All

   | 5 | 4 | 3 | 2 | 1 |

2. Is the length of the book appropriate for the age and stage of the child?
   Extremely Appropriate ⟵————————————————⟶ Not Appropriate at All

   | 5 | 4 | 3 | 2 | 1 |

---

Students might be asked to score a variety of children's books using this scorecard. The products with the largest number of points overall might then be selected to use with children in a reading activity in a preschool or library.

These selected criteria could also be measured via the use of a numerical rating scale. Figure 14-2 shows two items from a numerical rating scale that could also be used to evaluate a children's book.

In the examples above, the instruments have been used to measure an actual product, the book. They can also be used for projects created by learners. It is perhaps obvious that even when the object of assessment is a physical product, the measurement still represents cognitive or perceptual—perhaps even affective—skills. For example, a person's assessment of the product is influenced by how well it is written or how factual it is (cognitive outcomes), as well as how closely the values portrayed in the book match a person's own (affective considerations). It should be noted here that many instructors use a combination of process and product measurements as part of evaluation. Think about the middle school student who demonstrates an understanding of clothing repair, but whose fine motor coordination is not adequately developed to allow him or her to produce a high quality product. The learner could know, for example, how to replace the zipper in a pair of blue jeans and follow each step carefully, and still come out with a zipper that is crooked and lopsided! A measurement of process can yield very different data than a measurement of only product.

## MEASURING AFFECTIVE LEARNER OUTCOMES

A review of measurement and evaluation textbooks suggests that affective measurement has received a good deal less attention than the assessment of cognitive achievement. Methods for measuring changes in feelings are not as reliable as methods for measuring changes in doing or performing. And yet, it is possible to measure indicators or manifestations of affective outcomes. There may, of course, be inconsistencies in the manifestations and the causes of them. A particular action or reaction can result from a variety of stimuli.

Sometimes there is inconsistency because learners respond in ways they believe they should, not because of some actual affective change. Consider an instructional plan that calls for learners to become more accepting of disabled persons. An instructor may observe "accepting behavior" on the part of the learner—maintained eye contact, initiated conversation, some social appointment arranged—but is it an indication of a change in attitude or simply performance intended to please the observer?

Affective learner outcomes can be assessed in a variety of ways. One method is via direct observation. Learner behavior may be observed and recorded, and then inferences made about the cause of the behavior. Various types of instruments may be used during the observation. Numerical scales, graphic scales, and observer checklists can be used. Instructors may also develop instruments for conducting interviews (face to face). Other questionnaires and inventories ask learners to assess their own performance.

Unobtrusive measures involve directly or indirectly observing the behavior of learners without their being aware that their behaviors are being measured. An example of an unobtrusive measure might involve watching learners making food selections for lunch after a series of lessons on choosing nutritious foods. These observations might indicate whether, in fact, learners integrated the value for eating nutritiously into their own behavior.

## DEVELOPING AN EVALUATION PLAN

Most instructors enjoy being complimented after a session. Often, however, just knowing that learners enjoyed the learning opportunity is not enough. In many cases, it is both desirable and necessary to determine whether learners have, in fact, learned what was intended. This is especially true when how the learners use the information is critical. For example, a test or examination to determine whether learners correctly perform cardiopulmonary resuscitation (CPR) is very important when you expect that the learners may need to use CPR on someone who needs it.

There are some simple guidelines to follow in developing a test that will provide a measure of learner performance. Some of these steps may be accomplished as you determine learner outcomes; others will need to be completed as you develop an evaluation plan. An evaluation plan or **table of specifications** is a written matrix with the concepts to be tested on one axis and the learner outcomes relating to each concept on the other axis. The percentage of the test covering each outcome and concept are indicated in the matrix. It is best to write a table of specifications for any evaluation exercise so that it can be carefully followed when the examination is being constructed and can be easily modified for future examinations as needed.

The four steps leading to a comprehensive evaluation plan are:
1. Outline course content/determine objectives.
2. Specify the level of performance necessary.
3. Identify areas of emphasis in the examination.
4. Specify the number of items necessary.

## OUTLINING COURSE CONTENT FOR AN EXAMINATION

If you have carefully identified learner outcomes prior to writing an examination or test for a learning session, much of the first step in developing an evaluation plan is complete. Since specified learner outcomes are what you desire, then the test should be an attempt to determine whether learners are, in fact, able to demonstrate the desired learning outcome.

A sample structure for a table of specifications is found in Figure 14-3. As you can see from this plan, concepts or topic areas are listed on the left-hand side of the matrix. If you developed a concept outline for the learning session, you may simply reproduce that concept outline in this space. If, for some reason, you are developing the test plan after you have presented the instruction and you know that you failed to cover a segment of the concept outline, it should not be included in the evaluation plan. Obviously, learners cannot be expected to reach specified learner outcomes with which they have no experience.

## DETERMINING PERFORMANCE LEVEL

If you have invested time in developing detailed learner outcomes for a learning session, then you have already determined the performance level you expect from learners. Your learner outcomes indicate whether you expect learners to have memorized content, whether you expect them to actually be able to apply what they know to new situations, and so forth. You will have determined whether learner behaviors fall into the cognitive, affective, or psychomotor domain. You will, as well, have determined at what level within each domain you expect learners to perform.

In completing the second axis of the table of specifications, the levels of performance expected are listed across the top of the matrix. If you have learner outcomes that require your learners to be able to recall certain symbols or terms, then that should be one of the cells at the top of the matrix. Similar cells should be provided for all of the other levels of behavior called for in the learner outcomes. Figure 14-3 shows only those levels of behavior called for by the specified learner outcomes for this learning session: knowing facts and applying facts to a given example.

**FIGURE 14-3. Table of Specifications**

| | Cognitive | |
|---|---|---|
| Concept | Know Facts | Apply to Given Example |
| 1. Guide to Daily Food Choices | 20% | 30% |
| 2. Vitamins | 20% | 5% |
| 3. Minerals | 20% | 5% |

# DETERMINING AREAS OF EMPHASIS

Most people can recall taking a test in which all of the questions dealt with some obscure point only mentioned briefly by an instructor. The general reaction to such a test is, "Why didn't the instructor test on what we covered in class?" Tests that have not been carefully planned may not test learner outcomes in a desirable way because they do not emphasize the critical learning outcomes.

In Figure 14-3, the matrix contains an indication of what percentage of the test should deal with each concept at each level of learning. This step in the process of developing the evaluation plan helps to avoid the situation where a test is unbalanced and contains too many questions on one topic and not enough on another.

# SPECIFYING THE NUMBER OF QUESTIONS

The length of a test is determined by the amount of content that must be tested and the amount of time available to take the test. Obviously, there must be sufficient time allotted for taking a test so that the test can cover all of the areas specified in the evaluation plan matrix. It would be useless to test learners on only a part of the CPR process and then assume that learners passing the test can perform CPR! This may mean that the types of questions must be selected with some consideration given as to how long each type of question might take to answer.

When a great deal of content must be covered in a test that can only last for a specified instructional period, instructors may lean toward objective test questions that are quickly answered rather than essay questions that take more time. Even objective questions can take some learners a good deal of time to answer, however, so care must be taken not to include more questions in the test than can reasonably be answered by the slowest test taker. A good rule to follow is that one multiple choice item takes approximately one minute of time to answer.

After you have made some judgment about the kinds of questions you will be using and the probable number of questions that can be answered in the time available, you can use the percentages in the table of specifications to determine the number of questions you will need for each concept at each level. Your first approximation of how many questions you will need should be indicated on the examination matrix. You may vary the actual number of questions as you develop the test, but you should always maintain the percentages initially specified in the matrix. For example, if 20 percent of a test is to cover one topic and outcome, 10 items would be needed on a 50-item test; 20 items would be needed for a 100-item test.

The example given above relates to developing an evaluation plan for the commonly used achievement test where recognition and constructed items are primarily used. This same method can be used to develop other types of evaluation instruments as well. Rating scales, checklists, score cards and even ranking instruments may also be structured by using a table of specifications that specifies the content areas and learner outcome levels and the percentage weight of each area.

## CHOOSING APPROPRIATE EVALUATION TECHNIQUES

Two major areas should be considered when selecting evaluation techniques. Of primary importance is the learner outcome the instructor wishes to measure; however, practicality when evaluating selected learner outcomes must also be considered.

### Matching Learner Outcomes to Types of Evaluation

In the first part of this chapter, we discussed the relationship of the various types of measurement tools to the type of knowledge to be measured. Multiple choice items are ideal for measuring cognitive outcomes, but not psychomotor outcomes. Questionnaires may help to find out how learners feel about different issues, but may not reveal what they know or understand.

In the discussion of item construction, the point made earlier about the relationship of the level of outcome to the type of item used to measure the outcome was reinforced. The cognitive domain provides the best illustration of this principle. Outcomes of various levels may require different types of items. Measuring whether or not learners can evaluate, analyze, or synthesize content requires that learners have a chance to construct a response rather than identify a response. Recognition items are usually reserved for lower-level outcomes.

## WRITING MEASUREMENT ITEMS

It may seem that it takes a great deal of time to develop an evaluation plan for assessing learner outcomes, but this is a very important step. Considerable time must also be spent in developing the measurement items themselves. An evaluation instrument that is carefully constructed using a good plan and well-written items will give both instructors and students excellent information about how closely student performance matches desired learning outcomes. If careful construction of an evaluation plan is not followed by equally careful attention to the development of the specific test items, the evaluation is likely to do little to inform students about their learning strengths and weaknesses or instructors about the areas where instruction is adequate and inadequate. Well-written evaluation items take effort to construct.

Since well-constructed items are time-consuming to construct, instructors may wish to determine whether item banks are available. **Item banks** are collections of well-written items that have been tested for validity and reliability. Such banks may be provided as an addendum to a textbook or be available through other agencies or institutions. Item banks can provide a source of well-constructed items. However, the instructor has the responsibility of carefully selecting items from the bank that are valid for the instructional outcomes that have already been identified.

For all items, there are some general guidelines for construction that help to make the items both valid and reliable. All items should be presented without punctuation or spelling errors. They should also be clearly typed or handwritten and duplicated so that students do not miss items for extraneous reasons. In addition to these general rules, there are some specific practices that help in writing good test items. Below are some keys to writing good recognition, constructed, and performance items.

## CONSTRUCTING RECOGNITION ITEMS

Recognition items used to measure cognitive learning include true/false, multiple choice, and matching items. Each of these types of items requires the learner to select the correct answer from given answers or to recognize (rather than construct) a response. Following are some specific suggestions for writing well-constructed recognition items.

### Constructing True/False Items

True/false items are generally used when the content being tested is factual. They are inappropriate when the information being tested is not entirely true or false.

When writing true/false items, be sure that the statements you have written are factual statements that are unequivocally right or wrong. To accomplish this, base the items you are writing on established facts rather than upon opinions. For example, the true/false statement "Adults and children both need milk in their diets" may seem true. In fact, adults and children do not need *milk*, but do need the nutrients contained in milk. Lactose-intolerant individuals manage to obtain those nutrients without drinking milk.

In addition, you should avoid the use of words referred to as **specific determiners** such as *many, few, usually, almost, generally*, and *sometimes* (that are open to many interpretations and suggest that the item is true) and *all, always, no, never, none* (that suggest the item is false). Ambiguous qualitative terms such as *large, important*, and *better* should also be avoided. These words are cues that you have not written a completely *true* or *false* statement based upon fact.

It is easier to write good true/false items if you include only one concept in each question. When sentences contain two ideas, one true and one false, the statement is confusing to students and may only be testing the student's ability to unravel the ideas contained in it. In addition, you have no idea which concept was not understood when students give a wrong response to a true/false item containing two ideas. An example of this type of item is: "Warm colors make a room appear smaller, but pale tints have the same effect." Just reading this item makes a person feel confused!

If you are writing an item that is designed to measure whether students understand cause and effect, two ideas *may* be included in the statement (the cause and the effect), but the crucial element being tested should be contained in the second part of the sentence. The following is an example of a true item containing both the cause and the effect: "In healthy individuals, maintaining caloric intake and increasing caloric expenditure result in decrease in body weight."

Negative statements can be used in true/false items, but the negative words should be underlined or all in upper case letters to draw attention to them. The use of double and triple negatives in true/false items should be avoided. Double negatives only serve to make the item more difficult for the student to interpret. They do not help in determining whether learner outcomes have been met. Try answering the following item containing a double negative: "Piaget did not develop the concept that children do not go through a period of 'nonformal operations.'"

Instructors should also avoid writing true/false items using small, trivial bits of information. It is tempting to use word-for-word statements from the text or other learning materials in constructing true/false items. Generally, statements taken directly from learning materials are both trivial and ambiguous (because they are taken out of context). Although writing such items will swell the number of items, it will not likely help you assess whether or not students have achieved the desired learner outcomes.

In structuring the test using true/false items, there are some additional guidelines to keep in mind. First, a test that includes true/false items should contain at least 20-25 true/false items in order to counterbalance the 50 percent chance of guessing the correct response to an individual item. Further, there ought to be approximately equal numbers of true and false items arranged so that there is a random pattern of responses. If negative items are included, they should be grouped together at the end of the true/false statements. This grouping contributes to uniformity and keeps students from having to "shift gears" from positive to negative ideas. "Tricking" students into a wrong response is inappropriate and does not contribute to your understanding of the learner's progress toward learning outcomes.

Finally, provision needs to be made for clearly distinguishing the answers given by students. It is desirable to have students circle a *T* or *F* on the test or write a + or *0* in a blank provided. If students write *t* or *f* or *true* or *false* in a blank, it may be difficult to decide which answer they have written. See Figure 14-4 for a summary of desirable qualities of true/false items.

## Constructing Multiple Choice Items

Multiple choice items can be used to test a wide variety of learning outcomes and are a common type of test question for almost all levels of learners. In multiple choice items, a question or premise is generally presented in the "stem" of the item, and learners are asked to select the best response from a list of possible alternatives. Following are some specific suggestions for writing good multiple choice items.

## FIGURE 14-4. Desirable Qualities: True/False Item

**Items Qualities**

- Directly tied to desired learning outcome
- Test factual content
- Are unequivocally right or wrong statements
- Are based on facts, not opinions
- Avoid specific determiners: many, few, usually, almost, generally, sometimes, all, always, no, never, none
- Avoid negative statements, but highlight negative words when such statements are unavoidable
- Test significant rather than trivial information
- Are used in large enough numbers to minimize guessing effects

**Test Considerations**

- Include at least 20-25 items per test
- Use approximately equal numbers of true and false items
- Randomize responses
- Group negative items together at the end of the series of true/false items
- Have students circle the appropriate response

The "stem" (or introductory sentence or phrase) of the multiple choice item must be carefully written so that the learning outcome you wish to measure is the one you do measure. The stem of the item should present a single, important problem to be solved or question to be answered. It should be directly tied to the behavior specified in learning outcomes. One way to check whether you have included the main idea in the stem is to see whether someone can formulate an appropriate answer to the stem when he/she has not been provided with a list of responses. Compare the following two item stems:

A. Which of the following is true of newborns?

B. A newborn baby is tested for which of the following on the Brazelton scale?

In item A, a specific question is not posed in the stem. The item becomes a collection of true/false statements all relating to newborns. Item B does present a specific question in the stem and is the better of the two stems.

In well-written multiple choice items, the stem should be longer and more detailed, while the responses are shorter and less complex. This does not mean, however, that confusing phrases and nonfunctional words should be included in the stem to lengthen it and make it more complex. As with true/false items, use a negative stem only when it is important that the learning outcome emphasizes knowledge of a negative condition. If a negative word is used, highlight the word by underlining it or typing it in upper case.

There are a number of practices that can be used in constructing the responses for a multiple choice item that will make it more valid and reliable. The responses to multiple choice items are divided into two categories: the foils or distracters (incorrect answers), and the correct response. **Distracters** should be plausible answers to the stem. Distracters that are "silly" or completely implausible are not true distracters since no learner is likely to be tempted to choose them. In addition, they should be consistent grammatically with the stem of the item. Check nouns and verbs to be sure they are consistent with one another. Use a(n), is(are), and was(were) as necessary to make the stem and responses match grammatically.

All of the responses should be of approximately equal length, and, as noted previously, should be brief responses to the central problem stated in the stem. Responses to multiple choice items should not be a collection of true/false items that result when the stem is an incomplete thought. Further, all of the responses should be homogeneous. For example, if the correct response is the name of a person, all other responses should be names as well.

Multiple choice items that have at least four (and preferably five) responses are recommended (Popham, 1981). This number of responses helps eliminate guessing without making the item as complicated as one that has many more responses. Whether you decide to use four or five responses, the number of responses should be the same for all of the multiple choice items in the test. Be careful in constructing responses to one item that you do not inadvertently give a clue to the response of another item. Resist using the responses "all of the above" and "none of the above" just to end up with the number of responses you need. These choices should be used when it's important to emphasize the relationships between a number of correct responses (all of the same) or the fact that the one correct choice is not present (none of the above).

As with all types of items, the directions for multiple choice items should be clear. Learners should be clearly directed to choose the *correct, incorrect* (as in a negative item), *best choice*, or *best choices*. It is a good idea to use all upper case letters for the responses and to indicate that they should circle the correct letter (or letters) or mark them clearly on a computer answer sheet. Asking students to write the letter in a blank can lead to problems in deciphering answers. (In fact, it is amazing just how much a *B* and a *D* can resemble each other.)

Multiple choice items that show the responses in a column or "stacked" are easier to read than those where the answers are presented in a string. Finally, be sure there is no recognizable pattern to the correct responses in a group of multiple choice items. See Figure 14-5 for a summary of desirable qualities of multiple choice items.

## Constructing Matching Items

Matching items typically consist of two columns with items in the first column to be associated with those in the second. They are used to determine whether learners understand the relationships between two categories of items. These categories might be words and definitions, events and people, causes and effects, or examples and principles. Generally, the first column (the one on the left) contains the premises, while the column on the right contains the responses.

In developing matching items, it is a good idea for you to label the two columns to be used. For example, the first column might be labeled "Causes,"

## FIGURE 14-5. Desirable Qualities: Multiple Choice Items

**Item Qualities**

- Item is directly tied to a desired learning outcome
- Stem:
  - Clearly indicates a single problem to be solved
  - Is more complex than responses
  - Are negative only when absolutely necessary
  - Highlight a negative word when one is used
- Responses:
  - Relatively equal in length
  - Homogeneous
  - Are plausible
  - Are grammatically consistent with the stem
  - Are four or five in number
  - Use "all of the above"/"none of the above" rarely
  - Are stacked vertically

**Test Considerations**

- All items have the same number of responses
- Responses do not contain clues regarding other items
- Contain clear directions
- Ask students to indicate a response by circling or marking on a mark-sensitive sheet
- Contain no recognizable pattern of responses

the second labeled "Effects." Labeling the columns is useful for a number of reasons. First, it clearly establishes the basis for matching. As you write the directions for the item, you can refer to the column labels and help the learner to focus on the task. Second, it helps you, the test writer, to be sure you are maintaining homogeneity in each of the columns. You can quickly review each of the columns to be sure you have been consistent in formulating responses and premises that "match" the column labels.

In general, the premises ought to be longer than the responses, and, as in multiple choice items, clearly establish the premise. Responses should be brief phrases that are easily scanned as the learner attempts to match premises and responses. For example, definitions should be in the premise column while terms appear in the response column; researchers' findings in the left column, researchers' names in the right column. Responses should be listed in a logical order to make scanning easier, too. For example, measurements ought to be organized in ascending order (1/4, 1/2, 3/4, etc.) and times chronologically (several times a day, daily, monthly, annually). If no other logical basis for sequencing seems appropriate, the responses should be arranged alphabetically.

Matching is easier if the entire set of items appears on the same page and if there are not so many premises and responses in a single set that matching is cumbersome. It is recommended that 10-12 premises be included in any matching set. It is usual to have at least two extra responses to act as distracters. Directions should also state if responses are to be used once, more than once, or not at all.

In organizing the matching items on the test page, it is a good idea to provide a blank before the number of each premise. Learners should be instructed to write the letter of the correct response in the blank preceding each premise (or to clearly indicate the response on a computer response sheet if one is being used). As with other types of recognition items, be sure there is no recognizable pattern to the correct responses.

## Advantages and Disadvantages of Recognition Items

Recognition items have several advantages. They are relatively easy to score, primarily because they restrict student responses to choice among given answers. A single response is the "correct" response so little judgment is required for scoring. Further, recognition items test low-level cognitive objectives well. They isolate bits of information to determine whether students recall facts.

One drawback to recognition items is that good items take considerable time to construct. For example, most people can think of one or two distracters for a multiple choice item, but have difficulty generating three or four plausible, but incorrect, responses. (One way to generate incorrect responses is by using open-ended questions on a pretest.)

Another drawback is that students can select a correct response purely by chance. In items where learners must generate rather than recognize responses, chance plays a lesser role.

Finally, the levels and domains of learning that can be tested by recognition items are very limited. These items should be viewed as primarily testing factual knowledge. Figure 14-6 summarizes the desirable qualities of matching items.

**FIGURE 14-6. Desirable Qualities: Matching Items**

**Item Qualities**
- Item is directly tied to desired learning outcome(s)
- Item tests relationships between two categories of things
- Premises are longer than responses and are in left column; responses are brief and are in right column
- Columns are labeled
- Items within each column are homogeneous
- Responses are listed in a logical order

**Test Considerations**
- Entire matching item appears on one page
- Approximately 10 to 12 premises are in each matching set
- There are more responses than premises
- Directions clearly state the basis for matching
- Directions indicate whether responses are to be used once, more than once, or not at all
- Blanks for responses are located to the left of premises
- There is no response pattern

# CONSTRUCTING CONSTRUCTED RESPONSE ITEMS

Constructed response evaluation items are those items that require students to generate an answer rather than select the correct answer from ones given. They fall into two basic categories: short answer items and essay items. Following are some suggestions for writing good constructed response items.

## Constructing Short Answer Items

The most commonly used short answer items either require the student to fill in the blank or to generate a sentence or two in response to a question. Fill-in-the-blank or completion items require the student to complete a statement using a word or a few connected words (sometimes referred to as a **word unit**). Sometimes, the blanks to be completed are part of a diagram the learner is to label.

In developing completion items, it is important to be certain that there is only one possible right answer. This is sometimes difficult for a test developer to determine. Generally, asking another person to read the items and attempt to complete them can help you to determine whether the item is clearly written and requires only one response. In order to really provide a good test, however, you should be sure there are several *plausible* answers. When items only require a choice between such answers as "hot" or "cold" or "high" and "low" there is a 50 percent chance that students will be able to guess the correct answer.

As with all items, a completion item should test a specified learner outcome. To be sure that you are focusing on the desired learning outcome, leave out the significant word in a completion statement. Requiring learners to fill in trivial words only tests their ability to solve a word puzzle rather than finding out whether they have learned the information desired. Present the main thought of the item first (just as you do with the stem of the multiple choice item) and to leave the blank at the end of the statement. This helps the learner to focus on the main idea and minimizes confusion.

When constructing completion items, there should be only one blank in any item located at the end of the statement (as noted above). The blank may require that a word unit such as *"vitamin A"* or *"cooperative play"* be provided. If the answer is to be provided in a particular unit (e.g., pound, ounces or inches), specify the unit after the blank. As with multiple choice item stems, avoid using clue words preceding the response: use is/are, a/an, was/were.

In presenting the items on the test, be sure to use the same length blank for every item. In some cases, it helps to indicate where the missing word or word unit goes in the item with a very short blank, then have students write the word in longer (same-sized) blanks to the left of the item number. This format causes all of the answers to be in a straight line down the left-hand side of the page, making scoring easier.

It is tempting to use statements taken directly from a text or lecture notes to develop completion items. This should be avoided for two reasons. First, it is more difficult to be sure that there is only one correct answer. Even though the statement in a text may be true, it might be possible to use several different words and still have the statement remain true. Second, learners may be able to answer completion items taken directly from the text because they recall it from the reading they did. In this case, the instructor is only testing ability to memorize rather than comprehension of the material.

It may be desirable to have students label parts of an object in a test. This can be achieved by providing short answer items related to a diagram. All of the suggestions for constructing completion items that involve statements apply to labeling diagrams as well. In addition, the instructor should be certain that the diagram provided is simple and large and that the parts to be labeled are clearly numbered. It is wise to check each test paper to be sure that the diagrams have duplicated clearly and that arrows point to the distinct parts to be labeled. Directions should indicate the task to be completed (for instance, "Identify the numbered parts of the pattern piece by writing your answers in the blanks provided at the left.").

Sometimes it is useful to develop completion items that are associated in some way. Such items are organized just as matching items are except that the response column consists of blanks to be completed by the learner. For example, the left-hand (or premise column) might consist of the names of diseases caused by vitamin deficiencies. The right-hand (or response) column could then consist of blanks in which the learner had to supply the name of the deficient vitamin for each of the diseases. When writing such items, the instructor should follow the guidelines for both matching and completion items. See Figure 14-7 for a summary of desirable qualities in completion items.

## FIGURE 14-7. Desirable Qualities: Completion Items

**Item Qualities**

- Directly tied to desired learning outcome(s)
- Requires a single word or "word unit" response
- Requires a single correct response
- Responses are not trivial words or phrases
- Response should be the last word or word unit in the item
- If the answer is to be in a particular unit (pounds, inches, etc.), the unit desired should be specified
- No specific determiners, such as a/an, is/are, or was/were, appear before the blank

**Test Considerations**

- Same length blank is used for each item
- Provide blanks in which learners are to respond to the left of each item
- When using a diagram to be labeled:
  - diagram should be large enough to be clearly duplicated
  - parts to be labeled should be distinctly pointed out with arrows
  - directions should indicate the task to be completed

## FIGURE 14-8. Desirable Qualities: Short Answer Items

**Item Qualities**
- Item is clearly tied to desired learning outcomes
- Requires student to respond with a phrase or one or two sentences
- Item can be written as a complete question
- There is sufficient space for the learner response

Occasionally, you may wish to use a short answer item that requires the student to generate a phrase or one or two sentences. For example, you may wish to have the student define a particular word. In this case, the item should be written as a question instead of as an incomplete statement. Generally, a blank is provided in which the learner is to write the answer. As with completion items, there should be only one correct answer. See Figure 14-8.

## Advantages and Disadvantages of Short Answer Items

Completion and short answer items can help you to accurately assess knowledge of facts, principles, and processes. They require the student to actually generate a response rather than only recognize the correct response in a given set of responses. Most learners quickly become accustomed to completion items since they mimic the question-answer routine common in classroom learning. Further, they allow the instructor to test relatively complex cognitive learning in items that are easier to score than the essay item.

There are two major disadvantages to short answer or completion items. The first is that this type of item, even though quite powerful, cannot measure extremely complex cognitive achievement. Second, this type of item can cause scoring difficulties. Scoring problems can result when student handwriting is illegible or when incorrect spelling or grammar are used and the instructor must determine whether an answer is correct or incorrect. A detailed scoring key can assist with this particular problem, but not eliminate it completely.

## Constructing Essay Items

One of the most common types of constructed response items is the essay question. Although it can be used to assess lower-level learning outcomes, it is particularly useful in determining whether the learner can synthesize information and write coherently to express ideas. Thus, essay questions are particularly useful when learner outcomes require organization, generalization, integration, or expression of ideas rather than just memorization of factual materials.

Instructors may be tempted to write essay items for inappropriate situations because they take less time to construct. Most find, however, that essay items are much more time-consuming to score.

Once you have determined that an essay item is appropriate for the learning outcome(s) you wish to assess, be sure that the question elicits the behavior required. The question may pose a problem, describe a situation that requires response, or ask a direct question. It is helpful if the first words of the question clearly tell the student the form of the response required. Use "explain," "provide examples," and "contrast" rather than "discuss," "tell about," and "give your opinion." Try to keep the wording of the question to the point. If appropriate, indicate if there are any limitations or conditions on the response. For example, indicate if there are a certain number of examples needed ("Provide *four examples*...) or a specific author or expert whose opinion should be cited ("...of *Piaget's* conceptualization of learning").

Including extra credit or optional essay items should be avoided. All students should answer the same questions in a particular test unless there is some special circumstance, such as a make-up test, that necessitates using other items. As noted previously, reliability and validity are compromised when the items vary from test to test.

As essay items are developed, also create a clear and inflexible key to the scoring of the essay items. Such a key is easier to formulate if you write a trial response to the question yourself and use the points included in your response to formulate the key for the item. A procedure for scoring the test should also be developed. For example, score all of the first items on all of the tests, then all of the second items. Without such a key and procedure, the validity and reliability of the test are likely to be severely reduced.

In formulating an essay test, clear directions should precede each set of questions. These directions should include information about how spelling, penmanship, and punctuation errors will be handled. In addition, the numerical value for each question should be indicated, and the approximate time limit should be given. It is important to arrange the items in a sequence of increasing difficulty. Finally, there should be sufficient space provided for learner responses.

## Advantages and Disadvantages of Essay Items

Essay items offer the ultimate opportunity to test higher level thinking skills. Although they generally provide some structure for the learner response, learners are unlikely to "guess" their way to a correct response. Generally, written communication skills play a role in testing by essay item. Further, essay items don't take as much time to construct as do other, more structured items.

The primary difficulty with essay items is that they are difficult to score. Even with a well-structured key, the instructor may be influenced in scoring by the student's ability in written English, or even by his/her handwriting. Finding the key points in a narrative is more difficult than determining whether a student has responded correctly to a true/false item. It has been said that the less time spent in constructing an item, the more time needed to score it. This is certainly true when comparing essay items to more structured response items. Figure 14-9 summarizes some of the desirable qualities of essay items.

## FIGURE 14-9. Desirable Qualities: Essay Items

**Item Qualities**

- Item is directly tied to desired learning outcomes
- Requires student to synthesize ideas and coherently write responses
- First word of the item specifies the form of response required
- Item indicates whether there are conditions or limitations on the response
- Essay items are not "extra credit" or "optional"
- Inflexible scoring key is developed prior to test administration

**Test Considerations**

- Directions should clearly indicate how spelling, penmanship, and punctuation errors will be scored
- A numerical value and approximate time limit for each question should be indicated
- Arrange items in sequence of increasing difficulty
- Provide sufficient space for student response

# ORGANIZATION OF THE TEST

There are several factors related to the organization of the test that need to be taken into consideration in preparing it. They include the directions, the "mix" of items, item numbering and spacing, the key, and scoring.

The learner who will take the test should be provided with clear directions. The directions that are included at the beginning of the test should tell the learner what to do to respond to each item and on what basis to respond to the item. Is the learner to find the best answer, the right answer, or the answer based on his or her opinion?

Similar directions should be given each time the type of test item changes in the instrument. A test that includes multiple choice questions, true/false questions, and matching questions should include directions preceding each of these sections in addition to the general directions regarding the test.

As a general guideline, only three different types of items should be included in any one instrument. Similar types of items should be grouped together. For example, all short-answer or multiple choice questions should appear in the same section. A question in one section should not give clues to the correct responses in another section. These items are sometimes referred to as interdependent items. Interdependent items either provide the answers to one another, or the answer to one is necessary in order to respond correctly to another. These types of items should be avoided.

Instructors should include items that range from easy to difficult. Usually the easiest items on a test are placed first so that learners experience some immediate success. This gives them the confidence to proceed through the test.

All test items should be numbered consecutively. Do not begin again with "1" when starting each new section. Learners should have adequate room to respond to each question. It is sometimes desirable to leave a blank for each response in the left-hand column of the test. This allows learners to quickly check wnether or not they have responded to each item and allows ease of scoring by the instructor.

Instructors should pay attention to the spacing and arrangement of questions. A question that would be divided between two pages should be rearranged to fit onto a single page. There should be adequate white space on the page to make reading easy. A good reproduction method should be used so that the print is clear and easy to read. It may be helpful to provide a labeled space for the learner's name and any other required demographic data.

Instructors may also include information about the scoring or value of certain test items. For example, the point value of the questions and total points possible for the test could be provided.

Before learners take the test, instructors should prepare a key for the scoring of the test. This key should include sample answers to constructed response questions as well as answers for recognition items. Figure 14-10 summarizes important organization considerations.

---

**FIGURE 14-10. Desirable Qualities: Test Organization**

- There is labeled space for learner name
- Clear directions for test in general and for each specific section are provided
- There are only three types of items per instrument
- Similar types of items are grouped
- Items are numbered consecutively from the beginning of the test to the end
- There is adequate space for responses
- Response blanks are "grouped" for easy response and scoring
- Items are *NOT* split between pages
- Test is reproduced so that it can easily be read
- Point values for questions are indicated
- Key is prepared prior to test administration

---

## RATING SCALES, CHECKLISTS, RANKING TOOLS, AND SCORECARDS

There are a number of tools that can be used to measure outcomes other than the measurement items just discussed. Rating scales, checklists, ranking tools, and scorecards are especially useful for measuring products or performance outcomes that are in the psychomotor or affective domains.

## RATING SCALES

The **rating scale** is an instrument that lists the desirable attributes or qualities of a product or performance. With each characteristic is a scale used by the rater to indicate to what extent the attribute or criterion has been met. Numbers or descriptors can be used on rating scales.

The numerical rating scale has the advantage of being simple to use and providing easy-to-summarize results. When rating behavior (as contrasted to a product), the closer the rating is done to the performance, the more reliable it can be expected to be (Popham, 1981).

When constructing a rating scale, the instructor needs to begin by carefully and concisely describing the rating categories. Again, these may be specific qualities or characteristics of a product or of a performance. Consider the example of a rating sheet used to measure the extent to which a learner is able to operate a health-care appliance. The rating sheet would list all of the steps in using the appliance. For instance, steps, such as placing the blood pressure cuff at the right position, and establishing appropriate fit of the cuff, might be included. Each item on the scale should be stated at about the same level of specificity. Each item should be descriptive and concise enough that either a supervisor or another designated person could use the form for rating purposes. As often as possible, each item should be stated positively, rather than negatively. Avoid the use of items that describe what the learner doesn't do or what the product doesn't represent or contain.

The descriptive statements may be rated by either circling a number, word(s), or point on a continuum that represents the extent or degree to which that characteristic is evident. The numerical scale may simply use numbers to represent particular rankings, such as: 3 = best, 2 = pretty good, 1 = okay, 0 = does not meet criteria. Raters, for example, might need to determine the "fit of the pressure cuff": 3(good), 2(adequate), 1(not acceptable).

Bipolar adjectives are used when further description is desirable. Look at the example in Figure 14-11. In this example, raters still select a number, but the adjectives allow more detailed discrimination than the "good" to "unacceptable" model. It is usually desirable to invest the time to develop more detailed, objective measures.

Note in the example how the positive end of the scale is on the left, negative end to the right. There should be consistency throughout the instrument in the poles. The "good" end of the scale should come first (Guilford, 1954).

Construction of the graphic rating scale begins in the same way as construction of the numerical scale. Instructors first determine the qualities or characteristics to be measured. Rather than rely on numerical assignment, however, the graphic rating scale takes advantage of the visual image of a graph. Each given characteristic is presented along with a horizontal line on

---

**FIGURE 14-11. Bipolar Numerical Rating Scale**

Set up of the dramatic play area was
   a. organized ◄— 5 . . . 4 . . . 3 . . . 2 . . . 1 —► disorganized
   b. interesting ◄— 5 . . . 4 . . . 3 . . . 2 . . . 1 —► uninteresting
   c. theme-related ◄— 5 . . . 4 . . . 3 . . . 2 . . . 1 —► unrelated

**FIGURE 14-12.** Descriptive Graphic Rating Scale

| 1. Maintains organized records: | | |
|---|---|---|
| Highly Organized | Fairly Organized | Disorganized |
| 2. Posts detailed daily entries: | | |
| Highly Detailed | Includes Some Detail | Little Detail |

which the rater is asked to place an "X." Figure 14-12 is an excerpt from a descriptive graphic rating scale.

The guidelines for developing a good graphic rating scale are the same as those for developing the numerical rating scale. Statements or descriptions of characteristics should be concise and specific. The poles of the graph should be consistent. Space for comments is sometimes included so that raters can clarify or explain their responses per item. See Figure 14-13 for a summary of the desirable qualities of rating scales.

## Cautions in Using Rating Scales

While the rating forms described serve as tools for measuring products or performance against particular standards, there are cautions in the use of these tools. First, there is a tendency to forget the detail of performance unless the rating is done during or near the time of performance. Time is less of a factor when rating products.

Next, there can be concerns related to the training and preparation of the raters. If one person is rating all learners, there is likely to be consistency in the way items are interpreted and performances perceived. If, however, the same form is used by different raters, there may be inconsistency. Raters should be trained in the use of the instrument and allowed to practice. Practice allows raters to discover what types of deviations they may expect and what types of errors or misinterpretations are most likely.

**FIGURE 14-13.** Desirable Qualities: Rating Scales

- Measures qualities of products or performance
- Has concise rating categories
- Each item on the scale is at the same level of specificity
- Items are stated positively
- "Positive" end of the scale should be the same for each item (perferably at the left side of the scale)
- Sufficient space for comments should be provided

Another problem with the use of rating sheets may be the personal bias of raters. Individual raters may tend to be too generous (resulting in generosity error), too severe (severity error), or to view everything in the middle (central-tendency error) (Popham, 1981). These types of bias are more likely to occur if raters have not been given proper training for the use of the instrument or have not had opportunity to practice. The possibility of these types of errors exist, too, when learners are asked to rate themselves using self-report instruments. Learners may vary in the tendency to rate their own products and performances in too generous or too severe a manner or to see all aspects of their work as "just average."

A last frequent error occurs when the rater or instructor allows the overall impression of the learner to influence his or her rating. This type of error is known as the **halo effect** and biases the rater toward a favorable rating whether earned or not. The 4-H judge who knows that the young person has worked hard on his project, has won awards in the past, and wants to work with 4-H when he grows up may unintentionally view the project more favorably than it deserves. Rating products "blind" (without knowledge of the person who has done the work) is one way to minimize the halo effect. Another may be to purposefully reverse the order of the rating scale so that the rater will not casually circle all the positive positions on the left of the page.

## RANKING TOOLS

Ranking instruments are variations in measurement that are related to rating scales. A **ranking tool** is used to rank learner performance or products first to last, best to worst. The tool requires that evaluators make judgments by comparing individual learners or items within the group. In ranking, the evaluator would be given a list of criteria, then asked to rank products or performances based on those criteria. The method would yield the top three products or five best performances. This tool clearly has more limited power to provide various types of feedback than would the rating sheet. The ranking only gives feedback about relative position in relation to other learners rather than feedback on specific elements of the learner's performance. A rating scale could be used, however, to determine ranking. For example, the scores of learners from a rating scale could be used to determine the best three products or the five learners most capable on a given task (based on highest cumulative scores). This procedure would be likely to increase the reliability of the ranking procedure and would provide more learner feedback.

The first step in the development of ranking instruments is the same as for a rating scale. The instructor must determine on what criteria the rankings will be made. What qualities or behaviors characterize a desirable product or performance? Once these are determined, they should all be phrased as positive characteristics. These characteristics become the basis for the ranking as they do for the rating process. See Figure 14-14.

**FIGURE 14-14.** Desirable Qualities: Ranking Instruments

- Items in a group are ranked from first to last; best to worst
- Ranking is based on specified criteria
- Ranks are stated positively
- Sufficient space for comments is provided

# CHECKLISTS

Another tool commonly used in the evaluation of performance and products is the checklist. The **checklist** includes a list of desired behaviors and characteristics, and the rater simply checks the absence or presence of these characteristics. The instructor should attempt to write items that require the rater only to judge whether or not the behavior or characteristic is present, not to make qualitative judgments. The items should be at about the same level of specificity. The more general the items, the more opportunity for rater judgment and potentially, rater error. See Figure 14-15.

**FIGURE 14-15.** Desirable Qualities: Checklists

- Rater indicates *presence* or *absence* of particular characteristics, not variations in quality
- Items are at the same level of specificity

# SCORECARDS

The **scorecard** is a tool that can be used to measure either product or performance. The scorecard is used to rate or score the behavior of the learner or to rate or score the qualities of a product. Like the other tools described, the scorecard lists the desirable qualities or characteristics of a product or performance. Unlike the other tools, however, the scorecard *weights* each of these characteristics. Referring back to Figure 14-1 in this chapter, a scorecard was used in assessing a children's book showing how individual characteristics could be weighted. In that example, "appropriate illustrations" were valued or weighted at 30 points, while the "appropriate length" of the book was valued at 10 points. The capacity of the scorecard to allow raters to assign value to the criteria or characteristics is an added strength of the scorecard.

The guidelines for developing a scorecard are similar to those of other types of rating and ranking scales. First, the developer generates a list of desirable characteristics. Each descriptor should be grammatically consistent and about the same length as the others. Each should include a sufficient amount of detail to avoid inconsistency in rater interpretations. For example, "The floor plan contained logical traffic patterns" is a better statement of criteria than "good floor plan."

It is acceptable to include statements that describe what *should not* be included if this is critical to the product or performance. Look again at the children's book example. What if the book you were scoring had *all* of the required characteristics, but appeared to have strong racial or sex bias messages? Would it still be a "100 point" book? If the *absence* of certain characteristics or qualities is important, those, too, can be listed on the scorecard. In this example, one criterion might be, "Illustrations and text are free of all racial/sex bias."

Once the criteria have been established, each must be weighted. What is most important? What is least important? The developer can assign scores based on these judgments. This weighting allows you to consider proportionately all important characteristics, including details like neatness, correct spelling, materials selection, or others. These details need not carry the same weight, but can still be considered. This is easier with the weighted scorecard than, for instance, the 10-item rating scale.

All scorecard users should be trained for inter-rater reliability. If more than one judge will be used to look at student performance or student products, they should all agree on the interpretation of each of the points or characteristics. This is, of course, true with the use of any of the measurement tools that have been discussed. See Figure 14-16.

---

**FIGURE 14-16. Desirable Qualities: Scorecards**

- Measure product or performance
- Allow the rater to weight various characteristics to be scored
- Individual items are brief and about the same length as other items
- Items are concise and encourage consistent rater interpretation
- All critical items should be part of the weighted score
- Users should be assessed for inter-rater reliability

## PRACTICAL CONSIDERATIONS

While the primary guide to the selection of measurement items should rest on what type of content is being measured and at what level, some practical considerations must be acknowledged. The detail of the item and the time necessary to construct the items are of importance. In addition, there are some basic considerations in organizing a testing instrument and presenting it to learners that need to be taken into account.

## DETAIL CONSIDERATIONS

If observation is being used or performance measured, the more detailed and specific the instrument, the more objective the measurement will be. Consider, for example, a product evaluation used for youth cooking projects. One rating sheet might read: "Color - good/bad; Taste - good/bad; Texture - good/bad". Contrast this with a numerical rating sheet that combines some bipolar adjectives as seen in Figure 14-17.

**FIGURE 14-17. Rating Scale with Bipolar Adjectives**

TEXTURE:
Light, flaky   5 . . . . . . . . 4 . . . . . . . . 3 . . . . . . . . 2 . . . . . . . . 1   Heavy, not flaky

## TIME CONSIDERATIONS

Time is to be considered, however, when developing items. Probably the most time-consuming item to develop is the multiple choice item. Constructing good, plausible foils is difficult, but necessary in order to have a valid question. Multiple choice items are, however, fast and easy to score. Also easy to score are matching and true/false items. Essay and short-response items are quick to construct, but require a great deal of time and energy to assess. In general, items that take less time to construct take more time to score.

When two or more types of measurement items are equally adequate to measure a particular type of outcome (like recognition), it makes sense to choose the most efficient. Look at the following example of a learner outcome: "Learners will identify sources of Vitamin C." A multiple choice item could be constructed to measure whether or not students could recognize a source of Vitamin C when presented with one. This would require writing a question (stem), then creating four or five foils. Instead, the instructor might write a brief true/false question ("Oranges are a source of Vitamin C.") or incorporate the question into a matching set where students link Vitamin C to a food source.

## ELIMINATING CONSTRAINTS ON PERFORMANCE

Writing technically correct items that are carefully matched to the learner outcomes and that represent those outcomes fairly may be the most time-consuming aspect of measurement for the instructor. This time may, however, be poorly invested unless the measurement tool is organized in such a way that learners have a chance to respond to the best of their ability. This involves checking to make sure that the organization of the instrument does not include any barriers or constraints on performance.

# BIAS

Test instruments should be free of bias. Biased tests may yield results that can be unfairly interpreted. They may yield different scores for different subgroups because of linguistic bias, sex bias, or cultural bias. To review test items for bias consider the following:

• **Look for relevancy.** Determine whether the activities or examples reflected in the items are relevant to the life experiences of the learners. Test writers may include examples that require learners to have some understanding beyond the intent of the question. For example, a question that used a medical example with learners in nutrition or made references to regional landmarks to learners in another part of the country might hinder learners from understanding the real intent of the question.

• **Avoid wordiness.** Items should be written in a straightforward manner. Too many words, complicated phrasing or difficult vocabulary may hinder learners from responding as well as they might.

• **Items should be free of exceptional stimulation.** Sometimes a multiple choice question or case study contains so many details that it draws the attention away from the intent of the question. A case study, for example, that graphically described the injuries of a family involved in a head-on automobile collision might detract from the question being asked about the type of auto insurance that would cover the damages.

• **Items should be free of words or phrases that might be offensive to some learners.** Items that contain elements of sexual, racial, cultural or religious bias should be modified or eliminated. Setting up examples or illustrations where people in low-paying jobs are typically of one race or sex, or describing groups of persons as having negative attributes (always lazy, cheap, sloppy, or stupid) are ways in which this type of bias creeps into test items.

• **Be sure the meanings of all key words and phrases are shared by the test writers and the test takers.** Certain age groups or ethnic groups may have different connotations for the same word. Think about the different meanings for words like bad, cool, jammin', and trick. A difference in the interpretation of these words could create bias in a test item.

## SUMMARY

Good instructors understand the link between instruction and evaluation, and are committed to doing both well. Measuring learner outcomes is a complex process. There are a number of procedural and technical points that must be considered. Professionals should remember that the overall objective in measurement and evaluation is to determine to what extent learner outcomes have been achieved. This information will assist the instructor in instructional planning and in actual instruction. The aim of the instructor should be to develop a fair and reliable method for measuring what learners know and can do. This can best be achieved by following the guidelines discussed in this chapter.

— Match any measurement and evaluation plan to the stated learner outcomes.
— Match the selection of measurement instruments to the learner outcomes and to the purpose of the measurement.
— Match the selection of items on each instrument to the learner outcomes and to the purpose of the measurement.
— Follow development guidelines for the selected measurement instrument and each specific item.
— Organize and administer instruments in ways that minimize anxiety, confusion, and biases.
— Use measurement and evaluation data as a basis for instruction, instructional planning, and for feedback to learners.

## REFERENCES AND RESOURCES

Erickson, R.C., & Wentling, T.L. (1976). *Measuring student growth*. Boston: Allyn and Bacon.

Fink, A., & Kosecoff, J. (1978). *Evaluation primer*. Beverly Hills, CA: Sage.

Green, J.A. (1975). *Teacher-made tests* (2nd ed.). New York: Harper & Row.

Gronlund, N.E., & Linn, R.L. (1985). *Measurement and evaluation in teaching* (5th ed.). New York: Macmillan.

Guilford, J.P. (1954). *Psychometric methods* (2nd ed.). New York: McGraw-Hill.

Hamon, R.W. (1988). Educational evaluation: Theory and a working model. *Education, 108*, 404-408.

Nale, M.A. (1987). Student outcome assessment: An alumni survey approach. *Journal of Home Economics, 79*, 3-5.

Popham, W. J. (1981). *Modern educational measurement*. Englewood Cliffs, NJ: Prentice-Hall.

Smith, N., & White, W.F. (1988). The criterion and measurement problem in teaching. *Education, 108*, 385-392.

Stufflebeam, D.L. (1991). Professional standards and ethics for evaluations. In M. W. McLaughlin, & D.C. Phillips (Eds.), *Evaluational and Education at Quarter Century, 90th Yearbook of the National Society for the Study of Education, Part II*. Chicago, IL: University of Chicago Press.

Van Buren, J.B., et al. (1988). Nationally referenced assessment measure for undergraduate home economics students: Documentation of need. *Journal of Home Economics, 80*, 37-41.

Walsh, W.B. (1989). *Tests and measurements*. Englewood Cliffs, NJ: Prentice-Hall.

# 15

# PROGRAM EVALUATION

"What did learners like best about the program?" "Which instructional method was more effective in teaching this skill?" "Do learners who completed the program respond differently than learners who did not complete the program?" All of these questions express concerns about outcomes. In each of these questions, outcomes need to be measured and evaluated. However, the outcomes to be measured in each of these examples are not learner outcomes, but **program outcomes**.

When is program evaluation used? What tools are used to evaluate programs? How is a plan for program evaluation developed? Professionals in family and consumer sciences need to be as familiar with the answers to these questions as they are with questions about measuring the outcomes of learners.

## DEFINING PROGRAM EVALUATION

The term **program** can be used to describe a variety of learning situations of varying duration, structure, and complexity. "Program" can refer to a series of articulated courses that corporately comprise a program, like the family and consumer sciences program of a middle school or high school. A program may be a series of meetings of adult learners or a planned schedule of activities with adolescents. A program may also refer to a three-hour, one-time session or presentation or a two-day in-service education meeting. Professionals in family and consumer sciences are involved with many of these types of programs.

The process called **program evaluation** involves an assessment to determine whether or not the object of the evaluation (the program) has merit or worth. Whether the program consists of a series of related courses or a short, instructional episode, an instructional program may be considered worthwhile if its outcome or objectives are met, if the instructional activities proved beneficial to the learners, and if other unplanned outcomes of the program are positive (Fink & Kosecoff, 1979). The emphasis is, however, on the outcomes of the program or planned instructional episode(s), rather than the achievement of the individual learner.

## PROGRAM VS. LEARNER EVALUATION

When evaluating learners, the key question is, "What should the learner be able to do as a result of instruction?" In program evaluation, the evaluator asks, "What should have been the results or consequences of this program and what evidence is there that these occurred?" Program evaluation may further ask, "Are these outcomes worthwhile?" In program evaluation, the unit of analysis is the program or channel for instruction rather than the learner.

There are a number of similarities, however, between evaluating student performance and evaluating programs. The beginning point for both types of evaluation is objectives or statements of outcome. The instruments used to collect data about both sets of objectives or outcomes may be similar. Achievement tests, self-assessment tools, and performance tests may be used either in a program or student evaluation. Program evaluation, like student evaluation, may be conducted for a variety of purposes. It may serve as a check for how the program is doing (**formative evaluation**) or to appraise the effectiveness of the program (**summative evaluation**). Finally, program evaluation, like student evaluation, requires qualitative judgments about the desirability of certain outcomes and the levels at which these outcomes must be achieved to be deemed successful.

It may be helpful to use an example of a single program to compare learner evaluation with program evaluation. For example, in an in-service training program, the instructor will, of course, be concerned about whether or not the learners, after two days, have actually accomplished the learner outcomes. Can they use the nutritional analysis software? Can they conduct an interview with clients to solicit the information? Are they able to interpret the results to clients? These questions are all related to the intended outcomes for learners. The instructor may use performance testing, observational methods, or self-report strategies to determine whether or not these outcomes were met. However, there are other relevant questions about the meeting itself — program evaluation questions. Those might include: Did the meeting address learner needs? Was the content presented in a way that was helpful? Does the learner feel more competent now than before the training? (Perhaps the learners already knew the material beforehand!) Were learners comfortable during the meeting? In the learners' opinions, did the instructor create enthusiasm about the topic and keep learners interested?

It is not difficult to understand why an instructor might need to solicit program evaluation information, even for a program of limited scope and short duration like the one in this example. In this case, the instructor might be planning additional in-service training sessions and need to know whether the format selected suited the learners. A program administrator might want to know whether this meeting was really addressing the needs of the learners or if the instructors delivering the content were well received by the learners. For a variety of reasons, program evaluation information may be collected along with information about learner outcomes. The instructor may use performance testing, observational methods, or self-report strategies here, too, to answer questions not about the individual learner, but about the overall program.

Program evaluation at the macro level can be a complex and multi-level process that may involve skills beyond those regularly employed by instructors. For example, determining the outcomes of an entire human service program or exploring the impact of educational efforts can require skills in advanced research methodology and statistical analysis. While some of these skills are beyond the scope of this handbook, professionals in family and consumer sciences need to at least understand the role of program evaluation and the relationship between instruction and program evaluation. Professionals also need to understand the process of program evaluation and to be able to interpret program evaluation results. Finally, all professionals need to be able to conduct program evaluation at the micro level for those aspects of the program for which they have responsibility. Figure 15-1 contrasts program and learner evaluation.

**FIGURE 15-1. Program vs. Learner Evaluation**

| PROGRAM | LEARNER |
|---|---|
| The overall goal of program evaluation is to determine whether or not the program has merit or worth. | The overall goal of student evaluation is to determine whether or not students have made significant progress toward learning outcomes. |
| The basis of evaluation is *program* objectives. | The basis of evaluation is *learner* outcomes. |
| The emphasis is on *group* outcomes. | The emphasis is on *individual* outcomes. |
| A variety of data collection strategies and tools may be used. | A variety of data collection strategies and tools may be used. |
| Evaluation may be formative or summative. | Evaluation may be formative or summative. |
| Decisions based on the evaluation relate to the merit or worth of the program. | Decisions based on the evaluation relate to the success or achievement of the individual. |

# DETERMINING RESEARCH QUESTIONS

As has been suggested, program evaluation occurs at a variety of levels and with different degrees of formality. Some evaluations rely on intuition, opinion, or trained sensibility (Weiss, 1972). Other program evaluation models use a discrepancy framework that emphasizes identifying program standards and then determining whether or not a discrepancy exists between these standards and the actual program or program outcomes. The technical model discussed in this chapter is based on program evaluation as research. In this case, the tools and processes used in other types of research are applied in the context of program evaluation so that judgments can be made about the merit or value of programs. This approach is an extension of work over the past 30 years that has labored to perfect methods that would provide reasonable and sound evidence about the worth of social and educational programs. Evaluation as research is resource intensive, but "provides a rigor that is particularly important when: the outcomes to be evaluated are complex...; the decisions that will follow are important and expensive; and evidence is needed to convince other people about the validity of conclusions." (Weiss, p. 2).

The beginning point of program evaluation is the formulation of appropriate and credible research questions. Research questions in program evaluation are formulated to guide the assessment of the program. They are questions about the program that need to be answered in order to determine the merit of the program. As in other research efforts, they serve as a general guide to research design.

There are several considerations that need to be made in determining the research questions to guide program evaluation. First, look at the claims or stated purposes made about the program. Often these claims or statements of purpose or intent are written as program goals and objectives. If learner outcomes describe what learners should be able to do as a result of instruction, then program objectives describe what learners should be able to do as a result of the entire program. Program goals may also describe certain desirable aspects of the implementation or activity within the program. Program objectives are much broader than those written as learner outcomes. A parenting program, for example, might list as one of its outcomes that, "Learners will exhibit increased enthusiasm in their roles as parents," or that, "Learners will demonstrate competence in caregiving." These larger goals spawn the individual learner outcomes on which to base instruction. At the macro level they become the basis for assessing whether or not the program really has been successful.

Another potential source of research questions about the program may be the activities of the program. Sometimes we want to know how successful certain activities within the program were. For example, which instructional methods were most successful? Which experiences were most enjoyable? To what extent did learners participate in certain projects? Which assignments made the greatest impact? These questions have to do with the instructional activities of the program rather than the outcomes of instruction, but they may be important aspects of evaluating the merit of a program.

Those conducting program evaluation may also need to consult with administrators, sponsors, or funding agents in formulating research questions. What will these individuals require as evidence of program success? Perhaps their concern is whether or not learners in this instructional program perform better than learners in a contrasting program. For example, "How do learners in the family and consumer sciences/family health class compare with learners in the physical education/health class on a test of health knowledge?" Although the instructor may not have written a program goal related to doing better than other learners, the question may need to be considered as an aspect of program evaluation.

To obtain the significant research questions, Fink and Kosecoff (1978) suggest building a matrix called an *Evaluation Program Description*. This matrix includes a description of goals, the activities associated with each goal, and the evidence of merit for each goal and activity. Evidence of merit may include observed or measured gain in students' skills or testimony from learners or other professionals about changes in attitudes or behaviors. Figure 15-2 is an example of such a matrix for a high school-level pre-parenting education program.

The goals of the program are listed in the first column or "goals" column of the matrix. For most programs, these goals will probably be stated in some of the descriptive materials about the program. The evaluator needs to be

**FIGURE 15-2. Evaluation Program Description for Pre-parenting Program**

| Goals | Activities | Evidence of Program Merit |
|---|---|---|
| Increase knowledge of child development/parenting | Classroom activities and laboratories | Demonstrate significant gains in cognitive knowledge of child development/parenting |
| | | Demonstrate appropriate interaction/communication with children in the laboratories |
| Develop a realistic attitude about the parenting role | Laboratories | Demonstrate change in attitude regarding the parenting role |
| | Community work | Assist parents and families through volunteer experiences |
| Acquire attitudes consistent with those of a nurturing caregiver | Classroom discussions | Conduct in-class discussions |
| | Laboratories | Testimony of teacher regarding attitudes/behavior |
| | Community work | Students express attitudes about their roles consistent with those of a nurturing caregiver |

aware, however, of implicit or unstated goals of a program that everyone "assumes." Goal two within the example represents an implicit goal. While none of the written or official materials about the program state, "High school students in this program will learn what a tough job parenting really is," parents and teachers alike *hope* that this will be achieved. It is, in fact, a goal of the program. All of the goals of the program should be listed in the first column of the matrix.

In the second column are listed the program activities that are associated with each goal. In this example, there are planned classroom lessons and laboratories that are intended to bring about increases in knowledge of child development and parenting (goal one). The activities column of the matrix should list each effort that is planned to support each of the goals.

The third column, *Evidence of Program Merit*, describes the basis on which a person would determine whether or not individual goals have been met. You might construct this column by asking the question, "What would it take to convince you that the goal has been met?" For the first goal in the example, gains in cognitive knowledge and demonstrated behaviors would be evidence of increased knowledge in child development. Later on, the evaluator must decide *how* these would be measured or even if they're worth measuring. At the matrix building stage, however, it is critical to establish what is evidence of achieved goals or outcomes. Here again, the evaluator may need to consult with others related to the program. For the evaluation process and outcome to have credibility for an administrator, sponsor, or funding agent, there must be agreement on what the program is supposed to achieve (its goals) and what evidence will be required to establish its success (evidence of program merit).

Next, questions can be developed from the matrix. These questions are really research questions that help collect and organize the data that provide evidence of the success of the program. The following are examples of questions based on the example above:

- Did students demonstrate significant gains in cognitive knowledge of child development/parenting?
- Did students demonstrate good communication skills and interact appropriately with the children with whom they worked?
- Did students' attitudes change regarding the parenting role?
- Did students assist families and parents through volunteer work in the community?
- Did students participate in class discussion?
- Do teachers report evidence of nurturing/caring attitudes and behaviors of students when working with young children in the laboratories?
- As a result of their volunteer experience, do students express attitudes that are consistent with those needed to be a nurturing caregiver to children?

The research questions are linked to the program goals, activities, and the identified evidences of merit. There could be additional questions in the program evaluation that do not come directly from the originally stated goals and activities of the program. Again, sometimes these questions may be suggested by key people related to the program, generated by the "political" climate, or generated as a result of other research. For example, the instructor might want to know whether or not students who were enrolled in parenting education had significantly different attitudes about parenting than students *not* enrolled in the program. Whatever research questions are formulated and adopted, these questions become the basis for the evaluation. So step one in program evaluation is to *develop relevant research questions.*

## PLANNING THE PROGRAM EVALUATION

The next step in a program evaluation based on research is planning the evaluation. The following questions will need to be answered. What kind of data needs to be gathered? From whom will the data be gathered? When are the data to be collected? An evaluation plan includes determining an evaluation *design*, determining the *variables* that will be measured, and deciding on the *sample* for the evaluation.

The **design** refers to the format for the evaluation. There are several formats that can be used. One format is an **experimental design** where two randomly selected groups are used. One group is "treated" and the other is not. Both groups are tested and compared. True experimental designs are rarely used in education because it is difficult to work with groups that are truly random. There are also ethical difficulties in not "treating" the control group. Other designs are more suited to educational research. The **case design**, for example, allows the evaluator to look at a particular group of learners at a certain place in time. The evaluator may pretest the learners, and then posttest them after the "treatment" or educational program. The case design does not involve comparing the learners or sample to any other group, but rather looks simply at that particular group at a particular point. Another design, the **longitudinal study,** measures outcomes over a period of time to determine the effect of a program over time.

The **variables** in a program evaluation refer to the factors the evaluator chooses to consider or investigate as part of the evaluation. Some variables are *independent* or *fixed*, and others are *dependent* or *open* to change as a result of the program. For example, in the parenting program discussed previously, the gender of the students might be the independent variable, and test scores might be the dependent variable. The evaluator might want to look at the effect of the program on the test scores of male and female students. The evaluator is interested in the gender of the student (an independent variable) and test scores (dependent variable) as factors for consideration.

The *sample* refers to the learners who will actually be considered in the evaluation study. A sample may be a portion of the entire possible group of learners, selected in such a way that they actually represent all of the learners who might be studied. In an entire high school family and consumer sciences program, for example, the family and consumer sciences teacher might select 25 students to interview to determine what they enjoyed most about their family and consumer sciences classes. If these 25 students were selected so that they truly represented the enrolled population, the teacher could assume that their opinions reflected the opinions, in general, of all of the family and consumer sciences students.

Sometimes evaluators choose to involve all of the population. Professionals in extension, for example, generally ask all of the learners at a particular program to rate the program based on its effectiveness or their enjoyment of the program. Instructors must decide whether selecting a sample of the population would be appreciably more efficient, and still be effective.

The second step in program evaluation, then, is to *develop a plan for the evaluation*. To see how this step can be implemented, consider again the example of the pre-parenting program.

Assume that the evaluator in this example has decided to answer these research questions:

- Do students demonstrate significant gains in cognitive knowledge of child development/parenting?
- Did students' attitudes about child rearing change after the course?
- Are there differences in the attitudes about child rearing in students who have taken the pre-parenting course and those students who have not had the course?
- Are there differences in levels of cognitive knowledge in students who have taken the pre-parenting course and those students who have not had the course?

To answer these questions, the evaluator might decide upon a variation of experimental design. He or she could decide to compare the pre-parenting students and a group of study hall students. Since the evaluator doesn't have true random groups of students (the students weren't randomly placed into the class and into the study hall—they self-selected for a variety of reasons), he or she does not have a true experimental design. However, the evaluator decides it will suffice for his or her needs.

A pretest might assess knowledge about children and attitudes about child rearing (the dependent variables). The evaluator would then plan to posttest both groups at the end of the semester and compare not only the pre- and post-test scores of the students who were enrolled in the parenting class, but also compare those students with students who were not enrolled in the parenting class. This plan could provide data to answer the identified research questions for this program evaluation.

## DATA COLLECTION

The third step in a research-based program evaluation is *data collection*. In evaluating learner outcomes, the use of paper-pencil tests and other tools that could be used to collect data about performance or products was discussed. Performance tests, rating and ranking scales, interviews, questionnaires, and achievement tests are also used in program evaluation. The evaluation design in this example could involve the use of several types of instruments: for example, interviews, self-report measures, and achievement tests. The construction of the instruments used to collect data for program evaluation purposes follow the same guidelines as outlined in developing instruments for reviewing individual learner outcomes.

One data collection method not previously discussed for use in measuring learner outcomes is the archive review. An **archive review** involves collecting data from program-related documents, such as attendance or medical records. From this type of data collection, the evaluator can answer questions like: "Which program had the highest number of participants?" or "What was the most frequent childhood illness in February?"

The selection of a particular data collection strategy should depend upon the questions that the evaluator wants to answer and the type of design he or she has selected for the evaluation. If the research questions deal with the attitudes or preferences of learners, evaluators often use self-report as a strategy. Evaluators may use checklists, questionnaires, or rating scales as tools to collect these types of self-report data. Learners actually report how they feel or what they think so that the evaluator can answer questions like, "Have attitudes about child rearing changed as a result of the program?"

Paper-pencil tests may be used when evaluators need achievement data. For instance, to answer the question, "Did students demonstrate significant gains in cognitive knowledge of child development?", the evaluator might use a multiple-choice examination, both as a pre- and post-test.

Checklists, rating scales, and scorecards are often used to collect data about performance. If the evaluator, for example, wanted to rate the competence of learners' communication skills, the observer might use a rating scale.

The instruments used for program evaluation may look very similar to those used to measure individual learner performance, but the unit of study is the group rather than the individual. The third step in program evaluation, then, is to *select and/or develop tools for data collection*.

## DATA ANALYSIS

The final step in program evaluation is to *analyze and describe the data collected so that relevant decisions about the program can be made*. The instructor evaluating learner outcomes usually describes his or her findings using descriptive statistics, such as mode, mean, median, range, standard deviation, and frequency. These statistics are used to answer questions like, "What was the average test score?" "How many students answered #6 correctly?" "How many students scored at least 70 points?" Descriptive statistics may also be used in program evaluation.

Program evaluation, however, will probably require other statistical methods depending upon the research questions to be answered. Take, for example, the following research question: "Is there a significant relationship between attitudes about the parenting role and completion of the parenting course?" This question would require the use of correlation statistics that measure the relationship between two variables (the parenting course and attitudes). It is important for program evaluators to use appropriate statistical methods in the analysis of their data.

New computer software and technical assistance are available to the family and consumer sciences instructor who needs to conduct statistical analyses. While not all beginning professionals may have the necessary skills to conduct sophisticated statistical analysis, they can identify resources to assist them. Even the beginning professional should have a general understanding of basic uses of statistics to understand how research questions can be asked and answered.

## PRACTICING PROGRAM EVALUATION

Most family and consumer sciences professionals will not struggle on a daily basis with macro decisions about evaluation design and statistical methods. They will, however, need to be responsible for program evaluation. Consider again the example of the two-day in-service training program. This one-time, 16-hour program on the use of the computer for client nutritional analysis, needs to be evaluated.

The process for planning the program evaluation is much the same as in the more sophisticated example already discussed. The instructor begins by determining the purpose of the evaluation. What does he or she need to know? This requires the formulation of research questions. In the example, the instructor might identify the following as two of the research questions:

- Were learners satisfied with the format of the in-service training program?
- Did learners feel competent enough to use the nutritional analysis software as a result of the in-service program? (Note that how the learners *feel* about using the program is different than the competence they might *demonstrate* as a learner outcome).

After determining the research questions, the instructor must decide how to collect information on the questions. In the example above, the instructor decides to ask the learners directly. To collect the self-report data about their satisfaction with the program, the instructor decides to construct a short, open-ended questionnaire about how students liked certain aspects of the program, such as the demonstrations, practice time, lectures, length of the program, and use of simulation. To explore their feelings about using the computer program, a rating sheet with bi-polar adjectives that describe various feelings that might be related to using the software (excited/not excited, competent/confused, excited/reluctant) is developed. The construction of these instruments follow the guidelines outlined in the previous chapter on measuring learner outcomes. Figure 15-3 outlines the steps in program evaluation that have been described in detail above.

The use of a program evaluation instrument as just described is probably familiar to almost everyone who has ever participated in a formal or nonformal instructional episode. Sometime near the end of the session the leader

## FIGURE 15-3. Steps in Program Evaluation

- Develop relevant research questions.
- Develop a program evaluation plan that identifies the sample and evaluation design.
- Select and/or develop tools for data collection.
- Analyze the data collected and make relevant decisions about the program.

passes around evaluation sheets and asks participants to complete the forms and leave them at the end of the session. Sometimes these forms appear in registration packets or are distributed with handouts during the session. If the purposes of these evaluation tools is really program evaluation and the data from these tools will be used to make decisions about programs, then some guidelines for their development and administration should be kept in mind.

First, the instructor should be true to the program evaluation process and begin at the question stage. Too often instructors ask a little about everything—their instructional style, the quality of the lunch, the length of the breaks, how well participants enjoyed each of the speakers, etc. The questions asked need to be directly related to the research questions about the program. Unnecessary or rhetorical questions should be eliminated.

This doesn't mean that questions about room organization or lunch shouldn't be asked. It only means that instructors need to be certain that this is really the type of information that will help them determine how well the meeting or program actually met its intended goals.

Instructors should be careful, too, not to mix too many types of questions. Participants may become confused about just what they're being asked to evaluate if the questions or items hit upon everything from the personality of the leader to the sophistication of the computer software.

Next, the tools used should match the type of data to be collected. The information from open-ended questionnaires may be difficult to quantify or summarize. On the other hand, questionnaires may yield more detailed information and individuality of response that could be important. Rating sheets or checklists are usually convenient for participants, but limit the range and type of their responses.

Whatever tools are selected, participants should be given adequate time to complete the evaluation forms. If the forms are passed out at the very end of a meeting, participants may not give them their full attention. If instruments are sent to participants after the session or given out at the session with instructions to return them by mail, there may be a small return. If a later return is necessary, instructors should make the return of the instruments as convenient as possible, even to including stamped, addressed envelopes. It is recommended that time be built into the meeting agenda to complete the program evaluation instruments, and that participants understand that this task is an important part of the meeting. Obviously this time should be scheduled sufficiently late in the meeting to allow learners to have experienced most of the session, unless they are being asked to make an evaluation of particular parts of the meeting that have already occurred.

As with all instruments, there should be detailed directions for the learners. They need to know how to complete the forms. Consider whether or not learners need to identify themselves on the instruments. Participants may be reluctant to make negative remarks if they have to sign their names or if they have to hand the forms directly to the instructor. Decide how much privacy you need to allow participants and how accountable participants need to be for their responses.

The classroom teacher should consider using program evaluation strategies in addition to those typically employed for learner outcome evaluation. Teachers may want to consider what type of feedback would be helpful to them, just as they determine what type of feedback would be useful to students. Which instructional methods do students most enjoy? From which activities do they feel they learn most? Which teacher behaviors do they find most helpful? These are the types of questions that teachers may want to address periodically through the use of some type of program evaluation tool. As with the other types of evaluation, the results may be used for a formative purpose (to imp. ove or modify an existing program) or for a summative purpose — to help summarize or describe the outcomes of a program.

## SUMMARY

Professionals in family and consumer sciences are concerned with both learner outcomes and program outcomes. Program evaluation deals with whether or not intended outcomes have occurred, if the activities of the program are beneficial, and if other unplanned outcomes of the program are positive. There is a process for planning and implementing program evaluation that, in many ways, parallels the process for planning and implementing the measurement of learner outcomes. Professionals need to consider when to use program evaluation and how the data from those evaluation efforts will assist them in better communicating content.

## REFERENCES AND RESOURCES

Barak, R.J., & Breier, B.E. (1990). *Successful program review: A practical guide to evaluating programs in academic settings.* San Francisco: Jossey-Bass.

Borich, G.D. (1974). *Evaluating education programs and products.* Educational Technology Publications.

Crombach, L.J. (1982). *Designing evaluations of educational and social programs.* San Francisco: Jossey-Bass.

Fink, A., & Kosecoff, J. (1978). *Evaluation primer*. Beverly Hills, CA: Sage.

Harper, S. (1988). A model for program evaluation. *Education Canada, 28,* 18-23.

Judd, C.M. (1987). Combining process and outcome evaluation. *New Directions for Program Evaluation*, Fall, 23-42.

Kosecoff, J., & Fink, A. (1982). *Evaluation basics: A practitioner's manual*. Newbury Park, CA: Sage.

Posavic, E.J., & Carey, R.C. (1985). *Program evaluation: Methods and case studies* (2nd ed.). Englewood Cliffs, NJ: Prentice-Hall.

Tuckman, B.W. (1985). *Evaluating instructional programs* (2nd ed.). Newton, MA: Allyn and Bacon.

Tyler, R.W. (1991). General statement on program evaluation. In M.W. McLaughlin & D.C. Phillips (Eds.), *Evaluation and education at quarter century*, 90th Yearbook of the National Society for the Study of Education, Part II. Chicago, IL: University of Chicago Press.

Weiss, C.H. (1972). *Evaluation research: Methods of assessing program effectiveness*. Englewood Cliffs, NJ: Prentice-Hall.

# INDEX